Security Strategies and American World Order

I0127644

This book analyses security strategies in the American world order, systematically comparing Russian, Middle Eastern and European policies.

The main finding is that the loss of relative power has decisive importance for the security strategies of states, but that particular strategies can only be explained when relative power is combined with ideology and the probability of military conflict. Research on the unipolar world order has focused largely on the general dynamics of the system and the actions of the American unipole. By contrast, this book focuses on states that lost out relatively as a consequence of unipolarity, and seeks to explain how this loss has affected their security strategies. Thus, in essence, the book tells 'the other side of the story' about the contemporary world order. In addition, it makes an important theoretical contribution by systematically coupling relative ideology and relative security with relative power and exploring their explanatory value.

This book will be of great interest to students of international relations, security studies and foreign policy.

Birthe Hansen is Associate Professor at the University of Copenhagen.

Peter Toft is Research Fellow at the Energy Unit of the European Commission's Research Centre.

Anders Wivel is Associate Professor at the University of Copenhagen.

Contemporary security studies

Series Editors: James Gow and Rachel Kerr

King's College London

This series focuses on new research across the spectrum of international peace and security, in an era where each year throws up multiple examples of conflicts that present new security challenges in the world around them.

Security Strategies and American World Order

Lost power

Birthe Hansen, Peter Toft and Anders Wivel

Routledge
Taylor & Francis Group

LONDON AND NEW YORK

First published 2009
by Routledge
2 Park Square, Milton Park, Abingdon, Oxfordshire OX14 4RN

Simultaneously published in the USA and Canada
by Routledge
711 Third Avenue, New York, NY 10017

First issued in paperback 2014

Routledge is an imprint of the Taylor & Francis Group, an informa business

© 2009 Birthe Hansen, Peter Toft and Anders Wivel

Typeset in Times by Wearset Ltd, Boldon, Tyne and Wear

British Library Cataloguing in Publication Data
A catalogue record for this book is available from the British Library

Library of Congress Cataloging in Publication Data
A catalog record for this book has been requested

ISBN13: 978-1-138-87351-3 (pbk)
ISBN13: 978-0-415-46624-0 (hbk)

Contents

Illustrations

Figures

Table

Authors

Birthe Hansen, PhD, is an Associate Professor at the University of Copenhagen, Department of Political Science. She was a visiting scholar at The London School of Economics and Political Science in 2000, and is the director of a research project on unipolarity, democracy and the Middle East. She has published extensively on international security, terrorism and the Middle East, including *Unipolarity and the Middle East* (Curzon 2000), and *The New World Order* (edited with Bertel Heurlin, Macmillan, 2000). She is currently working on a monography on unipolarity (Routledge ftc.).

Peter Toft holds a PhD from the University of Copenhagen, Faculty of Social Sciences and has been a visiting scholar at Columbia University's Department of Political Science in 2004–05. His PhD dissertation (2006) compares and explains the strategies of six great powers who lost their great power positions in the wake of major wars between 1814 and 2006. He published the article 'John J. Mearsheimer: A Realist between Power and Geopolitics' in the *Journal of International Relations and Development* (2005). His research is focused on the international relations of the former Soviet republics, grand strategy, international security, realist theory, and energy politics.

Anders Wivel, PhD, is an Associate Professor at the University of Copenhagen, Department of Political Science. He has published articles in a number of journals including *Journal of Common Market Studies*, *Security Dialogue*, *Cambridge Review of International Affairs*, *Cooperation and Conflict* and *Journal of International Relations and Development*. He is co-editor of *The Geopolitics of Euro-Atlantic Integration* (with Hans Mouritzen, Routledge 2005).

Preface

Security Strategies and the American World Order: Lost Power explains the similarities and differences between the security strategies of Russia, Europe and the Middle East since the end of the Cold War until 2007. The book is the result of a three-year research project based out of the Department of Political Science, University of Copenhagen.

The empirical purpose of the book is to describe and explain the security strategies of the states that emerged from the Cold War as losers. The theoretical purpose of the project is to contribute to the contemporary development of realist foreign policy theory by developing a model for explaining the security strategies of states experiencing a relative loss of power. We focus on a *similar* condition, namely the loss of power, as well as the *un-identical* ways in which the states handle this condition in order to secure themselves in the world order.

Initially, it was the theoretical purpose that brought the three authors together. We shared an interest in realist theory: Birthe Hansen had created a model for unipolarity; Anders Wivel had created a model for regional integration; and Peter Toft was embarking upon the construction of a theoretical model for great power strategies after major wars. In the course of the research process, we discovered a mutual interest in the development of the American world order as well as a number of surprising similarities between the three cases under investigation.

Though each of us assumed the primary responsibility for writing the drafts for the individual chapters, we do not hesitate to forward this as a jointly authored text. The division of labour was as follows. Chapter 1 was authored jointly from the beginning; Anders Wivel drafted Chapters 2 and 4; Peter Toft drafted Chapter 3; and Birthe Hansen drafted Chapters 5 and 6. Each of the chapters was thoroughly discussed by all three authors and subjected to critical readings from colleagues in the IR research community to whom we also owe much thanks for discussing both the general and specific issues raised in the book. In particular, we would like to extend our gratitude to our colleagues in the International Politics Group at the Department of Political Science, University of Copenhagen, as well as Barry Buzan, Bertel Heurlin, Carsten Jensen, Knud Erik Jørgensen, Keir Lieber, Hans Mouritzen, Rick Fawn, Jean-Marc Rickli, Kajsa Ji Noe Oest and Sten Rynning.

For financial support, we would like to thank The Danish Social Science Research Council as well as the Department of Political Science, University of Copenhagen. For assistance at various stages of the research process, we thank Thomas Fahrenkrug, Christian Hald-Mortensen, Kasper Ly Netterstrøm, Bastian Schneider, and Jon Jay Neufeld. We would also like to thank our editor Andrew Humphrys and his competent staff at Routledge for their support and assistance.

Finally, we wish to extend our gratitude to one another for three years of good humour, constructive cooperation and companionship.

Birthe Hansen, Peter Toft and Anders Wivel, 2008

Abbreviations

ABM	Anti-Ballistic Missile Treaty
CFE	Conventional Forces in Europe Treaty
CFSP	Common Foreign and Security Policy
CIS	Commonwealth of Independent States
CST	Collective Security Treaty
CSTO	Collective Security Treaty Organization
EC	European Community
EDA	European Defence Agency
EPC	European Political Cooperation
ESDP	European Security and Defence Policy
ESS	European Security Strategy
EU	European Union
G7	Group of Seven
G8	Group of Eight
GATT	General Agreement on Tariffs and Trade
GDP	Gross domestic product
GDR	German Democratic Republic
GUAM	Georgia, Ukraine, Azerbaijan and Moldova
ICBM	Intercontinental ballistic missile
IMF	International Monetary Fund
INF	Intermediate-Range Nuclear Forces Treaty
ISAF	International Security Assistance Force
MENA	Middle East and North Africa
MIRV	multiple, independently targetable re-entry vehicles
NACC	North Atlantic Cooperation Council
NATO	North Atlantic Treaty Organisation
NRC	NATO-Russia Council
NSS	National Security Strategy of the United States
NTA	New Transatlantic Agenda
OECD	Organization for Economic Cooperation and Development
PfP	Partnership for Peace Program
PJC	Permanent Joint Council
PKK	Kurdistan Workers' Party

PLO	Palestine Liberation Organization
SCO	Shanghai Cooperation Organization
SDI	Strategic Defence Initiative
START	Strategic Arms Reduction Talks
TEP	Transatlantic Economic Partnership
UN	United Nations
UNPROFOR	United Nations Protection Force
UNSCOM	United Nations Special Commission
WEU	Western European Union
WMD	Weapons of Mass Destruction
WTO	World Trade Organization

1 Introduction

From loss to strategy

Since the end of the Cold War, the discipline of International Relations has largely focused on the strategy and behaviour of the big winner, the United States. This book tells the other side of the story: the tale of how those who lost have adapted to the new world order.

When the Cold War came to an end, a number of the Cold War losers shared in common a relative loss of power and influence in the new world order. They had to adapt. The three regions at the centre stage of the Cold War – the Soviet-Russian Empire, Western Europe and the Middle East (cf. Zakaria 1990) – produced a great number of losers. The losers chose to adapt their security strategies in very different ways. Our argument is that the choice of security strategies was not arbitrary; instead, it reflects patterns and systematic variations waiting to be explained.

Security Strategies and American World Order: Lost Power offers a general explanation for the strategy choices of otherwise very different loser states. The explanatory variables are relative power, relative security and relative ideology.

The book argues that the actors had limited room for manoeuvring because of the massive power gap to the United States. Our findings indicate that states have been inclined to pursue bandwagoning strategies in order to adapt to the current, unipolar world order if located in relatively secure areas, whereas a conflict-prone context favours balancing strategies. Furthermore, we found that ideological compatibility and the possession of nuclear weapons dampens the incentive to pursue hard balancing strategies.

Thus, our findings point to the explanatory value of general theory over particularistic studies of the adaptation process and the choice of security strategies. The findings are policy-relevant, both to the strategic discussions within loser states and to the attempts of the international community to deal with losers in the aftermath of dramatic international change.

The aim

The international systemic change of 1989 produced winners and losers. America, the only remaining superpower, enjoys unprecedented power and leverage to influence the global agenda. Germany, divided and severely constrained in its foreign policy options during the Cold War, is now reunited and a major political and economic force in most aspects of European politics. The states of Central and Eastern Europe, liberated from Soviet dominance, are now able to pursue their own foreign policy goals. China, for most of the Cold War locked in the bipolar conflict, now constitutes a potential Asian hegemon.

Conversely, the vast majority of states has lost strategic importance and foreign policy leverage. Russia, a former superpower, is now reduced to a regional power far less capable of influencing the global agenda. The former Soviet allies in the Third World and members of the Cold War non-aligned movement, enjoying a number of fringe benefits from the superpower conflict, are now politically and strategically marginalized. The European and Asian allies of the United States, highly important in the American containment policy against the Soviet Union during the Cold War, have lost strategic importance and political influence as well as relative power as a consequence of increasing US dominance over the international agenda.

The primary aim of *Security Strategies and American World Order: Lost Power* is to explain the grand strategy of the losers in the contemporary world order.

We characterize the contemporary world order as unipolar, because a defining characteristic is the asymmetric distribution of power leaving the United States as the only superpower: a unipole. Thus far, research on the unipolar world order has focused largely on the general dynamics of the system and the actions of the sole superpower.[1] In contrast, we focus on the states that lost relatively as a consequence of the shift from bipolarity to unipolarity and seek to explain how this loss has affected their foreign policy strategies and why they have chosen different strategies. This is important for three reasons.

First, in order to explain world politics, we must understand the challenges, options and choices of the losers as well as those of the winners. The continuous provocations of Saddam Hussein's Iraq prior to the 2003 invasion, the attempt of Iran and North Korea to develop nuclear technology, the war in Chechnya, and the rise in terrorist activity based in the Middle East and South Asia are all examples of losers seeking to adapt to the unipolar world order, but so is the desire of many European states to participate in NATO and the EU. Thus, it is impossible to assess whether the world is becoming a more peaceful or dangerous place to live in without knowledge about what lies behind the strategic choices and actions taken by the losers The hitherto rather narrow focus on the USA and the general dynamics of the system tells but a fraction of the story. Consequently, we have focused on telling the other side of the story.

Second, the losers face the massive task of formulating and implementing policies of adaptation to the unipolar world order. The adjustment process includes a shift in foreign policy strategy and military doctrine often combined with a restructuring of domestic society and a search for new allies and partners. Moreover, the adaptation strategy of the losers may pose a potential source of instability – globally, regionally or locally – and therefore constitutes a security threat to other states and the political order. Because of the complex nature of this process and the high risk of failure associated with it, solid empirical investigation based on a coherent theoretical framework of how and why losers adapt and why they choose one course of action over another is required in order to provide a better basis for political debate and decision-making. The analysis is therefore highly relevant at the policy level, supplying us with systematized information concerning the strategies and incentives of the losers and a coherent theoretical framework enabling us to explain their actions.

Third, the theoretical implications of *Security Strategies and American World Order* are equally important. The concept of unipolarity is currently the subject of scholarly debate in the discipline of international relations.[2] This is particularly true of the realist research programme, which traditionally focuses on the effect of the distribution of power on international and foreign policy. This focus, combined with the complexity and novelty of the new world order, has resulted in a rich and fruitful debate modifying and re-invigorating the realist tradition.[3] Of particular importance has been the specification of realist predictions of international outcomes and attempts at developing a theoretical understanding of how international structure affects foreign policy (cf. Elman 1996; Wivel 2005a). At the same time, however, realist theory development and empirical analysis have been biased toward the 'winners' of the new world order: the USA and its major allies and potential challengers. Accordingly, an important blind spot in the contemporary development of the realist research programme is how the losers of power, prestige and influence adapt to the contemporary world order.

In particular, we seek to answer two questions: 1) *How* have the states under investigation chosen to adapt to the American world order? 2) *Why* have they preferred one type of response to their new situation over others? Our realist point of departure also prompts us to raise a number of more specific sub-questions such as: How do changes in the international structure affect the foreign policy strategy of the losers? Why do some of them choose strategies bringing them on a collision course with the US and/or the international community, while others become American allies and support the status quo? Asking and answering these questions from a realist perspective challenges the current focus while simultaneously forwarding a constructive response to the challenge by providing theoretical and conceptual developments and empirical investigation complementary to contemporary research.

Theoretical framework

The proposed research project takes its theoretical point of departure in realist theory. Because realism – like most other perspectives on international relations – is a continuous work in progress with a myriad of different theories and models, it becomes necessary to specify the exact nature of the realist framework used here. Our theoretical framework is based on neorealist theory as formulated by Kenneth Waltz (1979).

We make four modifications to Waltz's theory. First, in accordance with most contemporary realists, we see the present international system as unipolar, i.e. with only one superpower. We assume the other range of responses of the other states to be restricted, because they have only one option for superpower align-ment: the United States.[4] Second, we assume that a state's response to a particular world order is influenced by the likelihood of military conflict. This likelihood varies widely across the international system and conditions the type of response from other states; in particular whether they choose balancing or bandwagoning strategies. We investigate one case of low likelihood of military conflict (Europe), one case of medium likelihood of military conflict (Russia), and one case of high-level military conflict (the Middle East). Third, we assume that a state's response to a particular world order is affected by its ideological distance to the great power(s). Ideological distance between the great power(s) and other states varies widely throughout the international system and affects whether states choose hard or soft security strategies. Fourth, in contrast to Waltz, we do not assume states to be 'defensive positionalists' (Grieco 1990: 10) primarily aiming to maintain the status quo via balancing strategies. We remain agnostic as regards the intra-realist debate on whether the general behaviour of states is most usefully assumed to be offensive or defensive.[5] Rather than assuming states to be either/or, we investigate how relative power, relative security and relative ideo-logy affect the choice of offensive and defensive security strategies. In effect, we view the choice between balancing and bandwagoning strategies and between offensive and defensive behaviour as empirical questions.

The four modifications are important to the contemporary realist debate. First, the dividing line between offensive and defensive realists has been central since the early 1990s.[6] Offensive realists assume states to continue to maximize their power with the ultimate aim of hegemony. As not everyone can maximize relative power at the same time, conflict is frequent in the international system. Defensive realists assume states to aim to secure their relative position of power in the international system but not to aim for hegemony, since this would prompt a countervailing alliance that might ultimately defeat the state. Rather than con-flicting interests, conflicts therefore result from overreactions and miscalcula-tions stemming from the anarchic structure of the international system. Rather than taking sides in this debate, we seek to add subtleties to it by investigating the exact conditions under which states choose one strategy over others.

Second, an important result of the contemporary realist debate has been to specify the implications of realist thought for the analysis of 'grand strategies',[7] which we understand as the strategic actions of states for making themselves secure.[8] Our conclusions add to this development of realist foreign policy theory by exploring how and why losers choose one grand strategy over another.

Finally, as mentioned above, the realist debate on the policy implications of unipolarity has thus far focused primarily on the winners, the United States in particular.[9] By applying realism to the analysis of states suffering a loss as a result of unipolarity, we will gain new insights concerning the policy options of losers as well as winners.

Thus, while our main intention has been to tell 'the other side of the unipolar story', this 'other side' has significant importance for the policy options of the United States, its allies and potential challengers.

Defining key concepts: what is a unipolar world order? What is a loser?

In addition to the neorealist starting point and the four modifications outlined above, a set of specific assumptions and expectations regarding the adaptation process of the losers of the unipolar world order is applied. The assumptions, concepts and expectations are refined and further elaborated upon in the following chapter; however, we start by outlining a number of preliminary expectations.

We define a unipolar world order as the combination of 1) a highly asymmetric distribution of power in the international system leaving one state significantly stronger than the rest (in the contemporary world order, this position is occupied by the United States); and 2) the political project of the unipole: in the contemporary world order, the American model for market economy, liberal democracy, human rights and horizontal non-proliferation of nuclear weapons (Hansen 2000a).[10]

We define a loser as an actor which has experienced a decrease in relative aggregate capabilities (Waltz 1979: 131), the loss of major political allies, and/or the loss of influence in terms of strategic importance as a consequence of a structural change in the international system. In accordance with our neorealist point of departure, we define a structural change as a change in the number of great powers.

Conversely, a winner is defined as an actor which has experienced an increase in relative aggregate capabilities, the addition of major political allies, and/or the increase of influence in terms of strategic importance as a consequence of a structural change in the international system.

In accordance with these definitions of losers and winners, we focus on the 'grand strategies' in the realm of security politics, i.e. the formulation and implementation of strategies necessary to preserve or improve the international position of the state.

All losers share a common challenge, because their strategic options are now fewer and less desirable than in the past. Unipolarity exacerbates this problem. The single superpower can be more selective concerning its commitments abroad than great powers in bi- and multi-polar systems, because it has no great power rivals. The lesser states must therefore generally work hard and provide for their own security and contribute to the maintenance of the stability of their geopolitical environment to a larger degree than in the bi- or multipolar order (cf. Hansen 2000a).[11] We expect the specific strategic content of this 'hard work' to be a function of the combination of relative power, relative security and relative ideology.

Methodology and research strategy

In accordance with contemporary realism, our methodological starting point is modified critical rationalism.[12] Critical rationalism provides a template upon which we modelled our research process. It tells us that we should begin by stating an initial problem, then suggests a trial solution and confronts the trial solution with empirical evidence. Finally, this process allows us to restate the problem based on the analysis and to repeat the basic procedure, though from a better starting point.

We choose the case study as our research strategy.[13] The case study is particularly suitable for this project, because it has a specific advantage over other potential research strategies when 'a "how" or "why" question is being asked about a contemporary set of events over which the investigator has little or no control' (Yin 1994: 4). We raise two main questions: *How* have the states under investigation chosen to adapt to the American world order? And *why* have they preferred one type of response to their new situation over others. The project certainly deals with contemporary events over which we have little or no control, since our main focus is on the foreign policies of states since 1989. Even though we go back in history, the primary aim is to substantiate and qualify our findings using secondary and already-known primary sources; not to discover hitherto unknown documents in the archives. In addition to written primary sources such as speeches and official documents and a rich and diverse range of secondary sources, our research relies on interviews with prominent area experts, academics, politicians and civil servants.

The most common objection raised against case study research is that the results of a case study cannot be generalized to other cases.[14] This is because there are often too few data points to control adequately for omitted variables, and because it is difficult to assess the relative importance of antecedent conditions that magnify the effect of independent and intervening variables. However, while it is true that case studies cannot be used for statistical generalization, i.e. generalization to a population or a universe, they can be used for analytical generalization, i.e. generalization to a theory as part of the theory development process (Yin 1994: 30–32). The basic idea applied here is that 'a previously developed theory is used as a template with which to compare the empirical results of the case study. If two or more cases are shown to support the same theory, replication may be claimed' (1994: 31).

The structure of the book

The rest of the book is divided in five chapters. Chapter 2 discusses our three variables: relative power, relative security and relative ideology. Based on this discussion, we formulate a theoretical model and deduce the expectations from the model, which we use to guide the empirical analysis. This analysis is conducted in Chapter 3 (Russia), Chapter 4 (Europe) and Chapter 5 (the Middle

East). Finally, in Chapter 6, we compare the security strategies identified and explained in the three case studies and assess the explanatory power of our theoretical model. We discuss the perspectives stemming from our conclusions for the development of realist foreign policy theory and the analysis of loser states and asses the policy implications of our analysis.

2 Explaining security strategy
A realist model of analysis

Unipolarity is the single most important condition influencing the strategic choices of states in the international system since 1989. However, whereas most states have adapted their strategies to the unipolar order, the content of these strategies varies widely. This chapter aims to provide a theoretical framework accounting for these variations, with a particular focus on the strategies the states pursue in relation to the unipole.

Our theoretical point of departure is contemporary realism. As noted in Chapter 1, realism, like most other perspectives on international relations, is a continuous work in progress with a myriad of different theories and models. In particular, the end of the Cold War and the subsequent critique of the (neo)realist perspective on international relations led to a proliferation of new realist approaches and theories. In addition to the conventional notions of classical realism and neorealism, the post-Cold War era has added at least 20 different 'realisms' to the tradition.[1] The new developments have allowed for more detailed studies of foreign policy; to the outsider, however, this has created a sprawling and often impenetrable intra-realist debate. It therefore becomes necessary to specify the exact nature of the realist framework, which is used here to derive our expectations.

We begin from structural realist premises (Waltz 1979). Structural realism is not a theory of state strategies per se; rather, it is concerned with the effects of international structure, anarchy, and polarity on international outcomes (Waltz 1996). Structural realists explain international relations in terms of rational states striving to survive in an anarchic international system. However, we cannot deduce state strategy from international structure alone. In order to explain strategies, we must understand the variations in the 'ability' and 'willingness' of actors to balance and bandwagon in the unipolar world order (Schweller 2004: 169).

We explore variations in the ability and willingness of states to pursue strategies of balancing and bandwagoning, thus enabling the theory to account for state strategies. In order to do so, we make four modifications to the original structural realist argument. First, in accordance with most contemporary realists, we see the present international system as unipolar, i.e. with only one superpower, a category apart from the original theory and still disputed by some realists. Building on the realist literature on unipolarity, we argue that unipolarity affects the ability of states to pursue balancing and bandwagoning strategies. Second, we add relative security to the model, arguing that the capacity and willingness of states to pursue strategies of balancing and bandwagoning is affected by the likelihood of military conflict. This likelihood varies widely throughout the international system and conditions the type of response to unipolarity by the states. Third, we introduce the concept of relative ideology, i.e. the ideological distance between the states analysed and the unipole. We argue that ideological distance influences the willingness of states to pursue hard and soft security strategies. Fourth, we view the choice between defensive and offensive state behaviour as an empirical question; not something we can deduce from our assumptions concerning the anarchical structure of the international system.

Relative power

What are the structural incentives for state strategy? This section outlines, first, the incentives for state action provided by the anarchic structure, and, second, the incentives provided by unipolarity.

Anarchy

We begin from the premise that the structure of the international system is anarchic. The defining characteristic of anarchy in realist theory is the lack of a monopoly on the legitimate use of force (Waltz 1979: 103–104). International anarchy implies that 'there is no overarching authority to prevent others from using violence or the threat of violence, to dominate or even destroy them' (Grieco 1990: 38). However, anarchy is not necessarily akin to chaos or a lack of order (Mearsheimer 2001: 30); it merely describes the organization of the units, thereby allowing us to deal with the dynamics of an anarchically organized system in contrast to those of a hierarchically organized system. These dynamics allow us to explain 'the recurrent patterns and features of international-political life' (Waltz 1979: 70).

Realism still requires specification as regards the exact influence and strength of the international structure on state strategy. Users of realism agree that international structure 'shapes and shoves' the actions of states (Waltz 1986: 343), though the structural forces may on occasion be successfully resisted; nonetheless, their general assumptions concerning international anarchy leave us little guidance regarding the particular state strategies (Wivel 2005a). Thus, even though some actions tend to be rewarded while other actions tend to be punished as a consequence of the anarchic structure, we can say little about the exact nature, timing and severity of rewards and punishments from anarchy alone. Moreover, some states may take their chances and take actions that are usually punished; some might even get away with it.

The primary insight about state behaviour to be deduced from the anarchic structure of the international system is that the lack of a legitimate monopoly of violence renders the anarchic international system a self-help system. Every state must focus on its own security and survival before anything else, because there is no guarantee that it will be rescued by anyone else. There is no effective police force to catch the violators of international rules and no efficient judicial system to punish them. This is what John Mearsheimer terms the 911 problem: 'The absence of a central authority to which a threatened state can turn for help' (2001: 32). Thus, while '[t]he domestic imperative is "specialize"! [...] [t]he international imperative is "take care of yourself"!' (Waltz 1979: 107).

How do states take care of themselves? In the absence of a central authority capable of protecting states against one another, each state focuses primarily on its own security and survival. Following the general logic of realism, we find that two aspects of this focus are particularly important.

The first aspect is that when every state ultimately depends on itself to take care of its own security, it worries about its relative power vis-à-vis other states. When there is no overarching authority to prevent states from taking advantage of each other and states cannot be sure about each other's future intentions, they tend to base their security strategies on power calculations rather than ideational factors. Stated succinctly, they cannot afford to base their foreign policy entirely on ideology or culture, as doing so would put their survival at risk. The international realm is therefore dominated by power politics.

The second aspect is that states typically face a collective action problem. Every state takes care of itself, but none is interested in producing collective goods, e.g. security, freedom and justice, prosperity, clean environment etc. which would benefit all of the members of the system. This problem is not specific to international relations; it is a general problem in large groups. As explained by economist Mancur Olson,

> [i]n a really large group, the typical individual receives only a miniscule share of the benefit of an action he or she takes in the group interest. This miniscule share does not typically motivate individuals in a large group to voluntary act in a way that is consistent with the common interest of the group.
>
> (2000: 77)

In international relations, realists argue, this problem is exacerbated by the risk of a rival state gaining a disproportionate share of the benefits from cooperative endeavours allowing it to boost its power and potentially in the future threatening the state providing the benefit.

The condition of anarchy also renders states cost-sensitive. On the one hand, the uncertainty stemming from the assumption that anarchy precludes 'optimizing behaviour guided by perfect foresight, knowledge, and wisdom', as is often associated with the neoclassical economist concept of rationality (Resende-Santos 1996: fn. 56). On the other hand, state actors are assumed to be rational in the sense that they are 'sensitive to costs' (Waltz 1986: 331). Thus, even though states do not optimize behaviour with perfect knowledge and the ability to forecast the consequences of each potential course of action, they make their choice 'for an alternative that is "better" and it is made from a set of only what already exists' (Resende-Santos 1996: fn. 56), and means and ends are evaluated in terms of their potential costs and benefits. Thus, we assume states to be rational in the sense that they 'possess consistently ordered goals, and that they select strategies with the purpose of achieving these goals in the largest possible measure' (Grieco 1988: fn. 1). In short, states 'are aware of their external environment and they think strategically about how to survive in it' (Mearsheimer 2001: 31).

Each state then faces a fundamental strategic choice between balancing and bandwagoning when confronted with a potentially threatening power (Walt 1987; Waltz 1979). Realists generally agree that an anarchic structure gives states a powerful incentive to balance power. The states that are not poles tend to

> flock to the weaker side, for it is the stronger side that threatens them. On the weaker side they are both more appreciated and safer provided, of course, that the coalition they join achieves enough defensive or deterrent strength to dissuade adversaries from attacking.
>
> (Waltz 1979: 127)

However, realists are less clear when it comes to defining the two terms. 'Although arguably the most frequently used term in the field of international relations, balancing remains an ambiguous concept', Randall Schweller writes in a discussion of the concept (2004: 166).

We define balancing as 'a strategy of foreign policy behaviour' (Paul 2004: 2), the purpose of which is 'under conditions of anarchy [...] to counter opposing power concentrations or threats' (Ikenberry 2002a: 3). In contrast, bandwagoning denotes a strategy for foreign policy behaviour aimed at supporting opposing power concentrations or threats under the conditions of anarchy (cf. Mearsheimer 2001: 139). Balancing and bandwagoning may be general or issue-specific, concentrating on changing particular aspects of a security order.

Balancing and bandwagoning are two very broad policy choices covering a number of different sub-strategies. Thus, in order to provide a more fine-tuned analysis, we draw a distinction between 'hard' and 'soft' versions of each of the strategies.[2]

- *Hard balancing* is behaviour where states 'adopt strategies to build and update their military capabilities, as well as create and maintain formal [and informal] alliances and counteralliances' (Paul 2004: 3; cf. Pape 2005: 47) in order to match the capabilities of the most powerful or threatening state.
- *Soft balancing* encompasses strategies based on 'coalition building and diplomatic bargaining within international institutions, short of formal bilateral and multilateral military alliances' (Pape 2005: 58; cf. Paul 2004: 3, 14) in order to raise the costs for the most powerful or threatening state to maintain its relative capabilities.

Mirroring these definitions of hard and soft balancing, this study employs the following definitions of hard and soft bandwagoning:

- *Hard bandwagoning* is behaviour in which states adopt strategies to build and update their military capabilities, as well as create and maintain formal [and informal] alliances and counteralliances in order to support the most powerful or threatening state (cf. Mearsheimer 2001: 139).
- *Soft bandwagoning* covers limited, tacit or indirect bandwagoning strategies largely through coalition building and diplomatic bargaining short of formal bilateral and multilateral military alliances in order to support the most powerful or threatening state.

This study addresses two fundamental points of criticism raised against the concept of soft balancing.

First, critics have argued that the 'criteria for detecting soft balancing are, on reflection, inherently flawed because they do not (and possibly cannot) offer effective means for distinguishing soft balancing from routine diplomatic friction between countries' (Lieber and Alexander 2005: 125).[3] As a solution to this problem, we treat soft balancing as part of a larger complex of concepts including soft balancing, hard balancing, soft bandwagoning and hard bandwagoning. This helps identify the content of soft balancing and how this content is distinguished from the content of rival strategies. We also specify when and how we expect states to engage in soft balancing as well as its strategic alternatives.

Second, the critics of soft balancing have argued there is an 'absence of a careful empirical analysis of the phenomenon' (Brooks and Wohlforth 2005: 75). We intend this study to contribute to a better understanding of soft balancing through detailed empirical investigation of soft balancing (and bandwagoning) in Europe, Russia and the Middle East. Doing so also allows us to address the related critique that there is no 'persuasive evidence of soft balancing' (Lieber and Alexander 2005: 125). Our study documents important empirical examples of soft balancing in the current unipolar world order and explains why soft balancing occurred and how it was distinguished from alternative strategies. It thereby adds to the already-existing literature documenting its importance (e.g. Art 2004; Walt 2005) while simultaneously revealing the continued relevance of its strategic alternatives.

Hard balancing, soft balancing, hard bandwagoning and soft bandwagoning may be used to further the security interests of a state. From anarchy alone, however, we cannot say when a state will opt for one strategy over the other. In order to move one step closer to answering this question, we must understand the dynamics of the particular power configuration in question. The next section therefore discusses the implications of unipolarity for the choice of strategy.

Unipolarity

> Polarity implies that within a definable system certain actors are so import-
> ant that they constitute "poles" against which other actors have to respond
> [...] Thus a polar actor is one which is so significant that its removal would
> alter the contours of the system.
>
> (Evans and Newnham 1998: 438–439)

What makes an actor 'important' or 'significant'? According to structural
realism the concise answer is 'power'. Three aspects of the structural realist con-
ception of power are worth stressing here. First, relative – not absolute – power
is decisive. In an anarchic system, it is the power of the state as compared to the
power of other states which matters the most, because this is what decides the
ability of the state to pursue both defensive aims (e.g. ensuring survival and preserving autonomy) and offensive aims (e.g. influencing or dominating the
actions of other states). Second, while most structural realists would likely agree
with Randall Schweller that relative power 'is composed of both material and
nonmaterial capabilities' (2006: 103), they find that the material capabilities are
the most important ones. For instance, John Mearsheimer distinguishes between
two types of state power: latent power and military power, both of which are
material. According to Mearsheimer, '[l]atent power refers to the socioeconomic
ingredients that go into building military power; it is largely based on a state's
wealth and the overall size of its population' (2001: 55). Kenneth Waltz makes
no such distinction between latent and military power, though he does stress the
importance of material power. According to Waltz, in order to be a pole, an
actor must achieve a high score across a number of different categories measuring its power capabilities: 'size of population and territory, resource endowment,
economic capability, military strength, political stability and competence' (1979:
131). Thus, an actor cannot constitute a pole in the economic sector alone
without also being a pole in the military sector: capabilities are seen as convert-
ible. Third, in the modern international system, states are the most powerful
actors; therefore, only the most powerful states can become poles. No other type
of actor is able to achieve sufficient capabilities to challenge the strongest states
(Gilpin 1996: 18–26; cf. Krasner 1999: 222–223).

Power politics play out differently, depending on the distribution of power
between states in the international system (Waltz 1979: 129–138). Polarity is
characterized as multipolar, bipolar, or unipolar, depending on the number of
poles in the international system. Each type of polarity has different implications
for state strategy. Structural realists argue that bipolar systems are more stable
than multipolar systems, but also that the two types of structure entail different
dangers. In a multipolar world, miscalculation represents the greatest danger to
international security, and the probability of conflict is impossible to calculate.
No state is strong enough to balance the others by internal means. Accordingly,
all must rely on external means of balancing, i.e. alliances. Since alliance patterns shift easily, today's friend is possibly tomorrow's foe, and it is unclear

who should deal with a threat when it arises. Dangers may emerge from multiple sources, not easily discernible in advance. By contrast, the two great powers in a bipolar world are mostly self-reliant. Compared to multipolarity, uncertainty and the risk of miscalculation are reduced in a bipolar world, because each great power can concentrate its efforts on focusing on its primary adversary. This entails the risk of overreaction, however, because of the intense monitoring of the adversary's every move (cf. Waltz 1988: 47).

The literature on the strategic implications of unipolarity is more ambiguous than the literature on bi- and multipolarity. At least two positions consistent with structural realism can be discerned from this body of literature, as epitomized in the contrasting views forwarded by Waltz (2000), that unipolarity is inherently bound to be balanced out and that multipolarity is already on the horizon, and Hansen (2000a), that unipolarity is basically robust, although not necessarily durable.

Realist representatives of the first position argue that unipolarity will inevitably lead to balancing and ultimately transform the system to multipolarity (Layne 1993, 2006a, 2006b; Waltz 2000). This position is consistent with structural realist balance of power theory and argues that it is most exhausting to be a superpower in a unipolar system, because other states attempt to balance the excessive power. They do so by external means, i.e. forming alliances, and by internal means, i.e. increasing their own power capabilities. Thus, the relatively faster growth of the power of other states and unipolar exhaustion gradually leads to a multipolar world. This will happen no matter whether the great unipolar power employs a benevolent or an aggressive foreign policy. It is the fact of the massive strength of the great unipolar power that makes other states perceive the unipole as a threat, not how it conducts its foreign policy or its national identity.

In contrast, representatives of the second realist position on unipolarity do not view balancing and multipolarity as inevitable effects of a unipolar distribution of power. This position can be divided into three analytically distinguishable (but often practically overlapping) arguments (cf. Layne 2006b: 14–16).

The first argument focuses on geopolitics: power may provoke a counter-alliance, but only if the great power in question is able to project its power on the territory of other states, i.e. credibly threaten an invasion (Levy 2004: 42; Walt 2005: 39–40; Wohlforth 2002a: 106–108). In international relations, power and incentive tends to wane with distance from the home base (Boulding 1962: Ch. 12). Thus, Wohlforth argues that '[b]ecause power – especially the power to take and hold territory – is difficult to project over long distances, the most salient threats and opportunities tend to be nearby' (2002a: 102; cf. Mearsheimer 2001; Mouritzen 1998). This is particularly true for those states that are not poles; unlike the poles, they can do little to change their threat environment by military conquest or strategies of political and economic dominance (Mouritzen and Wivel 2005: 17). Thus, many of the states that are not poles will be excessively concerned with their immediate vicinity to engage in systemic balancing. In the present unipolar order, the only superpower – the United States – is surrounded by oceans to the east and west and two relatively weak states to the north and south. The difficulties involved in projecting military power across oceans and over long distances means that potential challengers to the unipolar world order are less threatened by the power of the United States than they would otherwise be. Moreover, these potential challengers 'are clustered in and around Eurasia' (Wohlforth 2002a: 107), and therefore more concerned about the potential threat emanating from the power of each other than the threat emanating from the power of the United States.

The second argument focuses on the costs and benefits ensuing from attempting to balance the unipole.

> [i]n any system there is a threshold concentration of power in the strongest state that makes a counterbalance prohibitively costly. This is what it means to call a system "unipolar".
>
> (Wohlforth 2002a: 103–104, 1999)

According to Wohlforth, unipolarity by definition thus renders balancing virtually impossible, because the ability of states to pursue balancing strategies towards the unipole is severely limited by the asymmetric distribution of power. Balancing is always difficult because of the collective action problem in anarchy mentioned above: even if all states with the exception of the unipole wish for a balancing effort, they all have an incentive to pass the buck and let someone else endure the costs of balancing. In regard to systemic unipolarity, this problem is exacerbated because the overwhelming power of the unipole makes the costs of balancing high and the potential benefits doubtful. This is particularly important in the current era of unipolarity because of the strength of America: 'the United States' post-1991 dominance in military and economic power is unprecedented in modern history' (2002a: 104).[4]

Organizing collective action in anarchy is always difficult, as explained above. Defending the status quo by countering a rising power which may one day become a unipole may be possible only if buck-passing can be avoided (cf. Christensen and Snyder 1990). However, overturning a unipolar status quo is even more difficult than preventing it. As noted by Wohlforth, '[a]ll of the arguments in political science concerning the difficulty of overthrowing a settled, complex, path-dependent social equilibrium now work for, rather than against, the hegemon' (2002a: 106).

Finally, the third argument focuses on the combination of power and how it is used. All things equal, the overwhelming power of a unipole tends to provoke and worry other states. As noted in a recent analysis of American power, other states 'worry because the United States is strong enough to act pretty much as it wishes, and other states cannot be sure that Washington will not use its immense power to threaten their own interests' (Walt 2005: 74). However, the unipole may manipulate the dynamics and duration of unipolarity by signalling its intentions (Mastanduno 1999; Walt 2002a; Walt 2005). A unipole may prolong the period of unipolarity considerably by signalling its benign and non-threatening intentions to the other states. In contrast, if the superpower is perceived as aggressive, a coalition will form to balance it within a relatively short period of time. Thus, it is the exercise of power, not power itself, which plays a decisive role in the respective decisions of other states to ally with or against the unipole. In the current world order, the United States has successfully signalled to most states that it is not interested in conquering their territory. As noted by Walt, '[t]he United States may be self-righteous, overweening, and occasionally trigger-happy, but it is not trying to acquire additional territory' (Walt 2002a: 139). We build on this argument in order to explain state strategy during unipolarity, emphasizing the dual importance of both power and how it is used.

On balance, the asymmetric distribution of power provides a powerful incentive for states to balance, though just as powerful a restriction on their ability to do so. As noted by Stephen Walt in a discussion of the current world order,

> [b]y itself, therefore, the effects of power are probably indeterminate. America's current preponderance does worry other states and provides a modest incentive for them to balance, but it may also inhibit their willingness to take direct action to bring the United States to heel. By itself, therefore, power does not determine what other states are likely to do.
>
> (Walt 2002a: 136)

In essence, the asymmetric distribution of power in favour of one state is an important condition for the foreign policy and security strategies of all states in the international system (including the unipole) and a potential threat to most states in the international system (excluding the unipole); however, it does not provide unambiguous incentives to pursue specific strategies, nor can it explain variations between states.

Thus, we do not know when, how or why states choose to balance or bandwagon. We deal with these questions in the next section by discussing the effect of relative security on state strategy.

Relative security

State strategy in an anarchic international system is influenced not only by relative power, but also by relative security, i.e. the probability of military conflict (Brooks 1997). This is because states are 'sensitive to costs' (Waltz 1986: 331). They attempt to keep costs as low as possible and adjust their strategies according to the probability of conflict, i.e. behave in one way if the probability of conflict is high and another way if the probability of conflict is low. States face very different probabilities of conflict depending on their geopolitical location and adjust their strategies accordingly. This constitutes a modification of the original structural realist theory. 'For neorealists', Brooks writes, 'states are conditioned by the mere *possibility* – and not the *probability* – of conflict' (1997: 448; emphasis in original). Thus, '[n]eorealism holds that the possibility of conflict shapes the actions of states, who are seen always adopting a worst-case perspective' (1997: 446). In contrast to neorealists, but in accordance with so-called postclassical and neoclassical realists, we do not 'assume states employ worst-case reasoning; rather states are understood as making decisions based on assessments of probabilities regarding security threats' (1997: 446).

Relative security affects the propensity of states to balance or bandwagon in three ways. First, a high probability of conflict creates an incentive to balance, whereas a low probability of conflict creates an incentive to bandwagon. A high probability of conflict provides states with an incentive to focus narrowly on their short-term security and survival because of the self-help nature of the system. This leads to balancing behaviour, because, as noted by Waltz, '[s]econdary states, if they are free to choose, flock to the weaker side; for it is the stronger side that threatens them. On the weaker side, they are both more appreciated and safer [...]' (1979: 127). Neorealists expect the structural incentives to balance to be the same across the international system (cf. Waltz 1979: 121). However, the probability of conflict varies in different parts of the system. Furthermore, when the probability of conflict is low, the anarchic structure of the system induces states to opt for less costly bandwagoning strategies over more costly balancing strategies. As the probability of conflict reduces, rational states will shift their focus from the short-term to the long-term (cf. Brooks 1997). Applying John Mearsheimer's terminology, they will go from focusing on military power to focusing on latent power, i.e. 'the socio-economic ingredients that go into building military power' (2001: 55). Bandwagoning is the logical choice in this process, because it allows the state to obtain gains that can be used for strengthening future capabilities. As noted by Schweller, 'balancing is driven by the desire to avoid losses; bandwagoning by the opportunity for gain. The presence of a significant external threat, while required for effective balancing, is unnecessary for states to bandwagon ([1994] 1995: 251). Thus, whereas the aim of balancing is to protect the immediate security interests of the state, the aim of bandwagoning is to obtain values, which may be used for maintaining security in the future.

Second, the role played by the unipole in the probability of conflict is important. The unipole may play one of three different roles. First, the unipole may lower the probability of conflict for a state by providing security through an alliance and/or stationing troops; in this case, the state benefiting from the security provided by the unipole trades autonomy for security. In order to maintain its security benefits, it will have a strong incentive to pursue a strategy of general bandwagoning with the unipole. Second the unipole may increase the probability of conflict for a state by promoting a world or regional order against the interests of the state and attempting to coerce it to comply with key elements of this order. In this case, the state has a strong incentive to balance the unipole, although the state may choose to bandwagon in order to appease the superpower if hostility develops into a direct threat of invasion from the unipole. Third, the unipole may play a passive role in the security of a state, leaving it relatively free to opt for specific balancing and bandwagoning on a case-by-case basis.

Third, the destructive power of nuclear weapons allows the states possessing them to supersede the usual effects of the anarchic structure of the international system on state strategy (Waltz 1981, 1988). The international system continues as a self-help system in which every state is ultimately responsible for its own security. For nuclear powers and their rivals, however, the potential cost of military conflict has risen sharply. As explained by Waltz: 'In a conventional world, a country can sensibly attack if it believes that success is probable. In a nuclear world, a country cannot sensibly attack unless it believes that success is assured'. This has important consequences for security strategy, because

> [a] nation will be deterred from attacking even if it believes that there is only a possibility that its adversary will retaliate. Uncertainty of response, not certainty, is required for deterrence because, if retaliation occurs, one risks losing all.
>
> (Waltz 1988: 50)

We therefore expect nuclear weapons to enhance the relative security of possessor states. Nuclear powers are more secure and less affected by the security problems resulting from the anarchic structure of the international system than other states (1981, 1993). This has two consequences for security strategy. The first is that nuclear states are able to divert more resources to non-military sectors, because their nuclear arsenal allows them to spend less on conventional deterrence and continue to deter potential aggressors successfully. The second consequence is that domestic politics are allowed to play a greater role in the determination of security strategy than for other states, because the effects of the anarchic structure on state strategy are blunted by nuclear deterrence.

Relative ideology

It was noted in the above that states face a collective action problem in international anarchy: few states have an incentive to produce collective goods – e.g. security, freedom, prosperity, a clean environment etc. – which would be to the benefit of all of the members of the system. While no state is likely to produce these goods to all other states, great powers have an interest in supplying some collective goods to some states in order to manage their sphere of interest, i.e. to provide security in order to secure a stable order.

A unipole has an interest in maintaining a stable global order 'keeping the world "off balance"', i.e. maintaining the highly asymmetric distribution of power benefiting the unipole (cf. Walt 2002a). However, whereas power tells us something about the extent of the unipole's managerial tasks, it tells us little about the content of management. Part of this management consists of providing security to supporters of the unipolar order and at the same time providing 'insecurity' to those states challenging the unipolar order in order to keep the challengers in check and deter other states from challenging the order. As noted above, the unipole thus directly influences the relative security of the other states in the system.

Another part of the unipole's management of the system follows from the political content of the unipolar order. In addition to a highly asymmetric distribution of power in the international system leaving one state significantly stronger than the rest, a unipolar world order also consists of the political project of the unipole. In the contemporary world order, key aspects are the American model for market economy, liberal democracy, human rights, and the horizontal non-proliferation of nuclear weapons (Hansen 2000a: 21). Whereas power tells us where to look for external influence on state strategy, and relative security tells us about states' incentives to balance or bandwagon, the political project of the pole tells us which means security policy decision makers are likely to use to respond to this influence, i.e. about their willingness to employ hard and soft security strategies. In this manner, ideology functions as an amplifier of the effects of relative security. Relative security provides the main incentives for choosing either balancing or bandwagoning strategies, but ideology provides the major incentives for whether balancing or bandwagoning is hard or soft. This is because the political project of the pole influences the positive and negative sanctions that the pole is likely to exercise and therefore also the nature of the response to the pole's actions. Three factors are of particular importance (cf. Mouritzen and Wivel 2005: 20–22).

First, the *ideological distance* between the governing elites of the unipole and those of other states is of central importance, because – as noted by John M. Owen IV – '[u]ltimately, states balance [hard] against power that is being, or that they fear may be, used against them' (2002: 242). Thus, we expect states to be more likely to employ a strategy of hard balancing against a unipole with a rival ideology than a unipole with an ideology similar to its own. There are two reasons for this, both linked to relative security. The first reason is that conflict is more likely between two states with rival ideologies, because they tend to disagree on more issues than states with similar ideologies and because misperceptions are more likely between two states with rival ideologies than between two states with similar ideologies, because they present their interests in language tied to their ideological point of departure, which may inadvertently lead states with rival ideologies to perceive them as a threat, i.e. the fondness of American policy makers to speak of the spread of freedom and democracy may be intended as a promise to the world but perceived as a threat, which necessitates hard balancing, by those favouring alternative models of society. As noted by Hansen, '[l]iberal democracy and free market capitalism are centrepieces of the current US world order, and they are not welcome everywhere' (2000a: 21). The second reason is that the potential consequences of conflict are much worse for a state with a rival ideology than for a state with a similar ideology, because losing the conflict may force it to give up core values and possibly result in regime change. Conversely, we expect states to be more willing to employ a strategy of hard bandwagoning with a pole with an ideology similar to its own than with a pole with rival ideology, because there are fewer points of contention, ideological language is generally perceived as non-threatening for the states agreeing with it, and the consequences of conflict are less severe for states already committed to the same values as the unipole.[5]

Second, *ideological intensity* is of importance, i.e. the extent to which the unipole and other states stress the importance of ideology for strategic choice. The intensity may vary from a minimalist position ascribing little or no value to ideology as a guide for security policy to a maximalist position arguing that ideology should form the basis of policy choices. The importance of ideological distance varies with ideological intensity, thereby increasing and decreasing the effects on state strategy.

Third, the *ideological substance* of the order promoted by the unipole is important, because the core values of this order influence the use of positive and negative sanctions likely to be used against other actors (Mouritzen and Wivel 2005: 21). Two aspects of ideological substance are of importance, both concerning the incentive to employ a strategy of hard balancing vs. a strategy of soft balancing. Pluralist states tend to be less centralized than authoritarian states. Representatives of other states can therefore influence the decisions of a pluralist pole more easily through lobbying various interest groups and actors in the political system. This may be tied to actions of soft balancing, such as diplomatic declarations, voting in international organizations (such as the UN), or public diplomacy. We expect this to dampen the incentive to hard balancing, because the most damaging effects of policy decisions for other states may actually be modified through this political process (cf. Ikenberry 2001a). Furthermore, a pluralist ideology is likely to be more permissive than an authoritarian ideology. The United States and Soviet Union managed their hegemonies very differently during the Cold War. Whereas the Soviet Union used military intervention and replacement of governments as its primary sanctions if allies experimented with alternative models of socialism, the United States – although not a stranger to military intervention and *coups d'état* – allowed for greater diversity with distinct 'Asian' and 'European' models of capitalism to develop without American intervention and distributed many of its positive and negative sanctions through international institutions and diplomacy. These soft polices from the pole are likely to only provoke soft balancing. As noted by Robert Pape in a discussion of 'soft balancing in the age of US primacy', 'even though the overwhelming power of the United States may make many countries uncomfortable, none of the major powers fear being conquered or having their countries usurped' (2005: 55).

Our analysis is limited to strategies of the American world order. The ideological substance thus remains constant when comparing within and between case studies. We focus on general security strategies. Thus, ideological intensity is less relevant than it would be if we investigated a single case, e.g. the Iraq war or NATO expansion. Consequently, the focus of this study is on the effect of ideological distance on security strategy.

Explaining strategic choices in the American world order

Based on the discussions in this chapter, it becomes possible to forward a simple model of strategic choice in the American world order.

As a starting point, it is useful to be reminded of the conditions shared by all states in a unipolar world order. Anarchy creates strong incentives for states to focus on power capabilities and to evaluate their policy options in terms of potential costs and benefits. Thus, we expect state strategies to be significantly affected by the highly asymmetric distribution of power in a unipolar world order and states to evaluate potential strategies in terms of their expected costs and benefits. Unipolarity creates a strong incentive for states to balance the unipole; at the same time, however, unipolarity makes the potential costs of balancing very high.

From this starting point in international structure, we can now add the expectations following when combining relative power with relative security and relative ideology. Following the logic of the argument above, we expect the variations in our dependent variable, i.e. state strategy towards the unipole, to fit into four behavioural categories: hard balancing, soft balancing, hard bandwagoning and soft bandwagoning. Each strategy is a function of the combination of relative power, relative ideology and relative security.

States experiencing a high probability of conflict tend to use balancing strategies. This is because balancing offers the ultimate means of playing it safe in international relations. However, whether states opt for soft or hard balancing depends on relative ideology. We expect states experiencing a high probability of conflict and a long ideological distance to the unipole in the current world order to choose a strategy of hard balancing. To these states, the unipole constitutes a major threat to their security. While the costs of balancing are high, so are the costs of the unipolar order. Bandwagoning is counterproductive, because adapting to the interests of the most powerful or threatening state may place the security and survival of the states at risk. And soft balancing, although typically cheaper than hard balancing, only offers ineffective means in a security environment with a high probability of conflict due to the lower costs associated with diplomatic and institutional means compared to military means. We expect states experiencing a high probability of conflict but a short ideological distance to the unipole in the current world order to choose a soft balancing strategy. Such states benefit from the unipolar world order and can often rely on the support of the unipole if their security interests are threatened. Engaging in costly efforts involving hard balancing would therefore only serve to undermine their security interests by wasting money on unnecessary military developments. Nevertheless, these states do not have a security guarantee allowing them to bandwagon and will choose to play it safe by balancing, although softly.

States experiencing a low probability of conflict tend to use bandwagoning strategies. This is because bandwagoning allows the state to obtain gains, which can be used for strengthening their latent power capabilities and future military capabilities. As the probability of conflict diminishes, the focus of rational states will shift from the short-term to the long-term. However, whether states opt for soft or hard bandwagoning depends on relative ideology. States are likely to bandwagon hard with the unipole if there is only a short ideological distance between the two states. In this case, as explained above, communication is made easy by the use of a common ideological language, and the consequences of conflict are less severe for states already committed to the same values as the unipole. States facing a low probability of conflict are likely to employ a strategy of soft bandwagoning with the unipole if there is considerable ideological distance between the two states. The state serves its interests by obtaining the gains of bandwagoning, but it is reluctant to make a military commitment to the unipole because of the ideological distance, which renders communication difficult and the consequences of conflict more severe.

As noted above, the importance and effects of relative ideology will vary according to the extent to which the unipole and other states stress the importance of ideology for strategic choice, i.e. ideological intensity. For most states, however, the tendency towards hard balancing is dampened by the ideological substance of the unipolar world order allowing them to influence American policy making and to follow different politico-economic strategies in domestic society.

Figure 2.1 shows how we expect the interaction of relative security and relative ideology to produce incentives for different security strategies:

Case selection, analytical procedure and the scope of the analysis

Based on our theoretical discussion, we are now able to specify our analytical scope, case selection and the analytical procedure.

The scope of the analysis

The geographical scope of our analysis is the three regions at the centre of the Cold War: the Soviet-Russian Empire, Western Europe and the Middle East. This allows us to investigate three areas of continuing importance for order and security in international relations; at the same time, however, we say little about the consequences of the end of the Cold War and the shift to unipolarity for the security strategies of states located at the margins of the Cold War.

The temporal scope of our analysis is the time period 1989 to 2007, i.e. the first 18 years after the systemic shift from bi- to unipolarity.[6] This allows us to analyse how and why states coped with their post-Cold War related losses and the challenges from the new world order. Adaptation processes take time, and we are looking for trends, not only for events. In a historical perspective 18

Relative security/ relative ideology	Long ideological distance	Short ideological distance
Low probability of conflict	Soft bandwagoning	Hard bandwagoning
High probability of conflict	Hard balancing	Soft balancing

Figure 2.1 Relative security, relative ideology and expectations.

years is short, but we are not investigating historical patterns; rather, we are studying adaptations to the unipolar world order. Thus, 18 years is sufficient for our purposes of identifying and explaining security strategy.

Focusing exclusively on the unipolar world order has its pros and cons. A focus on the unipolar order allows us to analyse the strategies of states which suffered from loss of power related to a systemic change. This will contribute to our knowledge of unipolarity in general and at the same time provide specific knowledge about the losers and their strategic choices. At the same time, the specifics of unipolarity impose limitations on possible generalizations and prevent cross-polarity comparative analyses. In future research, comparisons between the security strategies of losers subject to different types of polarity is important, but here we aim at providing only one part of the puzzle of losers' strategic choices.

Our theoretical scope is realist. This allows us to construct and apply a systematic and theoretical coherent model; at the same time, however, it prevents us from exploring the importance of a variety of non-realist variables (e.g. those following from liberal, constructivist or foreign policy theories) and from identifying the full range of specifics regarding each case. Nevertheless, by analysing three different categories of losers, we aim at producing new knowledge about states that suffer relative losses related to systemic change – in the case of unipolarity – and which security strategies they choose.

The selection of cases and the procedural steps

Our cases are selected in order to provide variation regarding the independent variable: relative security. From the group with low probability of conflict, we chose the EU countries; from the group with a medium probability of conflict, we chose The Soviet Union/Russia; and from the group with a high probability of conflict, we chose three Middle Eastern states.

The types of cases also differ significantly: the Soviet Union/Russia constitutes a single actor internationally, while the EU and the Middle Eastern states represent groups of actors. Furthermore, the EU states are well integrated, while the Middle Eastern states have little mutual cooperation. This 'most different' set-up helps us isolate the effects of our preferred variables since variation across a host of variables cannot logically explain commonalities.

Because of the very different nature of our cases, our empirical analyses cannot be identical in their set-up. However, they can be subjected to the same procedure to allow for comparison and the accumulation of knowledge when compared to the theoretical expectations. Thus, we follow the advice of George and McKeown to formulate 'a theoretically relevant general question to guide examination of each case' (in Chapter 1 we formulated two general questions: 1) *How* have the states under investigation chosen to adapt to the American world order? 2) *Why* have they preferred one type of response to their new situation over others?). In order to define and standardize the data requirements of the study and deal 'selectively with only those aspects of each case that are believed to be relevant to the research objectives and data requirements of the study' (George and McKeown 1985: 41), we subject each set of cases to the same four-step analytical procedure.

The first step describes the loss: its size, character, context and relation to the systemic change of 1989. This step provides us with the baseline for the empirical analyses, and it provides us with a profile of the losses following from the end of bipolarity. To some states, a loss may prove devastating, because the state is generally weak in capabilities and unable to compensate for the loss or rebuild strength by other means. To other states, losing relative power or a powerful ally may turn out to be a bearable loss, because the losing state itself is relatively powerful and located in a relatively secure geopolitical environment. On the other hand, the loss of a powerful ally may corner a weak state in a hostile environment. Not all losses are related to the 1989-systemic change. Some states may be suffering losses as a consequence of other international developments, e.g. changes in their geopolitical environment as a consequence of domestic upheavals in neighbouring states or the acquisition of new weapons by regional rivals. It is therefore important to specify the extent to which and how the losses in question are related to the end of the Cold War.

The second step characterizes the nature of the states' adaptation to the unipolar world order. In order to do this, we analyse the position of the state on international security issues, state behaviour regarding important interstate dimensions, and policies regarding areas of strategic interest to the state. We focus on issues important in the shaping of the post-Cold War world order, globally and regionally, on issues on the agenda of the UN Security Council, and on 'hard' security matters, in particular those which involved active use of force by the US unipole. These are conventional criteria for assessing the abilities and commitment of the states when analysing state behaviour from a realist point of departure. In accordance with our rationalist analytical framework, we assume the adoption of costly strategies, in particular the use of armed force, to provide the most reliable indicators of state intentions. Some indicators are more relevant to some cases than to others. For example, position vis-à-vis international conflict has been of particular interest in the case of the Middle East due to ongoing conflicts and peace processes, but they also remain important in the case of Europe and Russia because of the importance of these actors for US implementation of policy. Institutions are particularly important in the case of European states, some of which have a long-time institutionalized cooperation with the US, but other forms also matter. Geopolitics is of special importance to Russia, which has managed a collapsing empire, but also in the Middle East, and even in Europe as the states faced the wars resulting from the collapse of Yugoslavia.

The third step identifies the patterns of the strategic response and discusses which combinations of strategic choices match the explanatory expectations. In effect, the strategies identified in the case studies are matched with the expectations summarized in Figure 2.1 above and discussed.

The fourth step explains the state strategies identified. Do relative security and relative ideology explain the security strategies? To what extent do they do so? And what remains unaccounted for?

In summary, each case study is subjected to the same four-step analytical procedure:

1   Were the cases subject to a relative loss/decline? This is measured in terms of the loss of powerful allies, military and economic support, political representation and influence and followed by a description of the character and the degree of the relative decline. Furthermore, the extent to which the loss was related to the systemic change of 1989 is also discussed.
2   How did the actors choose to adapt? What characterizes their security strategies for coping with the new world order in terms of bandwagoning (soft/hard) and balancing (soft/hard)?
3   Did the strategies of the case actors make up any patterns? The strategies are compared to features attributed to the case actors as well as to each other in order to search for similarities, differences and obvious patterns.
4   Why did the case actors choose to adapt as they did? While we cannot provide the full explanation in any of the cases, we are able to point to the predominance of factors over others and to assess the explanatory value of our variables.

This procedure allows us to characterize the losers and their losses related to the systemic change of 1989, to identify the losers' strategic options, and to explain their choice.

3　Russia

Introduction

The aim of this chapter is to explain adaptations in Russia's strategic behaviour to the American world order using the model spelled out in Chapter 2.[1]

Russia – viewed as the core of the former Soviet empire – stands as the single greatest loser of the Cold War. The Russian empire had been among the great powers since the seventeenth century; in its Soviet incarnation, it was one of the two superpowers in the Cold War era. But by the mid-1990s, Russia was no longer a superpower. In the words of political scientist William Wohlforth, Russia had undergone 'the steepest peacetime decline of any major power in recorded history' (2002b: 186). This decline was both absolute and relative. The decline in relative power position fundamentally altered the basis upon which Russia could pursue its national security strategy and its interests abroad in the new post-Cold War and unipolar American world order.

Steep relative decline put Russia in a real dilemma. On the one hand, Russia could attempt to refuse to accept American power and dominance and seek to oppose it vigorously with whatever means left at its disposal. However, this risked leaving it isolated and on a confrontational and dangerous course towards the unipole. Moreover, integration into the American-led world economic system would in many ways be both beneficial and necessary for Russia. Joining the American world economic system would allow it to rebuild its socio-economic and military-industrial base – a necessary prerequisite should Russia retain any hope of regaining a position among the leading global powers. However, unconditionally accepting the new international state of play was also risky, as it by no means ensured that the United States, facing little resistance, would be unable to seal its hold on the number one position and turn the international system into an American empire with Russia occupying an inferior position on the margins.

The content of an optimal strategy to deal with this dilemma is by no means self-evident. And, since the end of the Cold War, Russia has struggled to strike a balance between discord and collaboration in the American world order.

This chapter reveals that Russia adjusted to its new reduced international position by pursuing a bandwagoning strategy in the very early post-Cold War years. Russian cooperated closely with America in the early years after the end of the Cold War and agreed to settle into a new European and global security architecture largely defined by Washington. Since the mid-1990s, however, Russia increasingly moved towards soft balancing. Russia increasingly used diplomacy and international institutions to place bumps in the road to impede American plans. Russian defiance towards the US-led intervention in Bosnia, NATO expansion, the wars in Kosovo and Iraq, coupled with growing diplomatic coordination and cooperation with China and other key global players, may be viewed as evidence of this kind of balancing behaviour.

The baseline – Russia's loss of relative power

Soviet-Russia was in a process of relative decline in its relative international position since the mid-1970s. However, the knockout blow to Russian claims to superpower status came with the implosion of the USSR itself in 1991.

In 1980 the inner Soviet Empire covered 22.4 million sq km, making it seven times larger than India and two and a half times the size of the United States. By early 1992, Russian territory was reduced to its proportions in the seventeenth century (Hosking 1998) at approximately 17 million sq km. After 1991, Russia still covered a vast territory but was now 24 per cent smaller than in its Soviet heyday (*Encyclopedia Britannica* 1993). This territorial loss was problematic; with it, key strategic, industrial and agricultural regions (Ukraine, the Baltic countries and Belarus) in addition to key resources in Central Asia disappeared.

As a consequence of this territorial loss, Russia also lost important human capital, i.e. skilled labour. The Soviet population totalled approximately 266 million in 1980. Following the disintegration of the USSR, the Russian population dropped to approximately 143 million in the early 2000s, amounting to a decline of some 46 per cent, pushing Russia far behind the most populous countries in the world (see Table 3.1).

Population decline not only reflected the disintegration of the Soviet empire, it also demonstrated a serious long-term decline in general health standards in Russia. In the late 1980s, Soviet-Russia became the first industrialized country to record a drop in life expectancy (Feshbach and Friendly 1992: 273–274; Menon 2001: 180).

However, the real damage to Russia's international position was to be found in an ailing economy (Brooks and Wohlforth 2000: 14). Soviet gross domestic product (GDP) was approximately US$1.400 billion in 1985, making it the third largest economy in the world. However, the break-up and severe economic crisis of the late 1980s and 1990s implied that Russia's relative share of major power wealth plummeted.[2] While other major economies grew, the Russian economy continued to contract until 1999, which was the first year in which post-Cold War Russia saw real GDP growth. After 2000, Russian economic growth accelerated and displayed impressive growth rates of 5–7 per cent, greatly helped by rising oil and gas prices – Russia's main export commodities. Nonetheless, the other major powers were far ahead. In terms of the economy, Russia ranked dead last among the seven major world powers by 2005, down from third in the 1980s.

The military sphere was the sole area where the Russian decline appeared less pronounced. By 1992, it retained one of the world's largest militaries. However, the ailing economy implied that the Russian military capability was decaying due to lack of funding. Accordingly, the size of Russia's armed forces was reduced from almost three million personnel in 1992 to approximately 850,000 in 2005, behind China and the United States. Lack of funding for weapons research, investments and maintenance further undermined the Russian armed services, as did poor training (Lambeth 1995; Menon 2001: 181–183); however, Russia retained an impressive nuclear arsenal: it inherited a formidable nuclear arsenal with a secure second-strike capacity from the USSR.[3] As explained in greater detail above, however, Russia's second-strike capability also increasingly came under pressure due to cuts in numbers together with American technological advances in the nuclear sphere that Russia was incapable of matching.

On top of material decline, the relative power of Russia also suffered from social instability due to the chaotic Soviet break-up and tumultuous democratic transition. Political chaos started in earnest with the aborted coup led by old Soviet hawks in August 1991 and Mikhail Gorbachev's turbulent replacement with Boris Yeltsin, which was followed by a period of constitutional battle climaxing on 4 October 1993 with armed clashes between forces loyal to President Yeltsin and members of the old Supreme Soviet Assembly, which refused to disband (Aron 1993; Desai 1995; Duncan 1993). Cross-country separatism, organized crime and corruption were rampant and threatened the political cohesion of the country.

The political situation stabilized after the 1993 parliamentary elections and the implementation of the new Russian constitution. The centralization of political power under Vladimir Putin's presidency also increased the Kremlin's control over the regions of the country. However, political instability persisted in pockets of the country, particularly in Chechnya.

To sum things up, Russia's relative international position of power was significantly reduced by the early 2000s as compared to the mid-1980s. Table 3.1 provides an overview of developments in several of the material indicators of relative power.

Against the backdrop of this staggering decline in relative international position, how did Russia adjust its grand strategy in the post-Cold War unipolar period from 1989 until 2007? And why did it make the grand strategic choices that it did? To answer these questions, we first develop an explanatory hypothesis below concerning Russian behaviour based on our theoretical model. We then analyse the extent to which our expectations were borne out.

The model and Russia: theoretical expectations

The realist model of grand strategic behaviour forwarded in Chapter 2 leads us to examine elements in Russia's external environment rather than its domestic scene for explanations concerning Russia's strategy of adaptation. Our model

Table 3.1 The development of Russia's power resources, 1980–2005

	Military personnel	GDP	Population	Nuclear warheads
1980				
China	4,500	161	987	280
France	495	952	54	250
Germany	500	1,331	62	0
Japan	241	2,044	117	0
United Kingdom	329	763	56	350
United States	2,050	4,209	228	23,764
Soviet-Russia	3,568 (2nd)	1,256 (4th)	266 (2nd)	30,062 (1st)
1985				
China	3,900	268	1,071	425
France	477	1,036	55	360
Germany	478	1,411	61	0
Japan	243	2,409	121	0
United Kingdom	327	843	57	300
United States	2,152	4,907	238	23,135
Soviet-Russia	5,300 (1st)	1,474 (3rd)	277 (2nd)	39,197 (1st)
1992				
China	3,030	484	1,188	435
France	432	1,246	57	540
Germany	447	1,796	81	0
Japan	238	3,184	124	0
United Kingdom	294	978	58	300
United States	1,914	5,898	255	13,731
Russia	2,720 (2nd)	786 (6th)	148 (3rd)	25,155 (1st)
1995				
China	2,930	685	1,220	400
France	504	1,282	58	500
Germany	352	1,849	82	0
Japan	240	3,288	125	0
United Kingdom	233	1,075	59	300
United States	1,620	6,472	263	10,953
Russia	1,400 (3rd)	601 (7th)	148 (3rd)	14,978 (1st)
2005				
China	2,100	1,600	1,300	130
France	250	1,643	60	350
Germany	280	2,181	83	0
Japan	240	3,623	128	0
United Kingdom	210	1,415	60	200
United States	1,400	9,016	298	5,300
Russia	850 (3rd)	516 (7th)	143 (3rd)	5,830 (1st)

Sources: The figures on population size and military personnel are based on the Correlates of War (COW) dataset *National Material Capabilities* (version 2.1 and 3.02) provided by Singer *et al.* (1972) and Singer (1987). The figures on nuclear warheads are provided by Robert S. Norris and Hans M. Kristensen (2006). Population figures for 2005 and 2004 are compiled by the United Nations Statistics Division http://unstats.un.org/unsd/default.htm. GDP figures are provided by the UN Statistics Division available at http://unstats.un.org/unsd/default.htm. Military forces for 2005 are based on 2003 figures drawn from 'the Armed Forces of the World' database available at http://www.strategypage.com/fyeo/howtomakewar/databases/armies/default.asp.

Note
The figures are listed in the following units: population: millions of individuals; GDP: billions USD in constant 1990 prices; military personnel: thousands of individuals; nuclear warheads: number of single units. The figures 2005 in parenthesis for nuclear warheads in denote active arsenals.

basically posits that the anarchic structure of the international system induces states to worry about their relative position of power vis-à-vis other states and to be cost-sensitive in the sense that they base their security behaviour on cost-benefit analyses, although they lack perfect knowledge and ability to make exact forecasts concerning the consequences of each potential course of action.

As argued in Chapter 2, when carrying out cost-benefit analyses, states make a fundamental strategic choice between balancing and bandwagoning when faced by a potentially threatening situation. They also have a choice of whether to pursue each strategy in a soft or hard version. As explained in Chapter 2, the structural incentives, i.e. the unipolar distribution of power and specific alliance dynamics related to unipolarity, are indeterminate – at least to the extent that the unipole does not embark upon a clearly imperialist course. This is because, as explained by structural balance of power theory, the highly asymmetric global configuration of power in unipolarity creates a basic incentive to balance the unipole for all the major second-ranked states. Conversely, effective balancing is extremely difficult to achieve under unipolarity due to the massive power gap between the unipole and the second-ranked great powers.[4] Meanwhile, band-wagoning represents an attractive option that may provide benefits and protection. However, bandwagoning is potentially fraught with dangers of subjugation.[5]

Because the incentives of the unipolar international structure to balance or bandwagon are not clear-cut, how states choose between balancing and band-wagoning and whether they pursue each option in a soft or hard version depends on our independent variable, relative security, and our intervening variable, relative ideology, i.e. the political/ideological project of the unipole and how it suits other states. As explained in Chapter 2, a high level of relative security provides incentives to bandwagon, while low relative security levels provide incentives to balance. Relative ideology works as an amplifier, determining whether a state opts for hard or soft versions of balancing or bandwagoning. The greater the distance, the more likely it becomes that ideological conflict may antagonize relations between the unipole and other states, because different ideologies tend to prescribe distinctly different views on world order and relations among states, e.g. liberalism, Marxism or political Islam.

Based on this model, what would be our expectation in the Russian case? As explained above, Russia underwent a severe relative loss of relative power in the 1980s and 1990s. Although weakened, it nevertheless remained a considerable power factor in world politics and retained a formidable nuclear deterrent. More-over, in the early 1990s, Russia faced no serious geopolitical rivals that posed threats to its key security and economic interests. Thus, Russia's relative security was at a considerably high level at this point. We therefore expect Russia to bandwagon, because this was the more cost-efficient response in a situation in which state survival and key interests were not at risk.

By the mid-1990s, however, the relative security of Russia began to decline. NATO expansion into east central Europe and increasing US presence in the territory of the former Soviet Union increased the possibility of geopolitical rivalry in Russia's borderlands. More disturbingly, the Russian nuclear arsenal was slowly being undermined by a lack of funding, while the US modernized its capacity and proceeded with national missile defence programs. Combined, this threatened to render Russia's secure second-strike capacity obsolete over the long term. Accordingly, we expect that Russia would move away from bandwagoning and towards balancing from the latter part of the 1990s, because the decline in relative security raised the stakes associated with continued bandwagoning and made the costs of balancing more reasonable. Continued bandwagoning would be counterproductive, because unqualified acceptance of US supremacy would now leave Russia vulnerable and perhaps jeopardize its security interests. But should we expect Russia to pursue soft or hard strategies?

As explained above, the choice of the type of bandwagoning and balancing (hard/soft) a state pursues is linked to relative ideology in our model. In the early 1990s, Russia had only just begun to implement democratic and market economic reform that would adapt its domestic politics to the American liberal democratic project. The ideological distance to the American world order was therefore initially quite high. This ideological distance declined during the 1990s, as Russia democratized. Towards the end of the period under investigation, the ideological distance began to increase again due to democratic achievements being reversed to some extent during President Putin's second term.

Against this backdrop, we should expect soft bandwagoning in the early 1990s. At this time, ideological differences remained significant between Russia and the United States, spurring disagreement on many issues. Furthermore, Russia would likely face reprisals if the United States did not condone the outcome of the domestic reform process. We expect Russia's balancing to be soft – not hard – in the latter part of the 1990s and early 2000s, because the ideological gap between Russia and the United States narrowed considerably as Russia gradually democratized, removing many of the obstacles for cooperation related to rivalling ideologies. Figure 3.1 presents our expectations in schematic form.

The following analysis of Russia's strategic behaviour will reveal whether our theoretical explanation and the derived case-specific expectations were borne out. Before turning to the analysis, however, a brief outline of the general development in our two key variables – relative security and relative ideology –

	Relative ideological distance	
	Low	*High*
Relative security		
High		**Soft bandwagoning**
		Russia early 1990s until mid-1990s
Low	**Soft balancing**	
	Russia mid-1990s until 2007	

Figure 3.1 Expectations regarding Russia.

is in order to substantiate our expectations concerning how Russia would likely adapt using bandwagoning or balancing strategies in the first 18 years of the unipolar era.

Relative security

As recalled from Chapter 2, we argue that relative security in the contemporary unipolar era is primarily a product of two elements: nuclear weapons and the geopolitical role of the unipole towards a given state or region.

Nuclear weapons

Russia inherited a formidable nuclear arsenal with a secure second-strike capability from its Soviet predecessor.[6] This lowered the probability of the existential threats to Russia from other major states.[7]

Russia's continued ability to absorb a nuclear attack and remain able to launch a devastating counter-strike helped ensure that it was relatively immune to the kind of territorial conquest that befell previous vanquished great powers, e.g. the Tsarist Empire, Germany, Austria-Hungary or Ottoman-Turkey in 1918 and Germany and Japan in 1945.

However, two issues imply that the value of Russia's nuclear deterrent depreciated during the 1990s and the early 2000s. First, the quality of Russia's deterrent came under pressure due to the poor economic performance of the nation, thereby reducing the available resources for the strategic nuclear forces. This implied a sharp downsizing in the numbers of operational weapons and launch vehicles. At the same time, the United States improved and modernized its own nuclear systems, thus edging it closer to virtual nuclear supremacy (Lieber and Press 2006; *Moscow Times* 2006a).

The US decision in 2002 to construct a missile defence system also helped undermine Russia's second-strike capability.[8] In the short run, the implications for Russia's deterrent were minor, since it could easily overwhelm any nascent American system. However, the prospects of the development of missile defences could have long-term implications, since an operative system could render the Russian second-strike capability obsolete. This is especially the case in the unthinkable situation that the missile defence system be used in combination with an offensive US nuclear attack. In this case, Russia's ability to retaliate could be called into question (Lieber and Press 2006). In short, the robustness of the Russian nuclear deterrent and 'security guarantee' was increasingly coming under pressure.

The geopolitical role of the unipole

Although Russia's relative position of power came under pressure as a result of the end of the Cold War, the absence of serious geopolitical rivals – at least in the early 1990s – improved Russia's relative security.

The Bush I administration launched its doctrine of a 'New World Order' in 1989, the core tenet of which was that the United States no longer had to contain the Soviet Union (Hansen 2000a: 84–85) and was primarily concerned with preserving stability in the wake of the Soviet collapse. Thus, the United States did not seek to fill the power vacuum in Eastern Europe, Central Asia and the southern Caucasus that opened up as the USSR disappeared (cf. Goldgeier and Mcfaul 2003: 9–10).

By the mid-1990s, this was about to change. US actions increasingly challenged the Russian monopoly as the dominant power in its post-Soviet backyard as America committed to promoting and pursuing a certain regional order in Europe and Central Asia as part of its grand vision for a new world order after the Cold War. By 1994, it became apparent that the Clinton administration's new foreign policy concept 'engagement and enlargement' (Hansen 2000a: 84) implied that the United States was embarking on a much more activist global strategy (Layne 2006a: 25; Posen 2003: 6). After a few years of deliberations and uncertainty, the Clinton administration embraced a Wilsonian foreign policy strategy of spreading democracy and capitalism across the globe and with it an expanded American role to assist this development.

The vehicle for spreading liberal democracy in Europe according to the US model was NATO enlargement. NATO expansion implied an increased US military commitment to Eastern Europe through the invention of the Partnership for Peace Program (PfP) and the subsequent expansion of NATO membership to include former Soviet satellites in East Central Europe (Brinkley 1997: 120–123; Goldgeier and Mcfaul 2003: 11–12). The 'pre-emption' doctrine of the Bush II administration added to the Clinton doctrine, accepting the use of military force to carry out the goal of spreading democracy in addition to fighting terrorism and, importantly, preventing the rise of a peer competitor (Layne 2006a: 25–26, 214, fn. 58).

Accordingly, American presence and influence grew in East Central Europe, the Caucasus and Central Asia. The United States also increasingly began to rival Russia's traditional influence in those areas. Additionally, other regional powers such as China, Turkey and Iran vied for influence in the Central Asian region (Kleveman 2004: 3).

This collided with the view of the Russian political establishment of the former Soviet area as Russia's traditional sphere of influence in which Russia had vital national interests. Moscow perceived this area to be off-limits to third states, i.e. a Russian variant of the American 'Monroe' doctrine. Moreover, the Russian leadership preferred a neutral Eastern Europe (Aron 1998: 4–5, 23, 26–27).[9]

The United States sought to penetrate Central Asia by providing military and economic assistance to the newly independent states (*Kommersant* 2007d). However, it was the American war on terror in Afghanistan, launched in the autumn of 2001, that particularly heralded a distinct rise in US influence in Central Asia. As part of the war against Afghanistan, the United States established military bases in Kirgizstan and Uzbekistan. This brought US military forces into the heart of Central Asia (Kleveman 2004: 2; *New York Times* 2005). The United States also actively began championing new strategic pipeline projects for transporting oil and gas from the Caspian energy reserves that would bypass the extensive Russian monopoly pipeline network (Kleveman 2004: 8). Washington also actively sought to influence developments in the southern Caucasus by pursuing economic and military cooperation with Georgia (Kuzio 2002) and Azerbaijan (*Eurasia Insight* 2007, 2008). Washington therefore came to pose a challenge to the traditional dominant role of Russia in the post-Soviet space. This raised the stakes for conflicts of interest to erupt between Russia and the US unipole.

In terms of our theoretical model, the initial high level of Russian relative security leads us to expect Russian bandwagoning. However, as Russian relative security declined towards the end of the 1990s thanks to its diminishing nuclear deterrent and growing geopolitical challenges, Russian incentives to balance were growing."

Relative ideology

As explained in Chapter 2, we believe that the liberal democratic project promoted by the US unipole and the degree of ideological compatibility may influence whether balancing and bandwagoning strategies are likely to be pursued in hard or soft versions.

A comprehensive assessment of the state of Russian democracy is beyond the scope of this chapter. During the immediate post-Cold War phase, however, Russia was in a state of transition away from the Soviet one-party planned economic system towards pluralist democracy and a market economy. In Russia's case, the degree of ideological compatibility with (or ideological distance to) the US political project changed over the course of the 1989–2007-period. Boris Yeltsin initiated reforms aimed at introducing multiparty rule, free and fair elections, civil liberties and a market economy after his liberal reform team assumed power in 1991. The 1993-constitution codified the basic principles of democracy (Freedom House 2006) and introduced a federal two-chamber system with a directly elected president whose government must have the confidence of the lower house of the Russian parliament, the Duma. Moreover, the constitution divided political power at the federal level between the executive, legislative and judicial organs (Remington 2003: 96). By the mid-1990s, Russia had the formal structures in place for a democratic state.

However, the Russian transition to a *functioning* democracy was slow and uneven. While Duma elections in 1995, 1999 and the 1996 presidential election were generally deemed free and fair (Freedom House 2002), a civil society was slow to emerge and there were signs that the governing elites in Russia, especially under President Putin, sought to restrict the growth of a thriving civil society (Mcfaul 2002; *Moscow Times* 2006b; Urban 2003: 136–137). Moreover, while the freedom of the press and an active political opposition grew under President Yeltsin, civil liberties appeared to be receding under Putin, as federalism and the freedom of the press appeared to be waning (Freedom House, 2006, 2007a). Moreover, Russian politics under both Yeltsin and Putin continued to be less than transparent and running along informal and shady personalized relationships rather than via an open and transparent democratic process (Lo 2003), and political corruption continued to be widespread (*Transparency International* 2005). The heavy-handed handling of Chechen separatism also raises questions concerning Russian respect for human rights.[10]

However, concluding outright that Russia was an authoritarian state during the entire unipolar era 1989–2007 would be to go too far. Democratic achievements were made from 1993 to the early 2000s, and Russia was ranked as 'partly free' by Freedom House in this period (Freedom House 2007b). After Vladimir Putin's accession to power, however, Russian democracy began a process of falling back (Freedom House 2007a). Thus, from 2004/05 until 2007, Russia approached the threshold of being labelled as an authoritarian 'not free' society.

To sum up this brief analysis, the ideological distance between Russia and the US unipole narrowed until the early 2000s, when Russia was a 'partly free' society.[11] However, the distance grew somewhat wider again during Putin's second term; especially after 2004/05.

When the high level of Russian relative security in the early 1990s is combined with relatively great ideological distance at that time, we conclude that this gave incentives for Russian *soft* bandwagoning. Because of the relatively great ideological distance to the United States in the early 1990s, Russia did not have incentives for choosing hard bandwagoning thanks to the ideological gap, since it remained primarily authoritarian until 1993/04. When the relative security of Russia began to decline in the mid-1990s and this is combined with the fact that it approached being a liberal democratic society around the same time, this leads us to expect a Russian strategy of *soft* balancing. This is because the ideological distance to the US world order became relatively narrow. As democratic reform reversed under President Putin (especially after 2004/05), we would expect Russia to toughen its soft balancing and even move towards hard balancing. As our period of investigation ends in 2007, however, we refrain from evaluating this claim here.

In the following section, we analyse Russia's strategic behaviour between 1989 and 2007 in terms of balancing and bandwagoning. This will help us evaluate our theoretical expectations.

Russia's strategic behaviour 1989–2007 – balancing or bandwagoning?[12]

This section analyses whether Russia's strategic behaviour between 1989 and 2007 is best characterized as balancing or bandwagoning; and if so, whether these strategies were pursued in soft or hard versions. The analysis focuses on Russia's external relations with the key powers of the unipolar period, i.e. China, Japan, India, Europe and, above all, the US unipole. We also focus on

Russia's interactions with the other post-Soviet republics. We limit the analysis to these two clusters of states, because these were the states with whom Russia principally interacted and because they were the most consequential for Russian economic and security interests and Russia's strategic opportunities.[13] We begin with a brief summary of the legacy of Soviet grand strategy during the final years of the USSR.

From balancing to bandwagoning: Soviet strategy 1989–91

By 1989, Soviet-Russian security strategy had been undergoing a remarkable although gradual change for a couple of years. Since the late 1940s, Russia had pursued a hard balancing strategy against the United States. The USSR anchored the Warsaw Pact and propped up allies in the Middle East, Africa and Latin America. Moreover, Moscow maintained high troop levels in East Central Europe and pursued a nuclear and conventional arms race with the United States (Rich 2003: Ch. 23, 29–35).

By the late 1980s, however, it became evident that the inefficient Soviet planned economy could not sustain the arms race with the United States over the long run. The Soviet leadership under Mikhail Gorbachev subsequently attempted to end the arms race and sought détente in the Cold War. However, this did not imply that the Soviet hard balancing strategy against the United States was totally abandoned. Rather, by pursuing détente, the Soviet leaders allegedly hoped to free the resources required to invigorate the ailing Soviet economy and society (cf. Wohlforth 1995; Rich 2003: 496).

The first signs of a shift in Soviet policy became evident by 1987, when the Soviet Union and United States forged the 'Intermediate Range Nuclear Missile Treaty' (INF), in keeping with which both sides removed their intermediate-range nuclear missiles in Europe (cf. INF Treaty 1987).

In February 1988, the Soviet Union took another major step towards détente when Gorbachev announced that the USSR would end its ten-year long unsuccessful war in Afghanistan, which had fuelled American support for the Islamic fundamentalist Afghan mujahedeen fighters. Russian troops left Afghanistan by 2 February 1989 (Rich 2003: 521). Détente was also evident in the Soviet efforts to end the conventional and nuclear arms race by engaging in talks on a treaty to reduce conventional forces in Europe. This resulted in the 1990 'Conventional Forces in Europe Treaty' (CFE). Moscow also strongly supported the efforts to conclude the Strategic Arms Reduction Talks (START I) with the United States in order to reduce the vast number of strategic nuclear weapons piled up between the two countries. Importantly, these moves did not indicate bandwagoning, since military parity remained at the heart of Soviet policy; but they were the forerunners of later Russian bandwagoning.

Other elements in Soviet policy in the late 1980s indicated a number of key revisions and concessions that can possibly be viewed as intimations of soft bandwagoning. This was the case with Gorbachev's announcement in December 1987 that the USSR would unilaterally reduce its conventional forces stationed in Eastern Europe. Even more surprisingly, Gorbachev declared in December 1988 that the USSR would now accept that the Soviet Warsaw Pact allies in East Central Europe could decide their own political system (Ikenberry 2001b: 218–219, fn. 7); an American demand since the early days of the Cold War, which the USSR had previously resisted (Rich 2003: 308, 322–327).

Abandoning Soviet balancing against the United States and changing to soft bandwagoning became evident in 1989, as the USSR began making key revisions in its security strategy in line with American priorities. Crucially, on 21 September 1989 Soviet foreign minister Eduard Shevardnadze informed his American counterpart, James Baker, that the Soviet Union would give up its demands about how the United States developed its strategic missile defence initiative (SDI) (Rich 2003: 492), and Moscow no longer considered SDI as an obstacle to a START treaty. In doing so, the Soviet Union surrendered its long-time goal of nuclear parity with the United States, since Moscow accepted that the United States could possess nuclear defence systems that were beyond the reach of the Soviet Union (Hansen 2000c: 78). Elements of soft bandwagoning became even more evident in Soviet strategy in terms of the collapse of the German Democratic Republic in November 1989 (Rich 2003: 536). Moscow had crushed all previous public protests against the Communist regimes in Eastern Europe; in East Germany, Hungary, Czechoslovakia and Poland. In 1989, however, Soviet troops remained in the barracks and looked on as the German Democratic Republic (GDR) regime was swept from power, thus clearing the path for German re-unification. Although reluctantly so, the Soviet Union went along with German re-unification and a unified Germany that could remain within NATO. A long-time precondition for Moscow to accept German unification had been German neutrality (Rich, 2003: 330). Abandoning this condition meant the massive revision of Soviet security strategy. Equally astonishing was the Soviet acceptance of the US leadership in the international coalition to expel the Iraqi invasion of Kuwait in January 1991 (Rich, 2003: 504, 529–530); something that would have been difficult to imagine just a few years before. Moreover, to help build mutual trust after years of bitter rivalry and to manage the transition to a new security landscape after the Cold War, the Soviet government was positive towards proposals from NATO concerning the establishment of a North Atlantic Cooperation Council (NACC) in November 1991. The primary aim of the NACC was to serve as a consultative arena for discussions on European security, thereby helping to build trust between NATO and the Warsaw Pact (Bowker 1995; NATO 2004b: 82).

In short, in terms of balancing and bandwagoning, Soviet-Russian strategy changed from balancing to bandwagoning around 1989–90. As the Soviet Empire was beginning to unravel in 1990 and 1991, the USSR had thus switched to a grand strategy in line with the major American policy preferences (Goldgeier and Mcfaul 2003: 21). Soviet bandwagoning was of a soft variety, because although Soviet-Russia made key revisions in its security strategy in line with Western priorities, Moscow did not seek any close military relationship or alliances with the United States.

Abandoning bandwagoning: Russian relations with the major powers after 1991

During the 1992–2007 period, the Russian strategy towards the US world order may best be described as shifting from one of soft- and almost hard bandwagoning in the very early 1990s to one of soft balancing from the mid-1990s until 2007. In the following pages, we substantiate this conclusion by analysing key issues and trends in the interactions of Russia with the dominant states in the post-Soviet 1991–2007 period: the United States, its major European allies, China, India and Japan.[14]

Russia and the US unipole

During the first couple of years after the end of the Cold War and the Soviet dissolution, the Russian government of newly elected President Boris Yeltsin picked up where Gorbachev had left. Yeltsin's team of liberal reformers focused on transforming Russian society along western lines and deepened relations with the West. They pursued an almost unqualified pro-Western course which broke with Gorbachev's more conditional approach. Western advisors were thus invited to assist Russia in its difficult economic and democratic transition from a planned economy and one-party state towards a democratic country with a market economy (Goldgeier and Mcfaul 2003: 66–67). Moreover, the Yeltsin team even sought to establish a special strategic partnership with NATO, allegedly even hoping for some kind of Russia–US alliance (Goldgeier and McFaul 2003: 50, 53–54). Furthermore, Moscow pressed ahead with ratifying the Strategic Arms Reductions Treaty (START I) and was positive towards opening negotiations for a START II that would bring an end to the nuclear arms race (Falkenrath 1995: 119–120, 124). In terms of bandwagoning and balancing, there is little question that this strategy may be branded bandwagoning, as Russia aligned itself closely with the foreign policy positions of the United States and its NATO allies. Moreover, because the Russian government was contemplating forging a military alliance with the United States (not seriously considered in Washington, however) Russian bandwagoning even had traces of hard bandwagoning.

This 'honeymoon' phase did not last for very long, however. By 1994, Russia had abandoned its unqualified support for US objectives and began opposing US policies on a number of issues. The NATO strategy to end the Bosnian civil war was the first of such issues in which Russia took a decidedly different view than the United States in the post-Cold War order.

Russian opposition to the NATO use of force in Bosnia

Despite its previous acceptance of the US position on international security issues, Russia came to differ strongly with the United States and its NATO allies in 1994. Disagreement was rooted in the question about whether to exercise military might to bring the civil war in Bosnia to an end. In tandem with NATO enlargement, that was becoming ever more real at the same time disagreement over Bosnia reflected a shift in the Russian strategy of bandwagoning towards balancing.

Yugoslavia collapsed into its constituent parts in 1991/92. In Bosnia and Croatia, civil war broke out between ethnic Serbs, Croats and Muslim Bosnians. The longest fighting took place in Bosnia and Herzegovina. The EU and UN attempted to negotiate a peace plan, but this was rejected by the warring parties.

Preoccupied with its domestic transition, the Russian government assumed a relatively passive stance vis-à-vis the Yugoslavian crisis in its first phase during 1992–93. Russia supported all of the key UN resolutions, e.g. Resolution 713, which imposed a weapons embargo on Yugoslavia, as well as Resolution 743, which established a United Nations Protection Force (UNPROFOR) to protect civilians in the conflict. Moscow also supported Resolution 819, which called for the establishment of 'safe havens' (United Nations Security Council). Crucially, Russia endorsed UN Resolution 836 (1993), which expanded the UNPROFOR mandate to deter attacks, including the use of air strikes by NATO and other regional security organizations (UN Security Council).

By early 1994, fighting in Bosnia intensified and it became clear that UNPROFOR was unable to enforce the designated safe areas. At this point, the United States decided to become more actively involved. At a NATO summit in January 1994, Washington proposed to employ NATO air power to enforce the safe havens and force the warring parties to the negotiating table. The better-armed Bosnian Serbs were especially singled out as the main aggressor (Hansen 2003: 119–120; Rich 2003: 558; Rogel 1998: 35); however, this American proposal prompted strong criticism from Russia (Ballance 1995: 223, 237; Rogel 1998: 62–63). But Resolution 836 mandated the use of force under specified conditions, rendering the exercise of its veto in the Security Council impossible.

However, the Bosnian civil war revealed serious discord between NATO and Russia for the first time since the end of the Cold War. When NATO decided – despite Russian dissent – to carry out a series of air strikes against Serb positions around the Bosnian capital of Sarajevo in the spring of 1994 in line with Resolution 836, this resulted in very angry misgivings from Russian President Yeltsin (Ballance 1995: 238; IISS 1995: 95).

Despite this blow, Russia accepted an offer to join the United States and its NATO allies in a five-power 'Contact Group' on former Yugoslavia.[15] This brought Russia back into negotiations on the Bosnian conflict (McFarlaine 1999: 243; Rogel 1998: 64), though this did not mean that Russia now endorsed NATO air strikes. Instead, Russia used its seat in the Contact Group to continue its opposition to NATO military action in Bosnia and attempted to delay decisions, indicating elements of soft balancing in the Russian strategy and that bandwagoning was on its way out.

Despite Russia's opposition within the Contact Group, the United States continued to press for a hard-line strategy, and NATO issued more strikes. In the late summer of 1995, after a massacre in Sarajevo committed by Bosnian Serbs,

NATO sidetracked Russia and decided to launch a comprehensive air campaign (Operation Deliberate Force) to compel the Bosnian Serb Army to lay down its weapons (IISS 1995: 33, 100, 127–128). This proved effective, as the war came to an end in December 1995 upon the signing of the Dayton Peace Accords (Bjarnason 2001: 73; Rich 2003: 559–560; Rogel 1998: 37–40).[16]

Russia remained vigorously opposed to this course but took no concrete action, e.g. by supporting the Serbs with military equipment or financially (Ballance 1995: 158, 163). However, it is clear that by late 1995 Russia had distanced itself significantly from the United States and NATO. By vigorously opposing the preferred US/NATO solution and attempting to delay US/NATO action using diplomacy, e.g. within the Contact Group, Russia was embarking upon a course of soft balancing against the US unipole and abandoning its former strategy of soft bandwagoning.

NATO enlargement

Together with the Bosnian crisis, the decision to enlarge NATO into former Warsaw Pact territory represented a turning point in Russia's turn towards soft balancing. Coinciding with the increased US engagement in the Bosnian civil war in 1994, the American government under newly elected President Clinton had launched its foreign policy strategy of 'engagement and enlargement' (Hansen 2000a). This initiative made it clear that Washington, after some years of hesitation, had decided to pursue an activist foreign policy strategy.[17] This strategy included a continuation of the American continental commitment to Europe and North East Asia and foresaw the active promotion of US preferences for democracy and capitalism (and with it, US political influence) across the globe. The principle instrument for achieving this aim in Europe was the territorial enlargement of NATO into Eastern Europe.

NATO's mission had already been transformed and expanded in 1991 from its traditional Cold War mission as a purely defensive military alliance[18] into a pro-active mission conducting so-called 'out-of-area' operations outside the traditional Euro-Atlantic Area (Hansen 2003: 103; NATO 2001: Ch. 2). While possible NATO expansion into the former Warsaw Pact area had been discussed (Goldgeier and McFaul 2003: 184–185) in the very early 1990s, the US government had not spoken about this option very loudly. Instead, the Partnership for Peace Program (PfP) was launched in 1994, adding a military dimension and increased focus on the purely political process under the NACC framework (Bowker 1995: 82). The PfP envisaged a comprehensive program for closer military cooperation and association between NATO and all of the former Warsaw Pact countries (cf. NATO 2004b). The US government indicated the possibility of admitting new PfP participants from the former Warsaw Pact area into NATO, but made no clear commitment to such a course (Goldgeier and Mcfaul 2003: 186; Sergounin 1998: 35).

The Russian reception of the PfP was mixed. The leadership in Moscow increasingly feared that the PfP represented a first step towards full-blown enlargement (Dannreuther 1999: 151). After reassurances from Washington, however, the Yeltsin government decided to support the PfP, and Russia eventually also agreed to sign on in June 1994 (Dannreuther 1999: 152; Goldgeier and Mcfaul 2003: 183, 187). In terms of balancing and bandwagoning, this indicates elements of bandwagoning; even hard bandwagoning, since the PfP implied military cooperation, although no alliance per se. On the other hand, there was little question that Moscow did not want to see NATO get any bigger.

Shell shock spread in Moscow a few months later when NATO, after strong US pressure, announced that the alliance would be enlarged anyway. This provoked outrage in Russia (Dannreuther 1999: 152; Goldgeier and Mcfaul 2003: 187–189). The decision to enlarge NATO was confirmed by a NATO report in September 1995 that foresaw enlargement as virtually an open-ended process (Dannreuther 1999: 152; Heurlin 2000: 4; McFarlaine 1999: 242; Prizel 1995: 84). This firmly soured relations with Russia. Moscow signalled, as it did simultaneously in the Bosnia settlement, that it was firmly opposed to this US/NATO course of action. However, Moscow had few levers with which to do anything active to prevent NATO enlargement from proceeding; It could merely object. As will be discussed below, the decision to enlarge NATO coincided with active Russian diplomacy to improve relations with China, as the two Asian giants began to coordinate their policies and establish regional cooperation: the Shanghai Five process. This response indicates the beginnings of Russian soft balancing.

Enlargement was a done deal, however. It also initially appears as though Russia returned to soft – or even hard – bandwagoning in 1997, as Moscow accepted NATO's offer of a 'NATO-Russia Founding Act on Mutual Relations' and the creation of the Permanent Joint Council (PJC), which gave Russia 'special partnership status' with the Atlantic alliance. This was not the case, however; Russia continued its opposition to NATO's planned expansion into Poland, Hungary and the Czech Republic, which in the words of then-Russian Prime Minister Viktor Chernomyrdin was 'the worst and biggest mistake since the end of the Cold War' (quoted in Dannreuther 1999: 150, 152). Despite vocal Russian opposition, however, NATO enlargement was something that Russia simply could not prevent, since the PJC did not give Russia a veto – as stated by President Clinton (Dannreuther 1999: 147; Heurlin 2000: 4; Sergounin 1998: 36). In sum, Russia had turned its back on its earlier soft bandwagoning strategy by 1995 and began a strategy of soft balancing. Despite the strained Russia–NATO relationship over enlargement and NATO's exercise of force in former Yugoslavia, Russia continued to develop its economic partnership with the West. This became evident when Russia applied for membership in the World Trade Organization in 1996 (Sabelnikov 1996), indicating that there were limits to Russia's resistance to the US world order and that beginning soft balancing against the United States was primarily taking place on issues of military security.

US–Russian relations after the first NATO-enlargement

Russia's soft balancing against the United States in security matters became more pronounced in the late 1990s. The American-led war in Kosovo in 1999 and Iraq in 2003 in particular demonstrated Russian attempts to soft balance against the United States. By 2007, there were even indications that Russia's soft balancing could be on its way towards hard balancing.

NATO and the war in Kosovo

While Russia was committed to engage in the global economy built on the World Trade Organization (WTO) process, diplomatic relations between Russia and NATO deteriorated sharply in 1999. Again, it was the former Yugoslavia that was the focal point of disagreement. In 1998, civil war broke out in Yugoslavia's southern province of Kosovo. Ethnic Albanians representing the vast majority of the Kosovo population wanted to secede from Serb-dominated Yugoslavia. The Yugoslav government clamped down hard, and another human tragedy was a reality in the former Yugoslavia. In response, the UN Security Council passed two resolutions (1160 and 1199) condemning the Yugoslav Army's use of force and calling for a ceasefire. Both resolutions were supported by Russia; however, President Yeltsin made it clear that Moscow could under no circumstance accept any use of military intervention to solve the crisis (Goldgeier and McFaul 2003: 250). Nevertheless, as the bloodshed continued, NATO decided, after the failure of the Rambouillet peace talks between January and March 1999, that Russia should not be allowed to prevent NATO from intervention (Goldgeier and McFaul 2003: 251).

Between 24 March and 10 June 1999, the United States and its NATO allies launched a massive air campaign against the rump state of Yugoslavia (Serbia) to force the Yugoslav government to stop its heavy-handed policy in Kosovo and pull back its troops (Daalder and O'Hanlon 2000). The decision to strike was taken without a UN Security Council mandate, as Russia (and China) threatened to exercise their veto as permanent members of the Security Council to block a resolution mandating the use of force in Kosovo. This indicates that Russia soft balanced against the United States over the Kosovo issue, because Russia sought to thwart the American security goals in Kosovo by using institutions and entangling diplomacy. Moreover, Russia signalled the resolve to cooperate with China on this issue against the United States. Finally, Moscow suspended its cooperation with NATO in the Permanent Joint Council (Dannreuther 1999: 153; Paul 2005: 60–61), indicating that Russia distanced itself diplomatically from the United States and NATO.

However, in 2000, after the Kosovo low point, Russia gradually began to re-evaluate its anti-NATO stance and sought to patch up its relations with the United States (Dannreuther 1999: 147). The Russian government, now headed by newly elected President Putin, toned down its criticism of NATO's first round of enlargement. In return, it received promises from NATO that further enlargement would be postponed for the indefinite future. Moreover, Moscow was offered an upgraded version of the Permanent Joint Council named the 'NATO–Russia Council' (NRC). The NRC was a standing diplomatic forum for high frequency consultations and meetings between Russian and NATO officials at all levels, whereas the Permanent Joint Council was a forum of occasional meetings (Jensen 2003: 40–41, 51; Mangott 2000: 502; NATO 2004b).[19] This return to the NATO process indicates elements of soft bandwagoning in Russia's strategic behaviour.

The September 11 terrorist attacks and the war on terrorism

Elements of Russian soft bandwagoning became even more clear after the terrorist attacks against New York and Washington DC on 11 September 2001 (Wohlforth 2002b: 202–203). After the attacks, President Putin was the first head of state to call the US President to offer his condolences, also offering Russia's support in the fight against terrorism (Wohlforth 2002b: 205). Further along these lines, Moscow did not oppose temporary US military bases set up in former Soviet territory. The United States established bases in Uzbekistan and Kirgizstan for use in the American war against Afghanistan in October 2001 in order to destroy Al Qaeda training camps and topple the Afghan Taliban regime which hosted them (Freedman 2001; Wohlforth 2002b: 77–78).

Russia thus joined sides with the United States in the war against international terrorism – a war in which Russia itself was engaged in Chechnya. This indicates elements of Russian bandwagoning, though this bandwagoning proved short-lived. As the war against terrorism dragged on and US forces remained in Central Asia after the Taleban regime in Afghanistan had been toppled, the Russian government modified its support for US troops in the area and called for the withdrawal of the US presence in 2005 (Toft 2006: 159). There appeared to be much truth in the claim made by Kenneth Waltz that although the coalition against terror was a mile wide, it was only one inch deep (Waltz 2002: 353).

The news of NATO's decision in 2002 to undertake a second wave of NATO enlargement, including Romania, Slovenia and Bulgaria – and not least the three Baltic and former Soviet – republics by 2004 (NATO 2004a) also raised Russian frustrations (Berlingske Tidende 2004). The spirit of partnership between 2000 and 2001 dissolved, and Russia was back on the soft balancing track.

America's missile defence plans

Another contentious issue between Russia and the United States in security matters was the unilateral US decision to abrogate the 1972 US–Russia Anti Ballistic Missile Treaty (ABM) banning comprehensive missile defence systems.

When the question of a US national missile defence system re-surfaced in the late 1990s after some years of hibernation, Russia refused to revise the ABM treaty (Wilson 2004: 159). Although an embryonic US national missile defence system did not threaten Russia's nuclear arsenal in the short term, pursuing this path posed a potential long-term threat and sent a strong political signal of American resolve to gain a decisive lead over potential competitors (Wilson 2004: 159).

In 1998, when it became clear that the United States would formally commit to a missile defence system, Russia worked together with China. The two states issued a joint declaration in November 1998 stressing the importance of preserving the ABM treaty. In April 1999, the two nuclear powers issued another statement in support of the ABM treaty. In December 1999, China and Russia proceeded to sponsor a UN resolution calling for the maintenance of the ABM (Wilson 2004: 160). This diplomatic coordination with China through the UN institutional framework to make life difficult for the United States indicates soft balancing against the United States.

Russia apparently changed course on the missile defence issue in 2000. At a June meeting between Presidents Clinton and Putin, the two heads of state agreed to a joint declaration which in effect reversed Russia's opposition to amending the ABM treaty. This was not the case, however. Putin visited China in July, and the two leaders issued another joint statement, again declaring their support for the ABM treaty (Wilson 2004: 160–161). And in October 2001, Russia (along with China and Belarus) sponsored another UN resolution supporting the preservation of the ABM Treaty. This united Russian–Chinese stance did not prevent Washington's decision to abrogate the ABM treaty in December 2001. This action was labelled a 'mistake' by President Putin (Wilson 2004: 167–168). Moreover, Russia responded by rejecting the START II treaty that it signed in 1993 but never ratified. The START II treaty obliged the United States and Russia to reduce their strategic nuclear arsenals to 3,500 warheads each and destroy all ground-based Intercontinental ballistic missiles (ICBMs) with multiple, independently targetable re-entry vehicles (MIRVs). This favoured the United States, as the Russian nuclear deterrent predominantly built on this kind of land-based missile. This did not mean that Russia completely abandoned the nuclear disarmament regime (*Kommersant* 2007b); however, Moscow and Washington forged a new treaty in May 2002 (the Moscow treaty) obliging both parties to reduce their arsenals to between 1,700 and 2,200 warheads each (Wilson 2004: 168). This treaty initially appeared to favour the United States, because there was no verification mechanism or any milestones for reductions within the 2012 deadline. Unlike START II, however, the Moscow Treaty did not restrict the structure of nuclear forces of either side. This gave Russia the opportunity to deploy and produce ICBMs with MIRVs – which was much more cost-effective – 'than one warhead – one missile system'. After Washington's decision to abrogate the ABM treaty, Moscow announced its intention to begin production of a new generation of MIRV'ed missiles (*Kommersant* 2007e). This new generation of missiles, designed to overwhelm any US missile defence system, was beginning tests in May 2007 (2007b). In sum, the Russian opposition towards key US security preferences combined with diplomatic coordination with China on missile defence and the use of the UN to do so indicates elements of soft balancing by Russia. Russia's limited arms build-up, with the new generation of MIRV'ed ICBMs, also supports this interpretation.

The war against Iraq

America's war against Iraq in 2003 without a clear UN mandate was a watershed event in the post-Cold War era. Soft balancing was once again on the Russian agenda; and this time, Moscow found new ad hoc allies in Europe.

The US decision made in the autumn of 2002 to attack and disarm Iraq (cf. Gordon and Trainor 2006) provoked a flurry of diplomatic activity in the world's major capitals and at UN headquarters in New York. Together with France, Germany and China, Russia supported a UN Security Council veto to deny the US offensive coalition from having the legitimacy of international law in its arsenal of arguments to wage the war (Glennon 2003; Lemann 2003; Paul 2005: 58–59, 64–66). Although this attempt to stall American action using UN diplomacy did not prevent Washington from proceeding, the ad hoc alliance with France and Germany opened a new chapter in Moscow's relations with America's European NATO allies, who had bandwagoned with Washington up until that point (see Chapter 4). Russia's readiness to work diplomatically against the United States with other major powers indicated Russian soft balancing elements and demonstrated that Russia was prepared to exploit any potential cracks in NATO unity to wrest some US allies away from Washington.

After the height of the Iraq campaign in 2003, the US-Russia relationship remained troubled, not least over Russia's annoyance over the second wave of NATO enlargement into the Baltic area in 2004. Moscow also remained critical towards US interference in Central Asia and the Caspian basin as well as in Ukraine (*International Herald Tribune* 2004; *Moscow Times* 2004a; *Moscow Times* 2004b; *Moscow Times* 2005a; *New York Times* 2003).[20] Russia's soft balancing towards the United States was even hardened in 2007, after the United States declared its intention to set up parts of its burgeoning missile defence system in Poland and the Czech Republic. This provoked outrage in Moscow and was followed by Russian suspension of the CFE Treaty and threats to withdraw from the 1987 INF treaty and the stationing of Russian missiles in Belarus directed at the US missile facilities in Poland and the Czech Republic (BBC News 2007b, 2007c; *Kommersant* 2007b, 2007c).

Russian relations with the second-ranked major powers

As recalled from Chapter 2, in unipolarity, an effective countervailing coalition requires, by definition, the participation of all of the major second-ranked powers. This highlights Russia's actions towards Europe, Japan, China and India. If Russia was committed to a balancing strategy, as the evidence on Russia-US relations indicates it was, Moscow would have to woe these countries in order to pave the way for coalitions to form against the United States.

Europe

Europe constituted a natural focus for Russian foreign policy due to its proximity and economic importance to the Russian economy. European countries would also represent a great asset in any countervailing coalition against the United States thanks to their significant combined relative capabilities.

Shortly after the end of the Cold War, Russia began cooperating closely with the EU – both in the economic and political fields. In 1994, the EU and Russia agreed on a Partnership and Cooperation Agreement (PCA) to cover the 1997–2007 period (Shearman 1995b: 103–104). This agreement was both intended to facilitate economic exchange by lowering trade barriers on a number of goods and to establish a permanent political dialogue between the two (Mangott 2000: 502; Shearman 1995b).

Nevertheless, the positive partnership between Russia and the EU was slow to develop (Broadman 2004; Sidorenko 2004; *Moscow Times* 2006c; Webber 2007).[21] One of the most troublesome issues between the EU and Russia was the enlargement of the EU into Eastern Central Europe and the Baltic countries in 2004. EU enlargement created tensions – not least owing to Russian concerns for land access to its strategically important port in the Kaliningrad exclave on the Baltic coast.[22] After EU enlargement, Kaliningrad would be completely surrounded by the EU and complicate transit due to visa restrictions.

Shortly before the 2004 EU enlargement, however, Moscow and Brussels managed to strike a deal and arrive at a compromise after a series of prolonged negotiations (*Moscow Times* 2004d). Among the major European states Germany proved to be a special European partner for Moscow. The German government promoted Russia's case within the EU, and Berlin also went to great lengths to assist Russia's case in key international fora, such as the G7 and the International Monetary Fund (IMF) (Shearman 1995b: 98–99). Moreover, Russia and Germany agreed in 2005 to build an important gas pipeline under the Baltic Sea (Nord Stream) from Russia to Germany; despite strong objections from the Baltic countries and Poland (Larsson 2007; *Eurasia Daily Monitor* 2007). Moreover, as mentioned above, Russia cooperated diplomatically with both Germany and France, two of America's principle European allies, during the Iraqi crisis in 2002 and 2003. This demonstrates that Russia was interested in seeking good relations and to establish ad hoc alliances with some of the dissatisfied US allies against the policies of the unipole. On the other hand, Russia and the EU could not find common ground on a host of issues, which was reflected in the problems of renewing the Partnership and Cooperation Agreement (BBC News 2006a) after its expiration in 2006. This owed a great deal to the fact that a host of former Soviet satellites had been admitted into the EU in 2004. They had strong reservations about partnership with Russia. Moreover, Russian attempts to build up a political partnership with the EU as a whole on international issues was complicated by the fact that most European states continued to prefer bandwagoning with the United States (see Chapter 5). However, Russia's attempts to forge close relations with France and Germany in general and the co-ordination of policy during the Iraqi crisis are indicative of attempts at building soft balancing coalitions with Europe.

Japan

Russia did not substantially improve its relationship with Japan, America's other major former Cold War ally, in the 1991–2007 period. Moscow did attempt to do so, however. A major stumbling block preventing improvements to the Russo-Japanese relationship was the decades-old territorial dispute over the strategically important Kurile Islands. These islands were conquered by the USSR from Japan in 1945. Consecutive Japanese governments have demanded the return of the islands to Japan as a pre-condition for improved relations between the two countries. Russia has refused to do so thus far (Miller 1995: 142–143). If Russia really wanted to strike some sort of understanding or even an alliance with Japan, concessions on the Kurile Islands question are probably necessary.

Not much happened on this issue until 2005. By then, Russia changed its uncompromising position and hinted that it was prepared to consider a solution resulting in sharing the islands. Russia would consider returning two of the four disputed islands to Japan.

However, this was rejected by the Japanese government. Only the complete handover of all of the islands to Japan was acceptable to Tokyo (*Kommersant* 2007a). Nevertheless, the Russian offer was a significant first step towards Russian flexibility on the Kurile Island issue and showed that Russia was seeking to remove the stumbling blocks in the way for improving relations with Japan. Moreover, the Kurile Island question did not prevent growth in trade between Russia and Japan. Importantly, the negotiations were initiated in 2004 concerning the possible construction of an oil and gas pipeline for the transportation of Russian energy from Siberia to Japan (BBC News 2005).

In terms of balancing and bandwagoning, the Russian willingness to make some concessions on the difficult Kurile Islands question appears to play into the overall conclusion on Russian soft balancing, since Russia would have to budge, should it be able to bring Japan into some sort of anti-US coalition at some point. As in the case of Europe, however, achieving Japanese support for a common stand towards the United States was complicated by continued Japanese hard bandwagoning with the United States. What matters, however, is the effort on the part of Russia.

The Asian strategic triangle: Russia, China and India

The most successful and clearest Russian attempt to forge a like-minded coalition to counter-balance US dominance was made towards India and – especially – China. Compared to Europe and Japan – both Cold War allies of the Untied States – China and India were more forthcoming. China had problems of its own with the United States, and India had historical close ties to the Soviet Union.

Strategic partnership with China

During the 1989–2007 period, the Russo-Chinese relationship underwent a remarkable transformation, from bitter rivalry to an entente; one step from an outright alliance.[23] Not only did Russia and China agree to demilitarize their mutual border in Asia, they also quickly agreed on demarcating their mutual borders; something which had been unresolved for decades. Moreover, the two Asian giants established the Shanghai Cooperation Organization and agreed on a friendship treaty in 2001, which entailed close consultation in security matters. All of this was done in an atmosphere of joint criticism of the United States.[24]

As Russia's relations with the United States deteriorated in the mid-1990s, Moscow's relationship with China improved. This was remarkable, since Russo-Chinese relations had been at a freezing point during the Cold War (Bazhanov 1995: 160). In 1989 and the early 1990s, Russia fundamentally altered its approach towards China and initiated an outright diplomatic charm offensive to improve relations with Beijing (Bazhanov 1995: 171–172; McFarlaine 1999: 245; Wishnik 2001: 799). In the process, Russia made a number of concessions on a host of issues that had divided the two states for decades; most importantly on border demarcation (Wilson 2004).

During the 1990s, the Russian and Chinese governments agreed on a series of arms deals and both routinely expressed resentment towards a unipolar world in a series of joint statements (Wilson 2004). The Russo-Chinese rapprochement has led some analysts and pundits to conclude that Russia and China were forming an anti-American alliance.[25] Although this conclusion is premature, it is difficult to deny that Russia and China have stepped up their political and economic cooperation and coordinated their policies on a host of issues, including military security, and that it was often done in response to US policies (Toft and Oest 2007; Wilson 2004). It thus seems fair to conclude that Russia's China policy contributes to the general picture of Russian soft balancing towards the US world order.

The first tangible results of the improved Russo-Chinese relationship were the conclusion of a trade agreement in 1992 – mainly on arms exports from Russia to China – and the signing of a non-aggression treaty stipulating that Russia and China would not enter into unions and alliances aimed at harming one another (Bazhanov 1995: 165, 174; McFarlaine 1999: 245; *Moscow Times* 2003a). China then quickly became one of the best customers of Russian arms technology (Blacker 1998: 182–183).

At a 1994 summit, Russian President Boris Yeltsin and his Chinese counterpart, Jiang Zemin, announced their intention to build a 'constructive partnership' (Wilson 2004). This move coincided closely with the NATO enlargement decision and could be seen as a move to construct a geopolitical counter-weight to the United States. In 1996, 'Constructive Partnership' was replaced by 'Strategic Partnership', reflecting the ambition of both countries to improve their mutual relations even further. In 1996, Russia and China also founded the 'Shanghai 5' process.[26] The 'Shanghai 5' was established as an ongoing dialogue for confidence building after most of the border issues between China and Russia had been resolved. The 'Shanghai 5' was renamed the 'Shanghai Cooperation Organization' in 2001 and provided with a formal charter and provided with a secretariat in 2004. In addition to confidence-building, the organization was given a role in handling cross-border problems such as terrorism and organized crime. It was also a mechanism for discussing regional and international security (Toft and Oest 2007; Wishnik 2001: 799, 807). Although the organization did not qualify as a classical defence alliance, it did qualify in terms of an entente; the step before an outright alliance.[27] Moreover, the step-by-step development of the organization fitted a pattern of US geopolitical moves that increased American influence and military presence in the border regions of China and Russia (Toft and Oest 2007).

That the Russo-Chinese partnership was about global politics and not confined to regional issues became evident during the 1999 Kosovo crisis. In a classical act of soft balancing, Russia and China concerted their positions in the UN Security Council and threatened to veto the NATO decision to use air power to compel the Yugoslav government to withdraw its troops from Kosovo during the run-up to the NATO air strikes (Paul 2005: 60–62). Moreover, the American decision to bypass the UN Security Council during the Kosovo crisis was followed by the signing of a Treaty on Good Neighbourliness, Friendship and Cooperation between Russia and China in July 2001. The treaty could be interpreted as a burgeoning alliance. However, it primarily reiterated previous agreements already made in the 1990s. What was new was the ambition to further strengthen Russo-Chinese ties in a variety of areas, including in security and defence. Most importantly, the 1992 non-aggression pledge was upgraded in Article 9 of the 2001 friendship treaty that obliges the parties to consult one another in case of threats against the other (Wishnik 2001: 803).[28] This pledge falls short of an open commitment of mutual defence – the classical trait of a formal military defence pact. Moreover, Russian arms and energy exports to China remained at the heart of the relationship (Wohlforth 2002b: 193).

On the other hand, the clause on consultation is a classical trait of an entente, which may be viewed as a step towards a formal defence alliance (Toft and Oest 2007).[29] Moreover, the 2001 friendship treaty and the platform of the Shanghai Cooperation Organization could provide the foundations for a future, more formal defence alliance.

The possibility of a Russo-Chinese entente gained further credibility during the lead-up to and aftermath of the US invasion of Iraq in 2002 and 2003. This American move sparked renewed diplomatic coordination between Russia and China. As mentioned above, Russia and China were joined by Germany and France as outspoken critics of the US goal to disarm Iraq of its alleged weapons of mass destruction by armed force and to replace the Iraqi regime (Paul 2005: 65). Accordingly, they refused to accept a UN mandate authorizing the use of force against Iraq (Paul 2005: 64).

This was accompanied by the rapid development of the Shanghai Cooperation Organization's security agenda between 2003 and 2007 (Toft and Oest

2007; Wilson 2004). After the occupation of Iraq in April 2003, the Chinese and Russian governments sped up their joint activities in the Shanghai Cooperation Organization (SCO), which received a permanent secretariat in Beijing and its own budget. Moreover, Russia and China conducted a joint military exercise under SCO auspices in August 2003 (*Moscow Times* 2003c) (right after the US war in Iraq). In August 2005, Russia and China again conducted joint military exercises in Northern China; their largest to date. These exercises simulated an amphibious landing and involved 10,000 land, air and sea-troops (*Asia Times Online* 2005; *Moscow Times* 2005b; Toft and Oest 2007; United Press International 2005). Another major exercise was held in August 2007 (*Radio Free Europe* 2007).

Taken together, the evidence of Russian attempts at forging a partnership with China with a critical US core points to elements of balancing. Balancing with China was of a soft variety, however; there was no formal alliance or drawing of red lines, nor were there any signs of major coordinated arms build-ups. Moscow and Beijing primarily used diplomacy and international institutions to thwart the United States.

Strategic partnership with India

After some years of inattention, Russia also began devoting energy to cultivating a close political partnership with India in the latter part of the 1990s with a critical streak vis-à-vis the United States. This was reflected in the vision of former Russian Foreign Minister Yevgeny Primakov's of an Asian Strategic Triangle. Compared to the Russo-Chinese relationship, however, Moscow's partnership with Delhi was much more limited.

During the Cold War, India and Russia were informal allies. At the heart of the Russo-Indian alliance was especially Soviet military support in the form of arms supplies and political cooperation; not least to oppose China and the United States. The Soviet-Indian relationship was formalized in the 1971 treaty on 'Peace, Friendship and Cooperation' (Thakur 1995: 226–227; Walt 1988).

After the Cold War and the 1991 Soviet collapse, Russia neglected the Russo-Indian relationship. The new government in Moscow focused its attention towards the West and its domestic problems.

In 1993, Russia began revamping its India policy. The two Asian powers signed a Treaty of Friendship and Cooperation. Compared to the earlier 1971 treaty, the 1993 treaty was far less ambitious. It contained no commitments to security cooperation or even a clause concerning consultations in the event of a threat to the security of either country. Neither did it contain a non-aggression clause. However, the new treaty did call for 'regular consultations on all matters and for coordination in dealing with any developing threats to peace' (Thakur 1995: 225, 239–241).

Despite the 1993 treaty, Russia's India policy was not a high Russian priority until 1999 – the year of the Kosovo-crisis. After the Kosovo conflict, Russia attempted to inject new life into its relations with India, and Moscow managed to enlist Delhi together with China in opposition to the NATO bombing in Kosovo. Importantly, former Russian Foreign Minister Yevgeni Primakov attempted to form a so-called 'Strategic Triangle' including China and India (CNN 1998; Paul 2005: 63).

Following up on this idea, President Putin went to India in October 2000, where he signed a declaration of 'Strategic Partnership' with India. The leaders of Russia and India used this occasion to express their joint opposition 'to the unilateral use or threat of use of force in violation of the UN charter, and to intervention in the internal affairs of other states, including under the guise of humanitarian intervention' (quoted in Paul 2005: 63).

After the 2003 war in Iraq, Putin again travelled to India (December 2004) and signed a joint declaration emphasizing the Russo-Indian strategic partnership together with a number of agreements covering bilateral cooperation regarding space exploration, energy, navigation, visa services and banking (Kabila 2004). Moreover, Putin declared his support for India's candidacy as a permanent member in a reformed UN Security Council with veto rights (Kabila 2004).

In terms of balancing and bandwagoning, the evidence indicates that Russia sought actively to enrol India in some sort of diplomatic counter-US coalition along with China. There was no hard balancing involved, however, as the two nations did not forge an outright defence pact. Moreover, Moscow's attempts to enlist India in the ranks of the disillusioned were complicated by India's own policy of keeping its options open. At the same time as India and Russia revamped their relationship, New Delhi also began to move closer to the United States (Tellis 2006). Thus, Washington and Delhi struck a noteworthy deal on civilian nuclear energy in 2006 following years of American sanctions after India tested nuclear weapons in 1998 (BBC News 2006a; BBC News 2007a).

In short, the history of Russian relations with the United States and the second-ranked major powers between 1989 and 2007 demonstrates a shift in strategy vis-à-vis the US unipole away from soft bandwagoning to soft balancing. Soft balancing entailed that Russia sought to improve relations with other second-ranked major powers and forge ad hoc coalitions with them against particular US policies and to wedge some of the close US allies away from America's orbit (the EU and Japan). Russian attempts at reducing American influence and increasing its own were also evident in the Russian strategy towards its close neighbours in the former Soviet area. This is the subject of the next sub-section.

Keeping rivals out and the CIS onboard: Russia and its borderlands

Russian soft balancing in its relations with the major powers since the mid-1990s was supported by a regional strategy in the borderlands.[30] Much of Moscow's influence in the borderlands evaporated with the Soviet collapse in

1991. Already by late 1992, however, Russia began to demonstrate a borderland-strategy of preserving its remaining influence; and Moscow displayed efforts to regain influence in the borderlands. In particular, Moscow did not welcome other major powers gaining ground in this strategically important region.

For Russia, the borderlands have traditionally been highly important for economic, security and cultural reasons. Being a landlocked power with no clear natural borders, the strategic depth provided by the borderlands has served as a buffer zone for Russia. Although strategic depth is less important for defence in the nuclear age, the borderlands continue to play an important economic role; not least the energy reserves of the Caspian region and control over the transportation network for bringing oil and gas to world markets constitutes a vital component in the Russian economic recovery after the Soviet collapse. The borderlands also continue to play a role for security purposes, e.g. for avoiding instability in South Caucasus from spilling over to Russia. Moreover, they play an important role in a well-functioning Russian 'early warning' air- and missile defence system in relation to radar stations. The borderlands also play an important cultural role in Russian history and national myth (cf. Hoskings 1998). Finally, the borderlands represent the human and material resources necessary for Russia to someday return to superpower status.

It is therefore important to analyse Russia's borderland strategy for understanding its overall approach to the American world order. Bandwagoning would be evident to the extent that Russia would comply with possible American designs in the borderlands and in a comfortable attitude towards its loss of relative influence in the post-Soviet space. Balancing would be indicated by efforts to keep the influence of other powers at bay – especially the American unipole – as well as in efforts to regain political clout in the strategically important area.

Apart from the voluntary withdrawal of Russian troops in the wake of the Soviet dissolution in 1991–92 balancing elements aimed at restoring Russian influence dominated Moscow's post-Cold War agenda in that area. The method for restoring influence was not old-fashioned conquest, however. Instead, Russia applied more subtle and indirect methods of 'divide-and-rule', 'blackmail', and 'binding' (cf. Toft 2006). Russia primarily adopted an institutional approach within the multilateral framework of the Commonwealth of Independent States (CIS); a loose organization comprising most of the former Soviet republics. Moscow attempted to use the CIS structure to bind the other former Soviet republics politically to the Russian orbit. The means were beneficial agreements (carrots) using Russia's key position as the main provider of military security and economic opportunity in the former Soviet space. A bilateral approach was also employed, though primarily towards the former Soviet republics that were less susceptible to persuasion. In those cases, Russia used more heavy-handed methods, including blackmail and divide-and-rule.

The Commonwealth of Independent States

When the Soviet Union broke apart in late 1991, Russia, the Ukraine and Belarus formed the Commonwealth of Independent States (CIS) on 8 December 1991. The official purpose of the organization was rather diffuse, but there was agreement among the three founding states to establish a mechanism to facilitate working relations between the newly independent former Soviet republics in the wake of the disintegration of the USSR. Other former Soviet republics quickly joined. By 21 December 1991, 12 of the 15 former Soviet republics had joined the CIS. The three Baltic republics, Lithuania, Latvia and Estonia, remained aloof, however, as they became quickly associated closely with the EU and NATO. Georgia withdrew its membership in 1992 (Brzezinski and Sullivan 1997: 43, 47; Garnett 1998: 88–90; Webber and Sakwa 1999: 403).[31]

After the founding of the CIS, it became evident that Russia did not view the organization as a club of strictly equal members. Rather, it appears as though the Russian government perceived the organization as a tool for re-gaining political clout and leadership within the former Soviet space by promoting the CIS as a platform for some sort of re-integration of the ex-Soviet republics under Russian suzerainty (Brzezinski and Sullivan 1997: 44; Webber and Sakwa 1999: 384–385, 404). Consecutive Russian governments thus ensured that Russian personnel dominated all key CIS structures, including most of the lower levels of intergovernmental decision making. Russia also provided all of the key personnel for the CIS military and economic institutions. Moreover, the CIS presidency was dominated by Russia, despite the fact that the CIS founding agreement of 1991 called for a rotating chairmanship system (Garnett 1998: 88–90; Webber and Sakwa 1999: 387, 401–402).

The means to make such a voluntary 'binding strategy' work was to use Russia's unique opportunity to offer security guarantees and economic assistance to the very weak and sometimes failed former Soviet states in return for greater institutionalized political influence. In the security sphere of the CIS-framework, Russia promoted the so-called CIS Collective Security Treaty (CST) established in 1992. The CST was an asymmetric alliance establishing close military links between Russia and the CIS member states. In addition to Russia, the other members were Armenia, Kazakhstan, Kyrgyzstan, Uzbekistan and Tajikistan. Belarus, Azerbaijan and Georgia joined in 1993.

Within the CST, Moscow accepted a host of security responsibilities in return for special rights and access to equipment and base facilities (Møller 2007: 5). This institutionalization of military cooperation not only boosted Russian influence (Møller 2007: 7), it also amounted to the creation of a virtual forward Russian defence (Wohlforth 2004: 226). Russia suffered a set-back, however, when Uzbekistan, Azerbaijan and Georgia seceded from the CST in 1999 (Møller 2007: 2), but the hard core of ex-Soviet republics remained as members.

In 2001, Russia proposed a strengthening of the CST by deepening the CST with the creation of a 'Collective Rapid Deployment Force' based in Kyrgyzstan (*Asia Times Online* 2003). This would give Russia another important source of influence, as the reaction force would be under Russian command (Møller 2007: 5; Wohlforth 2004: 204). Moreover, Russia initiated an upgrading of the CST to a formal defensive alliance in 2003 (Central Asian Gateway 2006), renaming it the Collective Security Treaty Organization (CSTO). This further reflected Russia's quest for deeper military cooperation within the CIS framework. By binding a number of former Soviet republics, Russia stood to gain an important say in their security policies and could reduce their incentive to ally themselves closely with potentially competing regional powers, such as the United States, which began taking a more active interest in the former Soviet space after 9/11. Uzbekhistan's accession to the CSTO in 2006 (Møller 2007: 7) was a significant boost for Russia's efforts.

Russia's binding strategy was mostly successful in relation to Belarus. Belarus pursued a loyal policy towards Russia and was receptive to plans to create a Russian-led political union, plans that were launched in 1992 and 1993 (Garnett 1998: 73–74). Russia and Belarus agreed (in addition to the CST military agreements) to establish a monetary union that would introduce the Russian Ruble in Belarus. In 1995, a customs union was established as a first step towards this goal (Brzezinski and Sullivan 1997: 296–297, 306, 307, 311; Garnett 1998: 74). The customs union was extended to include Kazakhstan, Kyrgyzstan and Tajikistan in 1996 and 1998 (Jonson 2001: 101). In 1997 and 1999 the presidents of Russia and Belarus also signed documents committing the two states to form a confederate state, although progress towards that goal has proceeded at a glacial pace (Garnett 1998: 75, 76; *Moscow Times* 2005a; The Voice of America 1999).[32]

In short, Russia was able to maintain a significant number of the former Soviet republics within its political and economic orbit using the CIS institutional framework. This boosted its influence in the former Soviet area and helped crowd out the influence of potential major power rivals.

But Russia did not succeed in binding all of the former Soviet republics; rather, the CIS split in two camps: a pro-Russian block consisting of Belarus, Kyrgyzstan, Tajikistan and Kazakhstan, on the one side, and a US/NATO-leaning block comprised of Georgia, Ukraine, Azerbaijan and Moldova on the other (GUAM) (Kuzio 2000).[33] The US-leaning GUAM group led by the Ukraine argued that the CIS should not be a tool for re-integration but for managing a 'civilized Soviet divorce' (Buzan and Wæver 2003: 412–413; Garnett 1998: 88; Kuzio 2000; Webber and Sakwa 1999: 398–402; Wohlforth 2004: 229). Accordingly, the sceptics refused to participate in the key Russian-led CIS security arrangements and consistently sought closer association with NATO (Garnett 1998: 72, 88; Kuzio 2000: 84, 87; *Moscow Times* 2005f; Webber and Sakwa 1999: 407). This challenged Russian influence in the borderlands. However, in accordance with a balancing response, Russia did not sit idly by and allow key strategic borderland countries such as the Ukraine, Azerbaijan and Georgia to slip away easily.[34] Rather, it applied more heavy-handed methods of blackmail and divide-and-rule to maintain and regain a foothold and keep the influence of competitors at bay – especially the United States.

This balancing was soft, however, as it did not involve outright military pressure or intervention.

Russia vs. Ukraine

Ukraine, the largest and most important of the former Soviet republics, proved the most challenging to the Russian strategy to re-integrate the former Soviet Union under its leadership. Immediately after the Soviet break-up in 1991, it became clear that Kiev was unwilling to be subjected to Russian dictates. For instance, Ukraine disagreed on how to divide key Soviet-era military assets, including the Soviet nuclear arsenal and Soviet Black Sea fleet (Russel 1995). Like Belarus and Kazakhstan, Ukraine did initially declare that it would surrender its claims to the Soviet nuclear arsenal and adhere to the 1991-START I treaty as a non-nuclear state. In mid-1992, however, the Ukrainian government changed its mind (Dubinin 2004: 198–201, 204–208, 213–214; McFarlaine 1999: 243). At the same time, Kiev put forward demands for a 50–50 division of the Soviet Black Sea fleet and claimed full sovereignty over its base at the port of Sevastopol in open defiance of Russian policies (Dubinin 2004: 202, 205; Felgenhauer 1999: 2–4; Russel 1995). Ukraine also indicated that it saw the newly created CIS as an instrument of a civilized divorce; not as an instrument of re-integration with Russia (Garnett 1998: 88; Kuzio 2000; Webber and Sakwa 1999: 398–402).

In response to Ukraine's defiance, Russia threatened with economic sanctions in a blackmailing attempt to force Kiev to change its policy. Russia was in a good position to apply economic blackmail against Ukraine because, as a result of the Soviet planned economy, Russia provided 90 per cent of Ukraine's oil and natural gas, without which the Ukrainian economy would grind to a halt. Moreover, due to its poor economic performance after gaining independence, Ukraine depended on artificially low Russian energy prices and Russian willingness to accept growing Ukrainian energy debt. Finally, the Ukrainian economy depended on the transit fees it earned from the transport of Russian gas to Western Europe (De Nevers 1994: 47; Wohlforth 2004: 231).

The Russian blackmail against Ukraine became apparent during the 1993 negotiations in Massandra, where Moscow and Kiev attempted to settle the dispute over the Soviet nuclear deterrent and the Black Sea fleet question. At Massandra, President Yeltsin explicitly linked Ukrainian energy dependence and the nuclear and Black Sea fleet questions. Yeltsin proposed that Ukraine relinquish its claims to the nuclear weapons. In return, Russia would write off Ukraine's huge energy debt (Felgenhauer 1999; McFarlaine 1999: 237). Yeltsin's offer was a concealed threat, however. Coinciding with the Massandra-negotiations, Gazprom, the Russian state-owned gas giant, suddenly announced that it would raise the price of Russian gas to Ukraine. This move would seriously harm the Ukrainian economy and sent a clear warning to Kiev (cf. De Nevers 1994: 47). Whether this blackmail succeeded is difficult to say, because the United States was simultaneously intensely involved in negotiations with the

Ukraine in order to persuade it to give up its nuclear weapons (Goldgeier and McFaul 2003: 55–56).

Under heavy pressure from both Russia and the United States, the Ukraine eventually surrendered its position in 1994, falling more in line with Russian (and US) policy. Ukraine agreed to a compromise trilateral agreement on 14 January 1994, based on Russia's Massandra proposal reaffirming the denuclearization of Ukraine and a 50–50 partition of the Black Sea fleet, although in reality Russia obtained most of the fleet. In return, Ukraine would also receive 100 tons of fuel from Russia for its nuclear power plants (Globalsecurity.org 2007a). In the final 1997 settlement on the issue, Ukraine agreed to sell its share of the fleet to Russia in return for partial energy debt forgiveness (Garnett 1998: 86). Moreover, Russia could continue to lease key port facilities at the Sebastopol naval base for 20 years, and Ukraine pledged to remain within the CIS framework; though it stayed out of the security structures (Felgenhauer 1999; Garnett 1998: 88; IISS 1993: 52; McFarlaine 1999: 237).

However, Russia did not regain any strong measure of influence over Ukrainian politics. Kiev continued to distance itself from Russia and shirted towards the United States. In 2002, Kiev publicly announced its intention to move closer to NATO with the signing of a NATO Action Plan at the Prague summit in July 2002 (NATO 2002). And in 2004, the so-called 'Orange Revolution' brought a new pro-western leadership to power that made no effort to hide its intention of taking Ukraine in a pro-Western direction (Kuzio 2005).

Russia vs. Azerbaijan

Oil-rich Azerbaijan (along with Georgia) proved to be especially resilient to Russian influence in the post-Cold War period and leaned heavily towards US affiliation. The Baku government thus welcomed American influence and investments in its oil industry (Kleveman 2004: Ch. 2 and 5). However, Azerbaijan's war with Armenia over the Nagorno-Karabach enclave that was dominated by ethnic Armenians offered an inviting window of opportunity for Russia to regain a foothold in the area and weaken Azerbaijan in an act of classical divide-and-rule tactics.

Civil war broke out in Azerbaijan in late 1991. The eye of the storm was the Nagorno-Karabach enclave inhabited primarily by ethnic Armenians interested in being united with Armenia. Armenia actively supported the Nagorno-Karabachi insurgents (IISS 1993: 77; Menon 1998: 127–128). The Soviet Union had almost withdrawn its military presence in Azerbaijan by late 1991. When civil war broke out, however, Moscow quickly became involved as self-proclaimed and impartial mediator. Circumstantial evidence suggests that Russia was not exactly neutral. Moscow allegedly supported the weaker Armenian side in the conflict with money and militarily equipment despite its official policy of impartiality. Russian military units were also directly (but unofficially) involved in the fighting on the Armenian side (IISS 1993: 78; Kuzio 2000: 92, 97; Menon 1998: 130).

Russian support for Armenia should be seen against the fact that the Azerbaijani government explicitly sought to reduce Russian influence and proved a foot-dragging CIS member (Menon 1998: 129). A way of compelling Azerbaijan was therefore to ensure that the civil war continued until Azerbaijan was brought to a humbling defeat and agreed to a cease-fire in late 1993 (Menon 1998: 130) that effectively 'froze' the conflict.[35] Moreover, Moscow consistently opposed a number of peace initiatives, e.g. at the 1999-OSCE conference in Minsk, intended to break the deadlocked situation (*International Herald Tribune* 2003; Ismailova 2005).

To keep its bargaining chip, Moscow strengthened Armenia permanently by stationing a Russian force there (IISS 1993: 93–94; Kuzio 2000: 92; Menon 1998: 131–132). This also ensured Armenia's continued dependence on Moscow's security guarantees in view of a vengeful Azerbaijan. Armenia thus proved to be a core member of Russia's 'coalition of the willing' epitomized in two security treaties (1995 and 1997) allowing Russia to station between 12,000 and 15,000 troops to safeguard Armenia's territory (Menon 1998: 130).

The Russian strategy paid off to some extent. By 1997, Azerbaijan had changed its position towards Russia somewhat as Baku and Moscow concluded a formal treaty of 'Friendship, Cooperation and Mutual Security'. And Azerbaijan remained in the CIS. However, the Azerbaijani government continued its sceptical attitude towards Russia and the CIS (Buzan and Wæver 2003: 421; Kuzio 2000: 92; *Moscow Times* 2004a). Nevertheless, Moscow retained a presence and some political clout in the area in a situation in which it could easily have been crowded out by regional rivals such as the United States.

Russia vs. Georgia

Like Azerbaijan, Georgia also challenged Moscow's influence in the post-Cold War period. Tblisi pursued independence from Russian influence and continuously sought closer security ties with the United States (Menon 1998: 139; *Moscow Times* 2003b). Nevertheless, the civil war that broke out among Georgia's ethnic groups in the aftermath of the Soviet dissolution (King 2004) presented opportunity for Russia to re-gain influence. Instead of accepting its loss of influence and increased US influence, Moscow replicated the divide-and-rule formula successfully applied in Azerbaijan.

When civil war broke out in Georgia in 1991, Russia seized the opportunity and quickly intervened. It did so officially to broker a ceasefire; however, evidence suggests that Moscow enabled the South Ossetian and Abkhaz insurgents to effectively resist the Georgian government troops thanks to covert Russian financial and military support (Kuzio 2000: 97). By late 1993, the Georgian government troops were brought to their knees and Tbilisi agreed to a Russian-dictated ceasefire (Menon 1998: 139). The Georgian government signed a number of agreements that manifested Russian influence in Georgia. For instance, the ceasefire agreement brought in a Russian-dominated peacekeeping force to patrol the ceasefire line. This effectively divided Georgia and froze the conflict (Buzan and Wæver 2003: 409). Tbilisi also reversed its reservations about CIS membership (McFarlaine 1999: 239; Menon 1998: 140). Finally, Russia and Georgia signed a treaty of 'Friendship' in 1995 permitting Russia to station 25,000 troops in Georgia in four Soviet-era military bases for 25 years (Menon 1998: 139). In short, Russia seized the opportunity presented by the civil war to re-gain a foothold in Georgia.

However, Tblisi continued its efforts to reduce Russian influence. In 1994, the Georgian government unsuccessfully attempted to have the Russian-dominated peacekeeping force replaced by an international force less dominated by Russia (Buzan and Wæver 2003: 409; King 2004; *Moscow Times* 2004c). Georgia also became a key member of the US-leaning GUAM grouping within the CIS, and the country attempted to establish closer military ties with the United States and NATO (Buzan and Wæver 2003: 409; Kuzio 2000: 92). Finally, throughout the 1990s and early 2000s, Georgia continuously sought international support for the withdrawal of Russian troops from the country.[36] Georgia was partly successful; not least thanks to the fact that the United States established a base in the country in 2002 as part of the war on terror and provided military and financial assistance almost to the level where the United States may be said to be running the Georgian military (cf. Globalsecurity.org 2007b). Georgia also received US backing for its demand for the removal of Russian troops from the country (BBC News 2004). Nevertheless, Russia maintained its support for Abkhazia and South Ossetia and kept its troops in the country; at least until the time of writing (December 2007). By doing so, Moscow maintained an important lever against Georgia and avoided complete American domination.

In short, Russian soft balancing from the mid-1990s at the great power level was underpinned at the regional level. Instead of accepting the rising influence and preferences of outside powers – the US in particular – Russia sought to maintain and regain its influence in various ways in the strategically important borderlands. This balancing act was soft, however. Russia mostly applied subtle methods of binding and divide-and-rule rather than outright military occupation or open threats.

Conclusion

This concluding part sums up our analysis of Russia's strategic behaviour in the 1989–2007 period, comparing it to our initial theoretical expectations outlined in the second part of the present chapter. This enables us to answer how well our theoretical model explained Russia's post-Cold War grand strategy. The conclusion indicates a very strong convergence between our theoretical expectations outlined in the first part of this chapter and Russia's strategic behaviour. However, it also shows that the ideology variable proved somewhat less important than initially expected.

The disintegration of the Soviet empire between 1989 and December 1991 left the successor state – the Russian Federation – in a position of substantial relative loss measured in terms of most capabilities. The loss of territory was severe and territorial loss was accompanied by the loss of industry and other important economic resources. Most importantly, the Russian economy shrank significantly in both relative and absolute terms. Nevertheless, Russia did not disintegrate and retained substantial relative capabilities compared to most other states.

From our modified realist approach, we inferred two specific hypotheses regarding Russia prior to the analysis. We expected that Russia would initially choose soft bandwagoning. Despite its monumental relative loss in power, Moscow retained a high level of relative security thanks to its nuclear deterrent with an intact second strike capacity, and Moscow faced few geopolitical rivals in its borderlands. Bandwagoning was expected to be soft, however, because the political and economic reforms edging Russia closer to the liberal democratic order promoted by the US unipole first began to take root in the mid-1990s.

We expected Russia to change its soft bandwagoning strategy and shift towards soft balancing from the latter part of the 1990s, as Russia's relative security began to decrease due to questions increasingly being raised about the Russian second-strike nuclear capability and Russia facing an increasing number of geopolitical competitors in its borderlands in the late 1990s – not least the United States itself. But Russian balancing was expected to be soft – not hard. This owed to the narrowing ideological distance to the United States reducing the risk of ideologically generated conflict.

The empirical findings supported our expectations to a significant extent. As we expected, Russia did pursue bandwagoning from the late 1980s and into the first part of the 1990s. As we also expected, the Russian bandwagoning was mostly soft. But it did come close to being hard – especially in 1992 and 1993 – during the Yeltsin government's first years in power, where the new leadership briefly contemplated some sort of alliance with the US. This tends to contradict our model, which expects only states with close ideological affinity to the US liberal world order to opt for hard bandwagoning. On the other hand, the elements of hard bandwagoning were very brief.

Russia changed its strategy from soft bandwagoning to soft balancing around 1994–95. This was in line with our expectation concerning the decline in Russian relative security. As of the mid-1990s Russia distanced itself from the United States and began opposing a number of US policies, e.g. armed intervention in Bosnia, NATO expansion, intervention in Kosovo and the war in Iraq. At the same time, Moscow invested efforts in improving its relations with other major powers which could potentially form part of a countervailing coalition against the United States. Russia forged close security and economic relations with China, in particular, as well as seeking closer relations with India and the EU (especially Germany and France). It also sought to repair its relations with Japan. At the same time, Russia began pursuing a strategy of re-integrating the former Soviet territory under its leadership, thereby regaining influence in the strategically important borderlands and keeping rivals such as the United States at bay. In accordance with our expectations, Russian balancing remained soft, however. The reversal of democratic achievements under President Putin from around 2004–05, which increased ideological distance to the United States did not change this; at least in the period under investigation. This highlights the finding mentioned above that ideological affinity may be less important than initially expected. Despite growing ideological distance to the United States, especially after 2004–05, there were no discernable attempts of hard balancing, neither in the form of serious Russian military build-up nor in the formation of countervailing alliances. At the time of writing, however, it cannot be entirely ruled out that Russia's increasing security cooperation with China, e.g. in the Shanghai Cooperation Organization, could represent intimations of future hard balancing. To be sure, this conclusion on the ideology variable may be premature, as it must be seen against our rather rough measures on liberal democracy.

The main feature in the Russian strategy which our model could not account for was the brief interruption of soft balancing in 2001 and 2002 after the 9/11 terrorist attacks, where Moscow switched to soft bandwagoning during the first phase in the American war on terror. This shift proved short-lived, however, as soft balancing was again on the menu by late 2002. Nevertheless, the deviations from our expectations in 2001–02 as well as in the very early 1990s do highlight the limitations of a fairly parsimonious approach such as ours. To explain this shift in strategy, the personal influence and judgement of newly elected Russian President Putin and the special circumstances and opportunities surrounding the 9/11 terror attacks must be considered. Arguably, Putin eyed an opportunity to re-align Russia in the war against terrorism in terms of expectation of profits related to improved relations with the United States (cf. Kleveman 2004: 167).

Nevertheless, our sparse model based on structural realist logic in addition to relative security and the modifying effect of relative ideology appears to successfully explain a lot of Russian post-Cold War strategy although other social factors are clearly also at work. Ironically, our findings indicate that US policies were largely to blame for the Russian switch to soft balancing. Had Washington refrained from undermining Russia's nuclear deterrent and – not least – remained outside of the former Soviet Union, our conclusions suggest that Russia's grand strategic response to the post-Cold War order may very well have remained one of soft bandwagoning. Moreover, the logic in our model suggests that if the United States continues down that path (and if democracy is replaced with authoritarianism in Russia, as may become the case), then we are likely to see more Russian soft balancing and even hard balancing in the future. Sadly, this implies that we may expect a harsher and more hostile international political climate leaving the heyday of US–Russia cooperation in the early 1990s an all too brief interlude.

4   Europe

Introduction

'[O]n major strategic and international questions today, Americans are from Mars and Europeans are from Venus: They agree on little and understand each other less and less' Robert Kagan wrote a few years ago in one of the most influential analyses of the current state of transatlantic relations (Kagan 2003: 3). According to Kagan, the cause of transatlantic trouble is not to be found in events such as the attacks on New York and Washington on September 11, 2001, or the election of President George W. Bush; rather, such troubles are caused by a fundamental difference in their view of the world and the effectiveness, morality and desirability of using power to promote values and preferences in international relations.

As this chapter will reveal, Kagan's analysis captures an important aspect of European grand strategy in the American world order. At the same time, however, it downplays two equally important aspects. The aspect captured by Kagan is that the grand strategies of Europe and the United States differ as regards the means of statecraft. When should a state choose military power over bilateral or multilateral diplomacy in order to achieve its goals? Europeans and Americans have developed distinctively different answers to this question. However, two important aspects of European grand strategy are downplayed in Kagan's analysis. First, 'Europe' is not a unitary actor; rather, it is shorthand for the various national interests in the European region. These interests are occasionally expressed in concert through the EU, but often they are not. Regarding European grand strategy in the American world order, two positions can be discerned: an Atlanticist position, with Great Britain as the primary protagonist, and a Europeanist position, with France and Germany as the most important protagonists. The second aspect downplayed by Kagan is that Americans and Europeans fundamentally agree on the goals for the current world order. Their interests and values intersect more than they diverge, and they identify virtually the same set of challenges to these interests and values.

This has important consequences for European strategy in the American world order. The particular nature of the European political space – characterized by 'peace, domestic stability, the rule of law, cooperation, the transcending of national sovereignty, and agreed means for non-violent resolution of disputes' (Lieber 2005: 80) – and the fundamental values (democracy, human rights and economic freedom) and interests (Euro-Atlantic stability and prosperity, liberalization of international trade, reducing terrorism and preventing the spread of weapons of mass destruction) shared by Europeans and Americans render the European effort to develop a strategy to deal with security problems in the American world order very different from the efforts of actors perceiving the American world order as a threat to both their values and interests. On the one hand, Europeans are as reluctant as anyone else to accept dependence and American hegemony, leaving them with little choice but to accept the actions of the unipole, whether or not they disagree. On the other hand, the American world order is in many ways beneficial to the Europeans, allowing them to pursue their own particular interests while free-riding on the general provision of collective goods such as security and an international market created and maintained by the unipole. The content of an optimal strategy to deal with this position is by no means self-evident. Moreover, Europeans have struggled to define a common position in the American world order since the end of the Cold War.

On the one hand, the European position after the Cold War appears to defy expectations from balance of power theory. Europeans have worked closely with the Americans to reform and enlarge NATO, and the European Security and Defence Policy represents a supplement rather than an alternative to NATO. The European Security Strategy expresses many of the same goals as the American National Security Strategy, and European states have cooperated with the United States on military action in Afghanistan and former Yugoslavia. This appears to imply that the European states are currently engaged in traditional 'hard' bandwagoning with the United States, allying militarily with the strongest state in the international system. On the other hand, scholars have recently pointed to what they perceive to be a new kind of balancing: soft balancing. Instead of arms build-up or military alliances, diplomacy and institutions are used to balance the dominant power (e.g. Art 2004; Pape 2005; Walt 2002b), and the position of some European states on the war in Iraq, the International Criminal Court or UN reform may be interpreted as evidence of this kind of balancing behaviour. Unsurprisingly, '[a]cademia remains deeply split between' those 'emphasising overall and increasing divergence' and 'those insisting that convergence remains solid' (Howorth 2003: 13).

The aim of this chapter is to explain European strategic behaviour in the American world order. Thus, we employ the realist model for explaining security strategy constructed in Chapter 2 in order to answer two interrelated questions: What characterizes European strategic behaviour in the unipolar world order? And how is this strategic behaviour explained?

Is this model applicable to Europe? Even in the early 1980s, the EU – then the EC – was (in)famously described as 'less than a federation, more than a regime' (Wallace 1983). European integration has been both deepened and widened considerably since that time. Many observers of the region will agree with Buzan and Wæver that 'Europe is developing unique forms of political organization neither by replicating the state form at a higher level, nor by annulling the old order, but by mixing a continuity of sovereignty with new forms' (2003: 352). Even a realist such as Henry Kissinger finds that '[t]he emergence of a unified Europe is one of the most revolutionary events of our time' (2001: 47).[1] How does this fit with our realist assumptions of independent states behaving on the basis of their own cost-benefit analyses in an anarchic, unipolar international system? Neither institutionalization in general nor European integration in particular forecloses the use of realism as an analytical tool. Realists do not view institutions as independent variables causing state action; rather, they often perceive institutions as intervening variables between state interests and international outcomes, i.e. tools of statecraft (Grieco 1990; Mearsheimer 1994/95). Institutions, according to realists, are used to stabilize or alter the cost/benefit analyses of states (Jervis 1999). In particular, institutions alter the cost-benefit analyses of states by setting outer boundaries on the gaps in gains created by cooperation, by formalizing side-payments, and by creating voice opportunities for states to signal their concerns (Grieco 1990: 234). States use institutions to create rules of the game and a stable order in a system characterized by instability and insecurity owing to the anarchic structure of the system. These rules of the game may be used defensively as well as offensively, and they may be created and maintained by one state with overwhelming power or by states attempting to shield themselves from the effects of this overwhelming power (cf. Press-Barnathan 2005; Schweller and Priess 1997). Obviously, different states experience different costs and benefits from institutionalization. It is therefore only natural that they behave differently towards institutionalization reflecting their national interests (cf. Mouritzen and Wivel 2005). Thus, realists are neither surprised that European states continue to behave relatively heterogeneously, nor that the United States and European states alike have used and continue to use transatlantic and European institutions in their respective national interests (Grieco 1995; Mouritzen and Wivel 2005; Mowle 2004; Press-Barnathan 2005; Wivel 2004). For these reasons, nothing should prevent us from using a realist model for analysing state behaviour in Europe.

Two questions remain to be answered before we can proceed with the analysis. What constitutes 'Europe' in our analysis? And which dimensions of European behaviour are analysed? In our analysis, Europe is used as shorthand for the EU member states. The EU constitutes the most important institutional forum and the only candidate in the region for future superpower status. Today, the EU comprises most of the American and Soviet spheres of interest during the Cold War (including the former Soviet republics of Estonia, Latvia, Lithuania, Ukraine and Belarus). In effect, it includes what former American Secretary of Defence Donald Rumsfeld, termed 'Old Europe' *and* 'New Europe' during the transatlantic crisis over Iraq.[2] However, we do not focus equally on all European states. As realists, we focus on the 'big three' European powers: the UK, France and Germany. While none of these states are global powers and each of them has limited capabilities compared with the United States, they score relatively higher than other European states and therefore hold the power to transform Europe's political landscape (cf. Mouritzen and Wivel 2005).

Together, Germany and France constitute the engine driving the integration process through a series of grand bargains. Their combined – and to a large extent complementary (Pedersen 1998, 2002) – capabilities and their central locations on the continent allow them to decide the fate of continued European integration. The UK is Europe's strongest military power; developing a genuine European security actor without the UK would be impossible.

We analyse four dimensions of European behaviour: institutions, military strategy, military action and global governance. Institutions are central to any analysis of transatlantic relations. An institutional bargain is at the heart of the transatlantic relationship. Since the Second World War, both sides of the Atlantic have pursued their interests through institutions rather than military action in matters related to the governance of the Euro-Atlantic area. Military Strategy represents a second dimension of importance: strategies define goals and signal intentions. The EU member states first agreed upon a security strategy in 2003, but as a document on security policy agreed to by all member states, it contains vital information about European interests and likely behaviour in the unipolar world order. Military action is the third dimension, which is important because it tells us about the extent to which institutional and strategic commitments are implemented in the course of war, the ultimate determinant of the survival and prosperity of states. Finally, we focus on global governance in order to identify how the European states have responded to American policy at the global level.

Before turning to the analysis of these dimensions, a brief outline of the general development of Europe's capabilities and foreign policy options since the end of the Cold War is necessary in order to assess relative power and, thus, draw the baseline of Europe's international position in the unipolar era. This assessment answers the first of the analytical questions in our four-step analytical procedure presented in Chapter 2: Were the cases subject to a relative loss/decline? The assessment of European loss/decline is followed by, first, a discussion of which expectations for Europe may be derived from our theoretical model, and, second, an analysis of the four selected dimensions of European behaviour. This part of the chapter answers the second of the analytical questions in our four-step procedure: How did the actors choose to adapt? After the analysis, we identify the general patterns of European behaviour and seek to explain these patterns. This part of the chapter answers the third and fourth questions of our analytical procedure: Do the strategies of the case actors form any patterns? Why did the case actors choose to adapt as they did? Finally, the chapter is concluded.

The baseline: Europe as loser

The 1990s began with a European triumph. The Eastern European revolutions in 1989 and the subsequent collapse of the Soviet Union in 1991 effectively ended the Cold War, removing the main threat to transatlantic security over the past 45 years and implementing the central values expressed in the preamble of the North Atlantic Treaty: 'the principles of democracy, individual liberty and the rule of law'; 'stability and well-being in the North Atlantic area'; and 'the preservation of peace and security'. A year earlier, German reunification became a reality, thus removing the most important symbol of the division of Europe. In little more than a decade, the two primary institutions of the Cold War – NATO and the EU – were transformed and expanded to include most of the former adversaries in Central and Eastern Europe as equal members. Europe appeared to emerge as the primary winner of the Cold War.[3]

Soon, however, Europe's loss of power and influence as a consequence of the end of the Cold War became evident. The dissolution of the Soviet Union left the United States as the only remaining superpower. America enjoyed 'an asymmetry of power unseen since the emergence of the modern state system' (Walt 2005: 31). As documented by William Wohlforth in a comparison of the capabilities of hegemonic powers in the period 1750–2000, 'the United States' post-1991 dominance in military and economic power is unprecedented in modern history', it 'has the edge in every important dimension of power' (2002a: 104; cf. 1999). Thus, even though the enlargement of the EU has increased the territory, total GDP, total defence expenditure and population of the Union, the United States still possessed greater total GDP and GDP per capita, stronger economic growth, a lower inflation rate and lower rate of unemployment than the EU (cf. Heurlin 2005: 140). As exemplified by the failed attempt to create a European Constitution and the general stalemate in many areas of the integration process, the political coherence of the EU as a whole continues to be considerably less than that of any state in the Euro-Atlantic area.

Moreover, American power continues to grow. As one analyst commented at the beginning of the twenty-first century, the United States 'started the decade of the 1990s as the world's only superpower and then proceeded to have a better decade than any other power' (Ikenberry 2001a: 18). Thus, in 2005, the United States accounted for 48 per cent of the world's total military expenditures: $478.2 billion of $1,001 billion in constant 2003 prices (Stålenheim *et al.* 2006: 295 and Table 8.3; cf. Military Balance 2006). In comparison, the two biggest EU spenders on defence, the UK and France, each account for only 5 per cent of world defence expenditures (2006: 306). American relative spending is underlined by the fact that the UK and France are the second and third greatest spenders in the world, closely followed Japan and China, each accounting for approximately 4–5 per cent of world defence expenditures (Stålenheim *et al.* 2006: Table 8.3). Moreover, military spending in Europe continued a downward trend, whereas the American defence expenditures continued to grow. While France has increased its military spending, and military expenditures in Eastern Europe is growing, British expenditure and Western and Central European expenditures are generally falling. Germany and Italy are the third and fourth largest defence spenders in Europe, and both have decreased defence spending considerably in recent years (2006: 320–321). In the first few years after the Cold War, American defence spending was falling. It has grown in recent years, however, amounting to a 55 per cent increase from 1998 to 2005. In 2005 alone, American defence spending grew by 5.7 per cent, or $25.6 billion at constant

2003 prices, increasing the US share of total defence expenditure in the world from 47 to 48 per cent (2006: 301). This dominance is also reflected in the production of weapons. Fifteen of the twenty largest arms-producing companies in the world (excluding China), are American (Surry 2006).[4] In the future, the United States is likely to become even stronger. Thus, in 2005, the American government's defence research and development spending was 0.63 per cent of US GDP compared to approximately 0.24 per cent of GDP for the UK and France, which had the second and third highest ratios in the Organization for Economic Cooperation and Development (OECD). American defence research and development expenditure accounted for more than 80 per cent of total OECD expenditure and five times the total EU expenditures (Jane's Defence Industry (14 October 2005)).

Not only did Europe lose out in relative terms as the United States forged ahead; of equal importance was the European loss of strategic importance and the related benefits. The shift from bipolarity to unipolarity reduced the importance of the European continent for American security. During the Cold War, Europe was the 'strategic political "theatre"' of superpower rivalry (Hansen 2000a), with 52 per cent of American troops deployed outside the United States stationed in Europe during the second half of the twentieth century (Kane 2004a: 3).[5] After the Cold War, the importance of Europe to the United States started to decline. The collapse of the Soviet Union initiated a steady decline of American troops on the European continent from more than 300,000 when the Cold War ended to roughly 100,000. This represented approximately two thirds of the redeployment of US troops in the first decade after the Cold War, when the United States closed roughly 60 per cent of its overseas bases, in particular in Europe, East Asia and Latin America (Shimkus 2006). Nevertheless, considering the absence of a traditional military threat to NATO members, troop deployments were considerable.

The terrorist attacks on New York and Washington on 11 September 2001, increased the marginalization of Europe in the unipolar world order by revealing that the immediate threats to American security were of a very different nature than during the Cold War. Three closely related negative consequences followed for the Europeans. First, Europe no longer enjoyed the privilege of a being a region of unique importance for the Americans as during the Cold War, when Soviet expansion into Western Europe would have resulted in Soviet hegemony over the European continent that would have been unacceptable to the Americans. In the first decade following the Cold War, the Americans continued to focus on the threat from traditional great powers such as China, which was rapidly increasing its capabilities, and Russia, which was politically unstable and still possessed massive military and nuclear capabilities. After 9/11, the threat perception was dominated by 'terror, terror, terror' (Heurlin 2005: 193). In the National Security Strategy presented by President Bush in September 2002, Europe no longer occupied a special position. Second, new threats created the need for a new type of response. President Bush found that the presence of 100,000 troops in Europe was a relic of the long-gone Cold War security environment. Accordingly, the American Global Posture Review from 2004 presented a number of changes to fit troop deployments to the new security challenges by reducing the number of troops deployed abroad and focus on 'flexible forces that can be deployed on short notice to locations in the Middle East, Central Asia or Africa' (Shimkus 2006), meaning further American troop reductions in Europe. Third, the new threat environment had important consequences for American alliance and coalition building. In American eyes, the new threats necessitated a new approach to international cooperation summed up in the statement that, in general, the mission ought to determine the coalition; the coalition should not determine the mission, i.e. flexible ad hoc coalitions were preferred over stable and highly institutionalized alliances, and no ally would be allowed to veto American security policy. For European NATO members, this was equal to a marginalization compared to the past 50 years.

The marginalization of Europe in the unipolar world order was supplemented by increased transatlantic awareness of the issues separating Europe and the United States. For the past 60 years – in addition to posing a military threat to the survival of the states in the Euro-Atlantic area – Nazi Germany and the Soviet Union served as an antitheses to the liberal democratic societies of the West, reminding Europeans and Americans alike about the values they shared. Without them, Europe and the United States focused increasingly on their differences. The different views of the United States on the one side and Germany and France on the other side on whether or not to intervene in Iraq led to an intense conflict between the world's only superpower and the two states leading the EU-integration process. Moreover, it appeared as though this conflict was not unique; that it was merely the latest number in a long line of opposed positions on important security issues, including the proper roles of the EU and NATO as security organizations as well as relations and the division of labour between the two organizations, the Middle East peace process, strategies towards states such as North Korea and Iran, and the proper means in the fight against terrorism. The apparent severity of these crises was underlined by disagreements over issues such as the Kyoto Agreement and the International Criminal Court, as well as the role and governance of the UN and some of its agencies and programmes. These disagreements were coupled with an increased awareness of the many differences between the United States and European societies, including issues such as capital punishment, abortion, gun control, the balance between economic equality and economic freedom in liberal-democratic societies, and environmental politics. Divergences over the proper role of international institutions also emerged when Europe and the United States cooperated in the former Yugoslavia. At the same time, the Western European model of organizing domestic society was in crisis in the form of high unemployment rates and low economic growth. Unsurprisingly, most of the liberated states in Central and Eastern Europe, when reconstructing their societies after communism, chose socio-economic models much closer to Anglo-American societies than continental European societies, and the West European societies began reform processes influenced by American economic liberalism. In this sense, Europe suffered from a marginalization of its values as well as its interests.

The model and Europe: theoretical expectations

The realist model for explaining security strategy constructed in Chapter 2 provides us with the theoretical tools to address two interrelated questions: What characterizes European strategic behaviour in the unipolar world order? And how is this strategic behaviour explained?

Our model posits that the anarchic structure of the international system leads states to worry about their relative power vis-à-vis other states and to become cost-sensitive, i.e. base their security strategy on cost-benefit analyses despite their lack of perfect knowledge and ability to forecast the consequences of each potential course of action. When conducting cost-benefit analyses, states make a fundamental strategic choice between balancing and bandwagoning when faced by a potentially threatening power. We specify these very broad categories by distinguishing between four ideal types of behaviour: hard balancing, soft balancing, hard bandwagoning and soft bandwagoning. In each case, we accordingly assess the extent to which European behaviour can be characterized as balancing or bandwagoning and whether the behaviour was hard or soft. But what determines strategic choice? The asymmetric distribution of power in a unipolar world order creates a strong incentive to balance; at the same, however, time balancing is even more difficult in unipolar orders than in bi- or multipolar systems. From unipolarity alone, we can thus say little about the particular choices of states. Our model therefore singles out two additional variables: relative security and relative ideology, allowing us to specify our expectations regarding European security strategy 1989–2007.

As explained in Chapter 2, relative security affects the propensity of states to balance or bandwagon in three ways. First, a high probability of conflict creates an incentive to balance, whereas a low probability of conflict creates an incentive to bandwagon. After the Cold War, Europe has generally been characterized by a low probability of conflict. We would expect this to create an incentive for the European states to bandwagon in order to focus on obtaining values, which may be used for protecting security in the future. In short, the low probability of conflict creates an incentive for Europeans to focus on latent power, i.e. 'the socio-economic ingredients that go into building military power' (Mearsheimer 2001: 55) rather than military power.

Second, the role played by the unipole in the probability of conflict is important, more specifically whether the unipole lowers the probability of conflict (thereby creating an incentive to bandwagon), increases the probability of conflict (thereby creating an incentive to balance), or plays no significant role in the probability of conflict of the states (thereby leaving the states relatively free to opt for specific balancing and bandwagoning on a case-by-case basis). In the European case, the unipole lowers the probability of conflict by a continued commitment to NATO and the continued deployment of a considerable number of troops in Europe. Even though the number of American troops in Europe has been reduced significantly after the Cold War, and the strategic importance of Europe to the Americans declined both as a consequence of the demise of the Soviet Union in 1991 and as a consequence of the terrorist attacks on New York and Washington in 2001, the United States remains Europe's primary provider of hard security. This creates an incentive for European states to bandwagon.

Third, relative security is affected by nuclear weapons. Nuclear powers are more secure and less affected by the security problems ensuing from the anarchic structure of the international system than other states. There is no common European nuclear capability. Britain and France both have nuclear capability; however, the development these capabilities, in particular in the case of Britain, has been tied closely to the development of nuclear technology in the United States. As documented above, the United States continues to spend significantly more on defence research and development than any other OCED member state, including Britain and France. It is therefore unlikely that the two European countries would be able to compete with the United States in the development of military technology, including technology related to nuclear weapons. In sum, the possession of nuclear weapons allows the Europeans greater independence from the United States than would otherwise be the case, thereby dampening the incentive for bandwagoning, though without creating an incentive for balancing.

In regard to relative ideology, Chapter 2 singled out ideological distance as the most important dimension for this study. Ideological distance denotes the relative difference between the governing elites of the unipole and those of other states. We expect states to be more likely to employ a hard balancing strategy against a unipole with a rival ideology than a unipole with an ideology similar to its own. Conversely, we expect states to be more willing to employ a hard bandwagoning strategy with a pole with an ideology similar to its own than in relation to a pole with a rival ideology, as states with similar ideologies have fewer points of contention and the consequences of conflict are less severe for states already committed to the same values as the unipole. Moreover, communication is easier than between ideological rivals, because ideological language is generally perceived as non-threatening for the states agreeing with it. As argued in the preceding section, Europe has suffered from value marginalization on a number of issues in the American world order. At the same time, however, Europe and the United States continue to share a core of common values serving as the ideological basis for their societies, most importantly liberal democracy, human rights and market economy. As regards Europe, we expect this to create an incentive for hard bandwagoning. However, we would expect this incentive to be dampened over time due to the growing ideological gap between the United States and Europe on specific issues. To the extent that balancing takes place, the liberal pluralist ideological substance of the American world order creates an incentive for the European states to employ only soft balancing strategies.

Europe's strategic behaviour 1989–2007: balancing or bandwagoning?

This section analyses whether Europe's strategic behaviour in the period 1989–2007 is best characterized as balancing or bandwagoning when analysed in relation to four dimensions: institutions, strategy, military action and global governance.

Institutions

An institutional bargain reflecting the shared interests and values of the European states and the United States lies at the heart of transatlantic security relations since 1945. The core of the original bargain was the American supply of defence and money to maintain stability in – and aid recovery of – the European region after 1945, combined with the re-organization of Western Europe in terms of politics, economics and security affairs. As noted by Sloan, this understanding was 'based firmly on unsentimental calculations of national self-interest on both sides of the Atlantic, [but] it also depends on some amorphous but vital shared ideas about man, government and society' (2005: 1). The most fundamental aim was to contain Soviet power. The Second World War increased the Soviet population by 25 million and added 272,500 square miles to its territory (Davies 1996: 1062). As the sole great European power, the Soviet Union had increased its relative power and influence as a result of the war. Upon the conclusion of the war, 'Soviet dominance of Eastern Europe was a military fact, embracing a political reach of which the Tsars had only dreamed' (Walker 1993: 16). In 1949, the Soviet Union also ended the American nuclear monopoly.

The means to counter Soviet power and to contain further Soviet expansion into Europe were a combination of raw military power and international institutions. The military means were the stationing of American troops on the European continent; increased from approximately 120,000 troops in 1950 to approximately 400,000 troops in the mid-1950s, and remaining above 250,000 until the end of the Cold War (Kane 2004b). The institutional means were the Organisation for European Economic Cooperation, created in 1948 to promote European economic cooperation and facilitate the effective implementation of the Marshall Aid; the EU, enhancing European power by promoting the wealth of Western Europe through economic cooperation and trade; and finally, and most importantly, NATO, the primary transatlantic security organization committing its members to collective defence in case of attack on any alliance member. The development of this bargain since 1989 is important for identifying and explaining European strategy after the Cold War.

During the Cold War, transatlantic relations were shaped by the shared security interest of the United States and its European allies in containing Soviet power and maintaining the stability necessary for the economic and political reconstruction and development of Western Europe after the Second World War. After the Cold War, the dissolution of the Soviet Union reduced the costs of disagreement. Stated as succinctly as possible, during the Cold War, the high probability of conflict meant the costs of disagreement were potentially lethal for both the United States and its European allies; in the absence of any conventional territorial threat to either the United States or the European states, however, transatlantic crises can proliferate with little immediate consequence. As noted by Charles Kupchan, 'Europe and America have been fast friends for the past five decades in part because the Europeans have had no choice. They needed America's help to hold off the Soviet Union' (2002: 119).

By the end of the Cold War, when this particular help was no longer needed because of the dissolution of the Soviet Union and the Warsaw Treaty Organisation, it seemed possible that the United States would become disengaged from the region, leaving the great regional powers to maintain stability. This 'back to the future' scenario envisioned Europe as an unstable multipolar region with frequently shifting alliances, military conflicts and great power competition not unlike the situation prior to the Second World War (Mearsheimer 1990/91). In the absence of a common Soviet threat, the proponents of this position argued, the United States would shift its troops away from the region, and Europe would lack a common 'American pacifier' (Buzan *et al.* 1990; cf. Joffe 1984). Europeans and Americans disagreed not only on the strategy and institutional initiatives within NATO, but whether NATO ought to continue as the primary security institution. The UK wanted NATO to continue as the main security institution in Europe to ensure continued American commitment to European security. France favoured a European solution to the region's security problems by strengthening the WEU and creating a Common Foreign and Security Policy for EU member states. This view was generally supported by Germany, the other half of the Franco-German EU integration engine. Finally, the Americans sent mixed signals on the future security order: on the one hand, they wanted the Europeans to assume greater responsibility (economically, politically and militarily) for security in the region; on the other hand, they wanted to maintain their influence in the region, mainly through NATO (cf. Wivel 2000: 284–324).

The United States ultimately demonstrated a continuing commitment to Europe's stability and institutional order. In the first 15 years after the end of the Cold War, the United States successfully worked with the Europeans to ensure the stability of the region. Germany was successfully reunited despite initial scepticism among several European states that this would entail the risk of renewed regional instability. The United States continued to voice its support for the long march of the EU towards 'ever-closer union', despite this entailing the creation of a common currency and closer EU member state cooperation on foreign, security and defence policy. Despite the collapse of the Soviet rival, NATO was both reformed and enlarged, allowing membership to former Warsaw Treaty Organization members. Despite long-lasting confusion concerning which diplomatic, institutional and military means would most effectively bring a stop to the conflict in former Yugoslavia, peace and stability was eventually obtained and monitored in close cooperation between the United States, Britain, France, Italy and Russia in the Contact group for Bosnia and Kosovo.

This stable commitment to European security and stability gave the European states a strong incentive to bandwagon with America on security issues. As noted by one observer,

> if NATO can continue to assure the security of Western Europeans both from outside threats and even from internal ones, why should the Europeans bother to invest much of their scarce resources in defence, a policy area in which they have been content to under-invest for decades?
>
> (Haglund 2003: 224)

Thus, we should not be surprised that Europeans have not formed an alliance to counter American power but instead engaged in a prolonged effort to reform and enlarge NATO as long as NATO continues to serve the two core functions it has since 1949: protecting the national security of its member states and serving as 'the indispensable institutional, political and security policy oriented tool, which is knitting U.S. and Europe together' (Heurlin 2003: 46). The apparent 'triumph of transatlanticism' (Lansford 1999) tells us one important characteristic about European institutional strategy after the Cold War: there has been no hard balancing. However, the development of EU security and defence policy since 1990 provides us with a number of examples of soft balancing, in particular from Germany and France.

Efforts to develop an independent European security and defence policy have been significantly strengthened in the unipolar era by the Maastricht Treaty, which transformed the pre-existing European Political Cooperation (EPC) into the Common Foreign and Security Policy (CFSP) and eventually the European Security and Defence Policy (ESDP) and European Security Strategy (ESS) agreed upon in 2003. The major European initiatives in the post-Cold War era to create new institutional measures to handle the security challenges of the unipolar order include:[6]

The proposal to turn the European Community into a European Union with a common security policy in 1990–91

On 19 April 1990, soon after the Eastern European revolution in the autumn of 1989 but before the collapse of the Soviet Union, France and Germany proposed the most significant strengthening of the political elements of the European integration project since the founding of the EC: an aim, a procedure, and a timetable for turning the European Community into the European Union (Tervarent 1997: 44). The aim was to define and implement a common foreign- and security policy. The procedure was to call an intergovernmental conference for discussing political union parallel with economic and monetary union. The timetable suggested that the political and economic and monetary union should come into effect by 1 January 1993. At their Council meeting on 25–26 June, the EC member states decided to call an intergovernmental conference on political union to take place on 14 December 1990; the date on which the conference on

Economic and Monetary Union was scheduled to begin. During the second half of 1990, important discussions took place among the member states as they prepared for the Rome meeting of the European Council on 14–15 December. There was an emerging consensus on a number of the points in the Franco-German document of April. Most importantly, there was agreement on the aim of the Franco-German proposal: Europe needed a common foreign policy. This foreign policy was to be confined to 'vital common interests' and was to be achieved gradually. On 6 December, merely one week before the Rome summit, the Franco-German alliance reacted in response to the lack of a single European foreign policy voice in the ensuing Gulf Conflict with Saddam Hussein's Iraq since August and the growing European consensus about the need for a European Security and Defence Identity. This time, in a letter to the EU Presidency, they expressed a number of general principles and guidelines for the negotiations on the common foreign and security policy. In particular, they proposed a considerable strengthening of the Western European Union (WEU). While the proposals in the December letter were kept on a rather general level, they were followed by a substantial joint document in February 1991. The core of the document was a formal proposal to create a Common Foreign and Security Policy (CFSP) and to make the WEU the military arm of the EC by making it subject to directives issued by the European Council (Lansford 1999; Tervarent 1997). Thus, Europe was to have a defence policy as well as a foreign and security policy. The United States signalled its strong opposition to these plans and the Maastricht Treaty, which was completed by the end of 1991 and scripted cautiously to avoid provoking the Americans as well as reflecting the limits resulting from intra-European differences. Thus, while the Treaty stated that the EU ought to create a Common Foreign and Security Policy and the WEU would act as the Union's security organization until the implementation of the CFSP, it also stressed that the WEU did not challenge NATO (Article J.4).

The initiative to create a common Franco-Germany corps in 1992

On 21 May 1992, France and Germany announced a common Franco-German corps of 35,000 troops 'to enable the WEU to act in accordance with the directives of the EU by aiding in the defence of NATO territory, assisting in peacekeeping activities outside the NATO area, and assisting in humanitarian operations' (Kay 1998: 127). Moreover, Germany and France planned to deploy a naval force in the Mediterranean. This was perhaps even more controversial, because NATO was creating its own standing force in the region (Dorman and Treacher 1995: 54). This initiative addressed the gap between the lofty long-term ambitions to create a European Security and Defence Identity and the lack of common military capabilities. At the same time, the initiative constituted a response to the ongoing transformation of NATO. During the drafting of a new NATO strategy the previous year, France had formally taken part from the outset, 'but only participated when it became clear that major strategic decisions affecting the future of European security were being made in its absence' (Kay

1998: 61). Moreover, as it became clear that the new strategy would rival the WEU's monopoly on out-of-area missions, France had resisted that this aim should be present in the official documents, 'insisting that NATO should be maintained in reserve as a hedge against any new Soviet threat and not take on new missions' (1998: 62).

The Petersberg Declaration

Less than a month after the Franco-German initiative, on 19 June 1992, the WEU members met at Petersberg near Bonn. While the Petersberg meeting took its point of departure in the Franco-German proposal, it also moderated its practical implications significantly due to American opposition. The main task at the meeting was to enhance the operational role of the organization. Thus, the Petersberg Declaration issued at the end of the meeting stated that the military units of member states acting under WEU authority could be used for 'humanitarian and rescue tasks', 'peacekeeping tasks' and 'tasks of combat forces in crisis management, including peacemaking' (Petersberg Declaration 1992: Article II/4). Moreover, the WEU decided to deploy a naval force in the Adriatic. At the same time, however, it was stressed that the new operational tasks were only in addition to the common defence of Europe as stated in the Washington Treaty (Petersberg Declaration 1992: Article II/4). Moreover, there was agreement concerning a British proposal stressing that the WEU should not create its own command structures (Kay 1998: 128; Dorman and Treacher 1995: 54–55). While this revised European approach was clearly a reaction to the American success in limiting Europe's independence and operational abilities, it was also an expression of a more limited approach focused on filling the voids in the American security order in Europe rather than challenging the American position. Nevertheless, the Petersberg Declaration reinvigorated the WEU by stressing the need for operational capabilities and the West European intention to play a role independent of the United States.

The European Security and Defence Policy (ESDP)

In December 1998, after the lack of European success in the conflicts in former Yugoslavia, France and Britain proposed to reinvigorate the idea of a European Security and Defence Identity within the EU. The discussions and developments of a common security and defence policy continued during the summer and autumn of 1999 and also included a merger of the leading defence companies in the two countries. On 15 November, developments reached a high-point when the EU defence ministers joined the monthly meeting of the Foreign Ministers to appoint Javier Solana high representative for foreign and security affairs; to also appoint him as head of the WEU; and to discuss the creation of military and political decision-making structures for EU security and defence policy. At their December 1999 summit in Helsinki, the EU member states proceeded towards the creation of a 60,000-man-strong rapid reaction force by 2003. The Nice

European Council in 2000 asserted the objectives of the Common Foreign and Security Policy and sought to improve the EU's overall crisis management and conflict-prevention capability in support of it. It was emphasized that developing an autonomous capacity would enable the EU to carry out the full range of Petersberg tasks, and the military means necessary for acting autonomously were strengthened. The organization of the EU's second pillar was strengthened considerably by a specification of the command structure. The military capabilities allocated for European defence were specified, as each country (except Denmark) announced how many troops and what materials they would earmark for the ESDP. Contributions included a pool of more than 100,000 persons and approximately 400 combat aircraft and 100 vessels (Presidency Conclusions 2000, Annex I-VI). At the same time, agreement was reached on future planning and arrangements for EU-NATO consultation and a review mechanism for military capabilities. Decision-making procedures were revised to increase flexibility and effectiveness. The Constitutional Treaty agreed upon at the Brussels European Council in June 2004 strengthened this development by creating a Minister of Foreign Affairs combining the posts of High Representative of CFSP and external affairs Commissioner; by committing the members to a progressive framing of a common defence policy; and by relaxing the restrictions on flexibility in decision-making (cf. Missiroli 2004). This Treaty was not ratified due to popular opposition in a number of member countries. Most notably, it was rejected in referenda in France and the Netherlands in 2005; however, its replacement, the Lisbon Reform Treaty, signed by heads of state and government in the EU member countries in December 2007, continues the effort to strengthen EU foreign policy and security policy. In contrast to the Constitutional Treaty, a Minister of Foreign Affairs is no longer mentioned. Instead, the Treaty speaks of a High Representative of the Union for Foreign and Security Policy; in substance, however, little has changed. The ESDP was interpreted very differently by the respective EU members. As noted by Jolyon Howorth,

> [f]or the Atlanticist members of the EU (Netherlands, UK, Portugal and Denmark), ESDP was essentially geared to solving a serious burden-sharing crisis in the Alliance. For a group of countries less focused on NATO primacy (France, Belgium, Spain and Luxemburg), the project responded to an essentially European logic.
>
> (2003: 17)

For some countries, it therefore represented an attempt at soft balancing against the United States, whereas others viewed it as a prerequisite for maintaining a strong and enduring Euro-Atlantic relationship. The United States generally supported European attempts to increase its military capabilities so that it could act when the United States and NATO have no interest in involvement; at the same time, however, American voices stressed that the EU should avoid establishing political and military structures that would duplicate rather than complement aspects of NATO.

The integration of the European defence industry

Ministries of Defence are the main procurers of weapons. New equipment is not generally developed by defence firms independently, rather, it is commissioned by governments on the basis of a review of threats and strategic possibilities (Jones 2006a: 242–243). Thus, the defence market is closely tied to state interests. For these reasons, defence industry developments may provide vital information regarding state strategy. As documented by Seth G. Jones in a recent analysis, 'there has been a substantial increase in intra-European co-development and co-production weapons projects in the post-Cold War era' (2006a: 255). From 1981 to 1990, defence firms located in EU countries collaborated with American defence firms in 46 per cent of all co-production and co-development projects, with other EU defence firms in 43 per cent of all co-production and co-development projects, and with firms located outside the EU and United States in the remaining 11 per cent of such projects (2006a: Figure 1). After the Cold War, this pattern of cooperation has changed substantially in favour of intra-EU cooperation. From 1991 to 2000, defence firms located in EU countries collaborated with American defence firms in 31 per cent of all co-production and co-development projects, with other EU defence firms in 57 per cent of all co-production and co-development projects and firms located outside the EU and United States in the remaining 12 per cent of the projects (2006a: Figure 2). Examining mergers and acquisitions, the same pattern becomes discernible. Intra-EU mergers and acquisitions grew from 43 per cent of all mergers and acquisitions involving EU firms in the 1981–90 period to 57 per cent in 1991–2000. In contrast, mergers and acquisitions involving EU and US firms fell from 54 per cent in 1981–90 to 28 per cent from 1991–2000. Mergers and acquisitions involving EU defence firms and firms outside the EU and the United States grew from 3 to 15 per cent (2006a: Figures 1 and 2). This consolidation of the European defence industry succeeds a similar development in the American defence industry in the 1990s (Jones and Larrabee 2005/06: 62). One important turning point was in December 1997, when the UK, France and Germany agreed that they shared fundamental political and economic interests in restructuring the European defence industry (Mörth 2003: 83). In the summer of 1998, this was followed up by a letter of intent from the six largest European arms producers, France, Germany, Britain, Italy, Spain and Sweden, to increase the prospects of defence industry cooperation.[7] Further institutional underpinning was provided by the European Capabilities Action Plan, decided in 2001, in order to identify problems and potential solutions, and the decision made in 2003 to establish the European Defence Agency to aid the member states to streamline their defence capabilities to fit with the ESDP (Damro 2006: 140–144).

On the face of it, this development may be interpreted as soft balancing and even as an attempt at providing the essential prerequisites for future hard balancing. However, there is little evidence of this actually happening thus far. Rather, the development is in line with continued American calls for more equal burden-sharing between Americans and Europeans together with increased European defence spending (cf. Missiroli 2003: 5). With only limited economic capabilities, industrial cooperation is one means of increasing defence spending efficiency. Moreover, the United States has supported the creation of the European Defence Agency (EDA), and transatlantic partnerships continue to be important in the defence industry, although limited access to the American market means that collaboration among Europeans is often the only available option. American technological advances create interoperability problems, but the United States is unwilling to share the new technology with its European allies (Damro 2006: 138). In sum, the increased integration of the European defence industry reflects practical security and economics opportunities rather than any attempt to balance the United States.

In conclusion, there have been no European attempts at hard balancing the United States in the post-Cold War period. However, there are examples of soft balancing related to the development of an independent European Security and Defence Policy. Three characteristics of this development are worth noting. First, Germany and – in particular – France have been the main instigators of soft balancing via security institutions. The Franco-German partnership of the early 1990s presented clear alternatives to an American-led Europe. As soon as they were negotiated with Britain and other Atlanticist EU-member states, however, they were modified to a point where they no longer threatened American interests. Second, Europeans have been sensitive to American sentiments. The Europeans – including France and Germany – have reacted in a risk-averse manner, backing down from balancing initiatives whenever the United States signalled that its interests were at stake. Third, the choice between Atlantic and European institutions is no longer an either/or choice. As a consequence of the shift from stable alliance structures to more fluid coalition building – in NATO as well as the EU – the competition between the Franco-German and American security architecture has become less direct.

Strategy

Security strategies signal the intentions of one actor or party of actors, thereby shaping the expectations of others. It 'considers power capabilities, mainly but not exclusively military capabilities, and connects them to political ends' (Wyllie 2006: 168) and specifies 'when, where, for what reasons, and to what extent' force should be used (2006: 174). *The European Security Strategy: A Secure Europe in a Better World*, agreed to by the European Council in Brussels in December 2003, presents a common security strategy for EU member states and was negotiated and agreed to in the immediate aftermath of one of the most severe crises ever concerning the transatlantic relationship: the disagreement over Iraq in 2003. Thus, it may be considered a strong candidate case of soft balancing understood as 'coalition building and diplomatic bargaining within international institutions, short of formal bilateral and multilateral military alliances' (Pape 2005: 58; cf. Paul 2004: 3, 14) in order to raise the costs for the most powerful or threatening state to maintain its relative capabilities.

Two questions are central if we are to determine the nature of the European security strategy: 1) to what extent does the strategy allow the EU to act independently of the United States? And 2) to what extent are the goals and means of the European strategy diverging from the goals and means of the American security strategy?

Until quite recently, the notion of an independent European security strategy agreed to by all EU member states would have appeared not only utopian, but also unnecessary and even counterproductive. From the attack on Pearl Harbour on 7 December 1941, to the declaration by the leaders of Russia, Belarus and Ukraine on 8 December 1991, that 'the USSR had ceased to exist' and the subsequent creation of the Commonwealth of Independent States, Western Europe and the United States faced a common enemy. However, the more complex security order and the ensuing institutional development rendered the creation of a common EU strategy logical: if the CFSP were to function, member states needed to 'channel relevant components of their foreign and security policies through the EU. For this to occur, they must set common goals and agree on how to achieve these goals' (Toje 2005: 118). In the first decade after the creation of the CFSP, however, the EU member states only agreed on common strategies on a very limited number of issues (regarding Russia, the Ukraine and the Mediterranean region) and a few military missions. The EU initiated three of these missions (Operation Concordia in Macedonia, Operation Artemis in Congo and Operation Althea in Bosnia), while others were taken over from NATO or the UN.[8] As in the case of the ESDP, a crisis among the major EU member states was required to create the incentives for creating a common strategy. Discussions between the United States and its European allies over a potential invasion of Iraq in 2003 resulted in a public and dramatic split between EU members. Britain and the majority of the smaller EU member states allied with the United States, whereas Germany and France opposed the invasion. Following this crisis, the High Representative of EU Foreign and Security Policy, Javier Solana, was commissioned by the Council to write a strategic concept.

Does the ESS allow the EU to act independently of the United States in military affairs? The answer is no. The European Security Strategy stresses the continued importance of the transatlantic relationship, and it does not specify the means to act independently. As noted by Simon Duke, the ESS seems more like an 'inspirational sketch' than a full-fledged security strategy specifying actual goals and the means necessary to fulfil them (2004: 460). '[I]t does not really address questions as to when, where and for what reasons, and to what extent the European Union should use force' (Wyllie 2006: 174; Toje 2005: 120–121). The ESS identifies five 'key threats': terrorism, the proliferation of weapons of mass destruction, regional conflicts, state failure and organized crime (European Council: I The Security Environment: Global Challenges and Key Threats), but '[w]hich threats are the most salient, and which should be tackled first and with what degree of urgency is not addressed' (Wyllie 2006: 172–173). Discussing the strategic objectives of the EU, the document notes that the Union has been active in tackling terrorism, proliferation and regional conflicts and that '[c]onflict and threat prevention cannot start too early' (European Council 2003: II Strategic objectives). The ESS notes the importance of the EU neighbourhood policies, but places the greatest explicit emphasis on the importance of 'effective multilateralism', where 'international organizations, regimes and treaties [are] effective in confronting threats to international peace and security, and must therefore be ready to act when their rules are broken' (2003: II Strategic objectives). When it comes to policy implications, the document is general and without concrete advice. It talks about being 'more active', 'more capable', 'more coherent' and 'working with partners'. It argues that '[t]here are few if any problems we can deal with on our own' and stresses that '[t]he transatlantic relationship is irreplaceable. Acting together, the European Union and the United States can be a formidable force for good in the world' (European Council 2003: III Policy implications for Europe). Even though European leaders have since followed up on these issues – most notably regarding terrorism – they have failed to formulate concrete and operational policies and largely attempted to avoid controversial issues such as UN Security Council reform and Iraq, which would have proved ideal testing grounds for the general ESS statements.

Even if the ESS demonstrates neither the intention nor the capability of the Europeans to act alone, it might be argued that it represents a stage in a gradual development towards a more independent Europe by signalling a different set of goals and means than the National Security Strategy of the United States. If this is the case, it could point towards the beginning of soft European balancing of the United States. To what extent do we find evidence of this aspect of soft balancing in the ESS? In order to answer this question, we must examine the American National Security Strategy more closely.

The main goals of the American National Security Strategy presented in 2002 are to preserve the security and superpower status of the United States and to defend the liberal ideology of the United States and its allies against its enemies. In the words of the security strategy: 'to create a balance of power that favours freedom'. These goals were viewed as complementary, because using 'America's unprecedented power to remake the world in America's image' (Daalder and Lindsay 2003: 123) would allow America and its allies to create a world of states committed to peace and freedom with no inherent conflicts of interest. While stressing the need to continue to cooperate with other states to contain the spread of dangerous technologies to so-called rogue states, this strategy also stressed the American intention to act against emerging threats even before they are fully formed and that the United States would not hesitate to act unilaterally if necessary.

The ESS generally agrees with the American view of the present world order and its most dangerous threats. It recognizes 'the advent of a new strategic area' in the form of 'threats that are more diverse, less visible and less predictable than in the past' (Asmus 2006: 23). In contrast to Cold War security strategy, both documents are concerned with security threats from state and non-state actors alike rather than territorial defence. Both documents essentially focus on the same threats: terrorism, weapons of mass destruction, failed states and regional conflicts, although the Americans view terrorism as a much more urgent threat and the Europeans emphasize the importance of organized crime along with the other threats. As noted in a recent analysis, 'the NSS and the ESS share a generally common view of the nature of new security threats, a refusal to accept the international status quo, and a determination to change it' (Dannreuther and Peterson 2006: 2). Perhaps most radically, the EU acknowledges that 'we should be ready to act before a crisis occurs. Conflict prevention and threat prevention cannot start too early' (ESS 2003: II Strategic Objectives).

There are differences as well. The two documents demonstrate the dissimilar strategic outlooks of a global superpower, the United States, and regional powers, the major EU countries. Whereas the European Security Strategy (ESS) places special emphasis on building security in the EU neighbourhood, the NSS points to no region of specific importance. The two strategies also reflect the differences between a 'soft' security actor such as the EU and a security actor with a wide range of capabilities such as the United States. The ESS emphasizes the need for 'an international order based on effective multilateralism' (European Council 2003: II Strategic Objectives), and posits the intention of the EU to 'contribute to an effective multilateral system leading to a fairer, safer and more united world' (ESS 2003: Conclusion). Conversely, the NSS emphasizes a very wide range of means, including diplomacy, public information, cooperating with 'other main centers of global power' (The White House (NSS): VIII) and more direct means of meeting the new security challenges by transforming 'intelligence capabilities and build new ones to keep pace with the nature of these threats' and 'maintaining near-term readiness and the ability to fight the war on terrorism' in the short term as well as focusing on the goal 'to provide the President with a wider range of military options to discourage aggression or any form of coercion against the United States' (NSS: IX). This difference is also illustrated by the different structure of the two documents: the NSS is much more concerned about 'detailed action and tactics' (Dannreuther and Peterson 2006: 13), whereas the ESS focuses on 'softer' – and less operational – discussions of long-term issues influencing the security environment, e.g. economic development and inequality, in addition to more traditional security measures.

In conclusion, the fact that the Europeans now have a security strategy of their own is a sign of increased independence; however, the ESS is not a case of soft balancing. It does not allow the Europeans to act independently in security affairs and presents no alternative to the American perception of international order and threat environment. It is not a balancing strategy; rather, it is the strategy of a 'junior partner' following the general course of the superpower, but seeking to modify the content. The only aspect of soft balancing is the – somewhat vague – underlining of the importance of multilateralism. Taking into consideration the extent to which the Europeans have mimicked the American NSS, the ESS in general is best described as hard bandwagoning as defined in

Chapter 2: behaviour where states adopt strategies to build and update their military capabilities, as well as create and maintain formal alliances and counter-alliances in order to support the most powerful or threatening state (cf. Mearsheimer 2001: 139). But what happens when strategies are tested in military conflicts? The next section considers five military conflicts since the Cold War and assesses the European strategy in relation to the United States in each of them.

Military action

Five military actions since the Cold War have had a profound influence on the transatlantic relationship: The Gulf Conflict, Bosnia, Kosovo, Afghanistan and Iraq; each demonstrates something important about European strategy.

The Gulf Conflict 1990–91

On 2 August 1990, Iraq invaded Kuwait. Since mid-July, the invasion had been prepared through an Iraqi military build-up close to the border between the two countries. This build-up represented a reaction to Kuwait's reluctance to capitulate to Saddam Hussein's demands to Kuwaiti policy change made during the summer. All of Iraq's demands were tied to the poor Iraqi economy resulting from the war of attrition with Iran (1980–88). In particular, Iraq demanded that 1) Kuwait reduced its oil production, which was in violation of OPEC quotas, in order to drive up the price of oil; 2) the Iraqi debt to Kuwait should be reduced substantially; and 3) the border between the two countries should be redrawn, moving some of the most profitable oil fields from Kuwait to Iraq (Freedman and Karsh 1993: 42–63). As a reaction to the invasion, 35 states formally joined the American coalition against Iraq between August 1990 and January 1991. From the outset, the coalition goals were to impose sanctions on Iraq and deter an Iraqi attack on Saudi Arabia, though these goals were modified at least five times, each modification being initiated by the Americans or made as a unilateral American decision (Cooper *et al.* 1991: 401–402). The changes gradually transformed the goals of the coalition from imposing sanctions on Iraq to force it to withdraw from Kuwait and refrain from attacking Saudi Arabia over significant increases in troop strength, legitimization of the use of force by the UN, opening of an air war, opening of a ground war, and finally the decision to destroy most of the Iraqi military (1991: 402). Despite this transformation from relatively low-cost deterrence and sanctioning to outright war, no state left the coalition. Of the 36 countries in the coalition, eight were EU member states (Britain, France, Italy, Spain, The Netherlands, Greece, Belgium and Denmark) and five would eventually become members (Sweden, Poland, Hungary, Czechoslovakia – as the Czech Republic and Slovakia – and Romania). No EU state opposed the coalition or its actions; however, there were considerable differences between Britain France and Germany. Britain was far and away the most enthusiastic member of the coalition. Its military contribution included

43,000 troops, 75 warplanes and 15 ships and was the largest European contribution to the war and the largest British foreign deployment since the Second World War (Bennett *et al.* 1994: 53). Furthermore, the UK was the first country to support the American position, and British Prime Minister Margaret Thatcher continuously voiced her support throughout the conflict. France was Iraq's closest European ally with a considerable weapons export to the country: approximately one quarter of Iraq's total arsenal came from France (Freedman and Karsh 1993: 114). Despite this relationship, France supported sanctions and deterrence in the early stages of the conflict and made a significant military contribution to the war, even though French forces were slow to join the coalition war (Bennett *et al.* 1994: 59). However, France conducted its own diplomatic effort by dispatching French envoys to 24 different countries stressing the defensive nature of the French position and by endorsing a proposal linking Iraqi withdrawal to the Palestinian problem. At one point, France promised to attack only Iraqi installations in Kuwait (Cooper *et al.* 1991: 405). Throughout the build-up to the war, France thus demonstrated its independence from the United States, even engaging in diplomatic efforts detrimental to the American effort to drive Iraq out of Kuwait without any compensation. Once the fighting began, however, France participated in air combat as well as ground operations under American leadership. Germany was the only major EU power not to contribute militarily. German officials continuously stressed their preference for diplomatic efforts rather than military action, and Germany, like France, linked the solution of the conflict to other security issues in the Middle East (Bennett *et al.* 1994: 65–66). Although Germany was preoccupied with reunification and the Germans pointed to important historical and constitutional reasons for not participating militarily, their position met considerable American scepticism (Cooper *et al.* 1991: 403–404). However, Germany made a substantial economic contribution towards covering some of the expenses endured by the United States and Britain as a result of the conflict. In conclusion, the European states ultimately bandwagoned with the United States, though with France combining hard bandwagoning with soft balancing (in different phases of the conflict) and Germany combining soft bandwagoning and soft balancing (in different phases of the conflict).

Bosnia

In 1991, Croatia, Slovenia and Bosnia shifted toward independence from the Serb-dominated central Yugoslav government. This triggered a Serbian response in the form of military and paramilitary forces deployed to protect Serbs in the breakaway republics and to obstruct the disintegration of Yugoslavia. The EU sought to mediate when Slovenia and Croatia declared independence in June 1991 and succeeded in negotiating an armistice in early July. Later the same month, however, civil war broke out in Croatia between Croats and the Serbian minority, which enjoyed the support of the Serbian military. Slovenia and Croatia were recognized by the EU after strong German pressure, but 'left

Bosnia the choice of seceding or accepting vassal status within a Greater Serbia', leading to a deep split between the Muslim majority favouring independence and the large Serb minority rejecting it (Calleo 2001: 304; cf. Peterson 2003: 89). The conflict quickly escalated into a war of ethnic cleansing perpetrated by the Serbian leadership in Bosnia with the support of the Yugoslav army, and the Bosnian Croats joined the battle over Bosnia's future. The Muslims were helpless, as they had no military, and European leaders decided to intervene in 1992 by deploying 6,000 troops in Yugoslavia. These troops had some effect, but were far too weak to lead to a solution to the conflict. The United States was initially reluctant to become involved, as this was viewed as a European security problem to be solved by the Europeans. When America finally got involved, they rejected the peace plan developed by Cyrus Vance working for the UN and David Owen working for the EU dividing Bosnia into ten 'cantons' each controlled by either Serbs, Croats or Bosnian Muslims. While the EU countries worked for a solution based on UN forces and UN sanctions, the United States was violating the UN policy of a weapons embargo against all three groups in the conflict by supporting the Muslims and Croats and took the lead in the NATO bombings of Bosnian Serb positions. The United States took the lead, but it was strongly supported by France and Britain (Lundestad 2003: 250–254). As the conflict broke out, European leaders saw it as 'the hour of Europe, not the hour of the Americans', as noted by Luxembourg's Prime Minister Jacques Poos (quoted in Stirk 1996: 257). While this statement may sound like the initiation of soft balancing of the United States, there was little to balance at the time, as the Americans were reluctant to become involved. Nonetheless, EU success could help marginalize NATO. Moreover, as the conflict developed, it exposed the weakness of the EU as a security actor and the continued European dependence on the United States. As noted by Art, 'Bosnia demonstrated to the Europeans their collective impotence, their difficulty in prevailing when the United States opposed their policies, and consequently, their need for U.S. political participation and military power' (2004: 191). In conclusion, Bosnia may have started out as a vague attempt at soft balancing, but it ended up as hard bandwagoning.

Kosovo

In 1998, Serbian military and police forces killed at least 1,500 hundred Albanians and 400,000 were driven away from their homes. After strong diplomatic pressure, the Serbs temporarily stopped. In late 1998 and early 1999, however, the Serbs resumed their campaign against the Albanians. In response, NATO conducted a 78-day high-tech air campaign without a UN mandate to stop the atrocities. The air campaign, combined with intense European diplomatic efforts, successfully pressured Serbia to agree to a peace plan based on NATO-defined conditions: all Serbian forces had to leave Kosovo, and a NATO-led peacekeeping force would ensure stability until Kosovo had created its own democratic institutions fit to take over (Sloan 2005: 103–104). The Kosovo air campaign represents a remarkable case of European hard bandwagoning with the United States. There was no UN mandate, even though the European allies would have preferred it, and the Europeans, in particular Germany, worked hard to follow-up with a diplomatic effort. In contrast to Bosnia, the Europeans acted together and successfully in terms of diplomacy and economic aid although, as Peterson notes, '[a]n arguably necessary, if insufficient, condition for European solidarity in Kosovo was the Clinton administration's stubborn insistence on it' (2003: 90).[9] This does not mean that Kosovo was without transatlantic disagreements, e.g. whether to begin with a massive attack or build up the attacks gradually; whether to limit the military involvement to air strikes or put troops on the ground as well; whether to strike at the Serbian leadership or the Serbian troops. However, the Europeans did not question the need to strike or the legitimacy of striking without a UN mandate. The most important threat to the transatlantic relationship appeared to stem from a growing gap between American and European capabilities as a result of much more advanced American military technology. As in the case of Bosnia, European weakness was exposed.

Afghanistan

Only shortly after the attacks on New York and Washington on 11 September 2001, the US government identified the Taleban Afghan regime as an important threat to US security because of its links to the Al Qaeda network. On 7 October 2001, a widely supported 'Coalition of the Willing' under American leadership began an air campaign. On 22 December 2001, a new Afghan interim government began its work supported by an International Security Assistance Force (ISAF). NATO took over the command of ISAF in August 2003, making it the first NATO operation outside Europe. Military action in Afghanistan has been relatively uncontroversial in terms of political support, but it has not been unequivocally successful. The security environment remains unstable, which is largely due to the lack of resources allocated by the US-led coalition. No peace settlement has been reached, and 'the amount of troops, police and financial assistance has been among the lowest of any stability operation since the Second World War' (Jones 2006b: 111). After the attacks on New York and Washington in 2001, NATO invoked Article 5 of The North Atlantic Treaty for the first time ever, which states 'that an armed attack on one or more of [the allies] in Europe or North America shall be considered an attack against them all'. Despite this act of solidarity from its European allies, the United States decided to lead a 'coalition of the willing' in Afghanistan. This allowed America to bypass the political and military authorities in NATO, though the Europeans nevertheless supported the American mission and made no serious attempt to play an independent role. In contrast, they provided a large part of the troops in Afghanistan, although subject to American criticism that the Europeans were not providing enough troops and sources to the mission.[10] In conclusion, Afghanistan represents a clear case of hard European bandwagoning with the United States.

Iraq

Iraq undoubtedly represents the most important crisis in post-Cold War transatlantic relations. After 9/11, Saddam Hussein became viewed by some US government officials as both constituting a state symbolizing efforts to proliferate weapons of mass destructions and as part of the terrorist problem. From early 2002, the United States worked systematically to convince its allies that regime change was necessary. The United States presented its case against Iraq in the UN; however, as it became clear that legitimizing military action against Iraq through the UN was impossible, the Americans decided to act through a 'coalition of the willing' despite strong opposition from NATO allies Germany and France.

The public and dramatic split between European countries renders it impossible to discern a 'European' strategy on the issue. France and Britain – the only two EU member states also members of the UN Security Council – disagreed fundamentally about the necessity of invading Iraq. Britain played an active role in the lead-up to the war, working closely with the United States in its – ultimately failed – attempt to convince a majority of UN Security Council members to vote for a resolution legitimizing military action against Iraq. The heads of government of eight European NATO and EU members – Britain, Italy, Spain, Poland, Portugal, the Czech Republic, Hungary and Denmark – also published a letter in European and US newspapers supporting the American position. In addition to these countries, The Netherlands, Ireland and most Central and Eastern European countries supported the war. In contrast, France and Germany used the fortieth anniversary of the Elysée Treaty to express their ambition to see Europe as an international actor, and French President Jacques Chirac reacted angrily when most Central and Eastern European countries supported the American position by stating that their support was 'childish' and 'dangerous' and they had 'missed a great opportunity to shut up'.[11] In addition to France and Germany, EU members Belgium, Luxembourg, Greece, Austria, Sweden and Finland opposed the war.

Three observations suggest that the transatlantic split was less dramatic than it initially appeared. First, though some of them strongly opposed the war, European governments agreed that the sanctions against Saddam Hussein had hurt the Iraqi people without undermining the regime. The French President supported UN inspections and seemed open to military action if weapons of mass destruction were to be found. He even played an important role in securing unanimous UN Security Council approval of resolution 1441 supporting the American position by publicly voicing his support and working diplomatically to secure the support of Syria, a rotating member of the Security Council at the time (Rynning 2005: 140 and 212, endnote 65). The issue for the European opposition to the war was not to prevent inspections of Iraqi military facilities or to hinder their effectiveness, but to give the UN inspectors more time. Thus, the European countries opposing the war did not oppose the American policy goals (to free the Iraqi people and defuse the Iraqi security threat), but their means.

This was consistent with the ESS discussed above, which expressed the European support for the American world order and a general appreciation of the same threats as the Americans while placing greater emphasis on multilateralism and less on military action than the Americans.

Second, Europeans and Americans have often disagreed over the Middle East while at the same time containing their differences in a manner allowing them to preserve the core functions of the transatlantic relationship: the security, stability and wealth of the Euro-Atlantic area. Iraq is no different from these previous disagreements. In regard to Iraq, a large number of different issues interacted, rendering it a special case rather than an example of the current state of transatlantic relations, because it 'involved taking positions on, *inter alia*, the choice between war and peace, the legitimacy of military action, democratic control, the nature of the transatlantic relationship, the viability and future of the UN, stability in the whole Middle East region, and the effects on the world economy' (Crowe 2003: 535). Accordingly, little can be said about the position of either side on European or global orders in general or the transatlantic relationship in particular by studying European and American politics in this area. Moreover, Europeans and Americans appeared equally eager to mend fences after the dispute over Iraq and not let this particular disagreement spill over to other issues. The ESS issued shortly after the crisis reflected a European desire not to provoke the Americans, and the Americans and Europeans ultimately agreed that NATO ought to play a role in Iraq by training to help the Iraqis establish a military academy as well as military headquarters and a defence ministry (Rynning 2005: 129–131). The Americans were also eager to reconcile. As argued by Bailes, '[a]lready by mid-2004 the USA had "walked back" into cooperation with the UN, NATO and the European states – including those which had offended it worst in early 2003 – on a range of dossiers, by no means limited to the need for wider assistance in Iraq' (Bailes 2005: 23).

Finally, as noted above, this was not merely a transatlantic split, but also a European split. This raised the stakes for all European countries and provided them with a tremendous incentive to contain the consequences of the disagreement.

Nonetheless, two strategies become clearly discernible when examining the major European powers: one pursued by Germany and France followed by a number of smaller states represents soft balancing by seeking to create a diplomatic coalition of resistance against the American policy towards Iraq; the other strategy followed by Britain and a number of smaller states constitutes hard bandwagoning by allying with the most powerful state and adapting their security policies in accordance with the US position.

Global governance

In contrast to any of the European states (and any other states in the international system), the United States is a genuine global power with interests throughout the world. Unipolarity allows the United States to pursue these interests with less restraint than during bipolarity. As noted by Robert Jervis, 'the United States is acting like a normal state that has gained a position of dominance' (2005: 92). This position of dominance has important consequences for US foreign and security policy (2005: 92–96). American power is no longer checked by Soviet power – or any other comparable power – in the international realm. American foreign policy is therefore now less affected by external restraints (Waltz 2000: 29). In particular, the United States has been able to expand its foreign policy goals from attending to its national security problems stemming from the rivalry with the Soviet Union during the bipolar era to goals aiming at shaping international relations in accordance with American interests and values – i.e. spreading liberalism and democracy – in the unipolar era. Thus, the US focus has shifted from the short term to the long term. Finally, 'the world is the hegemon's neighbourhood' in the sense that a unipole has an important stake in the world order and interests in most parts of the international system (Jervis 2005: 94–95). In essence, as unipole, the United States has system-wide interests and the power to pursue them.

The global interests of the United States are neither matched by the European states when acting alone or through the EU. Even though the EU has increased its international presence, it is first and foremost a regional institution focused on the stability and prosperity of the European region. Thus, in the unipolar world order, Europe must 'work hard' to maintain the strong American military presence in the region and accept that a) other states and regions compete with Europe for attention and support from the unipole; and b) Europe must increase its own contribution to the security of the region, as the United States has a more limited interest in the region than during bipolarity (cf. Hansen 2000a). At the same time, the system-wide interests of the unipole mean that the United States is highly unlikely to abandon Europe. The United States will remain, but it will not always listen.

'The United States', as noted by Smith and Steffenson, 'has always been the most "significant other" of the European integration project in the world arena' (Smith and Steffenson 2005: 343). When it comes to the specific content of the current world order, the EU member states work closely with the United States on a number of issues but disagree on others. Here we examine European behaviour concerning the global security order and the global economic order, because these are the two issue areas with greatest importance for the security and survival of states.

Global security order

Europeans and Americans have a long history of cooperating on global security issues including, most prominently, the two world wars in the first half of the twentieth century and the subsequent Cold War conflict with the Soviet Union. Cooperation has continued and even intensified on some issues in the unipolar world order. Both during and after the Cold War, Europeans and Americans have typically cooperated either through NATO or the UN supplemented by coalitions outside these institutions. NATO was the cornerstone of transatlantic security cooperation during the Cold War. After the dissolution of the Soviet Union, NATO was transformed and expanded. Membership increased from 16 to 19 to 26 states. Moreover, despite their differences, Europeans and Americans agreed to transform the organization to conduct out-of-area missions and focus on a broader range of security challenges, in particular after 9/11. Transatlantic cooperation in NATO was supplemented by cooperation in the UN. The United States played a decisive role in the creation of the UN, and France, the UK and a number of small European countries were also founding members of the organization, which the United States dominated in its first 15 years existence. Over time, however, a number of divergences made an impact on the US-European relationship as regards the global security order. Prominent examples include the 1956 Suez crisis and Israel's foreign policy (in particular in the 1973 October war) in the Middle East and the Vietnam War in East Asia, as well as differences over which strategies to pursue towards the Soviet Union (cf. Gordon and Shapiro 2004: 23–31).

Nevertheless, cooperation continued. The beginning of the unipolar era witnessed a surge in US-European cooperation on conflict resolution and humanitarian issues, though cooperation in the UN suffered from the subsequent decline in American willingness to pursue many of their security interests through the UN. Still, even though the George W. Bush administration proved to be 'fundamentally suspicious of treaty-based approaches to the promotion of international security' (Malone 2003: 91), the American and European commitments continue to the institution as a central forum for debates on global security and occasionally also as a tool for action (Personal interview with Helle Dale). Informal consultations between the United States and major European powers have always been part of the relationship, with Britain enjoying a privileged role often described as a 'special relationship'. During the Cold War, the United States, Britain, France and Germany met to discuss Berlin issues. After the Cold War, the four powers have cooperated on nuclear diplomacy with Iran (Cameron 2006: 59–60) and in the Contact Group for Bosnia and Kosovo, also including Russia and Italy, which took over after the failure of the UN and the EU in the Balkan conflicts in the 1990s (Wivel 2005b: 400).

Despite continued cooperation on global security, Europeans have challenged the US position on three different issues. First, Europeans have adopted a different stance on multilateralism in global security affairs. The Europeans consistently and uniformly stress the importance of multilateralism. They point out that in the ESS, they 'are committed to dealing peacefully with disputes and cooperating through common institutions' (ESS 2003: Introduction) and underline their intention to 'contribute to an effective multilateral system leading to a fairer, safer and more united world' (ESS 2003: Conclusion). Multilateralism may not always be possible – as in the case of Kosovo 1999 – but acting outside international law and institutions is the exception, not the rule. The NSS sees a more limited role for international institutions: the United States will rely on international organizations '[w]herever possible' (NSS: III Strengthen Alliances to Defeat Global Terrorism and Work to Prevent Attacks Against Us and Our Friends), but will always be ready to take over when they fail and American leadership and capabilities are needed. As noted by Cameron, '[i]nternational institutions are presented as playing a mere supporting role' (2006: 51). The differences should not be overemphasized. The two first American presidents in the unipolar era both supported the role of strong international institutions in the international security order. The Bush Senior and Clinton administrations both 'sought to improve US relations with the UN and other multilateral institutions' and the Bush Senior administration even positioned the UN Security Council 'at the centre of its vision of a New World Order, and obtained UN support for both the 1991 Gulf War and its 1992 decision to commit US troops to a humanitarian intervention in Somalia' (Pollack 2003a: 121). The Clinton administration played a decisive role in the enlargement of NATO, and although the United States has remained critical of aspects of the UN, they continue as the organization's greatest single sponsor and play an active role in the NATO reform process.

Europeans have also challenged the relatively narrow American military approach to security problems with a more comprehensive approach stressing a long list of different measures inside and outside the military sector as important for the future of global and regional security. Thus, EU enlargement was perceived by EU member states as a means of projecting the stability and security of Western Europe to Central and Eastern Europe, thereby contributing positively to the global post-Cold War security order. Also, 'Europeans have preferred to offer states accused of supporting terrorism positive incentives to reform their behaviour. Trade, diplomacy and cultural contacts have been viewed as more likely instruments than the threatened use of force to modify the errant behaviour of governments in countries such as Libya, Iran and Syria during the 1990s' (Rees and Aldrich 2005: 915). This broad security agenda is also reflected in the issues promoted by the EU member states when acting as a bloc in the UN (cf. Laatikainen 2003). Again, the differences should not be overemphasized. The NSS stresses that the United States is willing to support 'moderate and modern governing' as part of its policy against terrorism creating liberal and democratic societies (NSS: VII), and support for economic growth and free trade (NSS: VI) are each awarded an entire chapter in the NSS.

Finally, Europeans have challenged the American approach to the war on terror. This difference largely follows from the two preceding differences. In the war on terror, the United States views the contribution from international organizations as marginal and sometimes potentially damaging the effectiveness of American policy, although they acknowledge the importance of their allies, e.g. Canada and European countries. The American administration strives to produce a 'balance of power that favours freedom' (NSS: I) and 'will not hesitate to act alone' (NSS: III), sometimes pre-emptively, if American security interests are threatened. As argued by Sean Molloy, this puts the Europeans in a difficult position, because 'the Bush administration has on one hand offered the European Union a place at the centre of the war on terror, while at the same time insisting on America's right to act unilaterally and pre-emptively. The European Union thus has been caught between its advocacy of the rule of law in global politics and its support for America in the fight against terrorism' (Molloy 2006: 70). The European reaction to this situation has – perhaps not surprisingly – been mixed. On the one hand, Europeans have presented a shared vision in the ESS for fighting terrorism by arguing that the threat from terrorism requires a response based on 'a mixture of intelligence, police, judicial, military and other means' (European Council 2003: II Strategic Objectives). Conversely, Europeans have done little to make these very general directions operational let alone allocating the necessary means for their implementation. Furthermore, as noted above, the ESS does not present an alternative vision from the American NSS; rather, it merely presents a modification of some of its points. The individual states have therefore been left to balance or bandwagon with the United States on a case-by-case basis.

To what extent may the European challenges to global American security governance be perceived as a case of balancing? Clearly, no hard balancing has taken place, as the Europeans have failed to establish a military alliance. The emphasis on multilateralism and a less hierarchical order of means may be seen as a case of soft balancing of the present American security strategy, particularly regarding the war on terror. Nevertheless, the lack of detail in the vision and the lack of resources allocated to achieve it severely limits its prospects of success to the extent that such an alternative vision exists. In sum, European behaviour can hardly be regarded as soft balancing of global American security governance in general, but rather as soft balancing of particular aspects of this order attempting to modify the American strategy rather than replacing American dominance.

Global economic order

The transatlantic relationship constitutes a cornerstone in the global economic order of central importance to long-term European security interests. A number of high profile trade disputes over e.g. steel, export subsidies, anti-dumping and genetically modified organisms have not prevented a dramatic increase in transatlantic trade and economic cooperation in the unipolar era. Despite the extensive media coverage of these disputes, they only represent 2 per cent of total transatlantic trade according to an estimate from the European Commission (Europa – Internetportalen til EU (2007)). The EU and United States combined account for approximately 50 per cent of global GDP and world trade, and the two are now each others' most important trading partners since a doubling of the volume of transatlantic trade in the 1990s (Pollack 2003b: 67). The United States and EU are the primary actors in international trade negotiations. This became evident in the Tokyo Round of General Agreement on Tariffs and Trade (GATT) negotiations 1973–79 (Grieco 1990), in the Uruguay Round negotiations 1986–93 (Piening 1997: Chapter 1), and has been the case right until the most recent WTO trade negotiations. EU exports to the United States after the turn of the millennium have become more constant with a small reduction of exports from 2002 to 2003 and a steady rise from 2003 to 2005. EU exports currently amount to approximately €250,000 billion, as was the case in 2001. US exports to the EU have been falling from around €180,000 billion in 2001 to around €150,000 billion in 2005, although exports have been rising moderately since 2003 (European Commission (2007)). In addition to trade, the mutually high levels of direct foreign investments secure around 3.5 million jobs in the EU and roughly the same number in the United States (Pollack 2003b: 67).

The transatlantic economic relationship is highly institutionalized, and the EU has generally supported the long-term American goal of creating a market place in Europe, the transatlantic area and globally. In the 1970s and 1980s, a number of US congressional leaders promoted the notion of a Transatlantic Free Trade Area, and the idea gained momentum in the early 1990s as a consequence of the successful Uruguay Round negotiations of GATT, the end of the Cold War, and increased regional cooperation in Europe and the Americas (Duesterberg 1995; cf. Soskice 1998; Reinicke 1996). A transatlantic free trade area has yet to materialize, but the EU and the United States have both continued to pursue a strategy of ever-deeper institutionalization. The creation of the World Trade Organization was a result of the Uruguay Round, which also reduced tariffs and made important progress in contentious areas such as agriculture, telecommunications and heavy electrical equipment (Duesterberg 1995: 253). Negotiations continued, leading to agreements in 1997 on telecommunications services, information technology products and financial services. The WTO has agreements for goods, services and intellectual property as well as a dispute settlement mechanism, which dealt with approximately 300 cases in its first eight years, the same number as the total number of cases dealt with by GATT during its entire existence (1947–94), and the approximately 150 WTO members now cover 97 per cent of world trade (World Trade Organisation). The EU and the United States have been the main actors in developing the organization and have been on the same side for most of the recent unsuccessful Doha Round, attempting to negotiate an opening of agricultural and manufacturing markets, although the breakdown of negotiations in July 2006 led to mutual accusations between the United States and Europe over who was to blame for the failure (BBC NEWS 2006b). In addition to the United States and EU playing central roles in the WTO, there has also 'been a dramatic increase in both formal and informal co-operation among the authorities of the US and the EU, in the framework of agreements such as the 1995 New Transatlantic Agenda (NTA) and the 1998 Transatlantic Economic Partnership (TEP)' (Pollack 2003b: 81). In regard to economic development in the Third World, Europeans and Americans basically agree on the policies of international financial institutions, the World Bank and the International Monetary Fund. Both organizations are heavily influenced by the United States (Woods 2003), but there is no European attempt to create alternative institutions or speak with a single voice in an institution such as the IMF (cf. Smaghi 2004). In conclusion, there is no evidence of balancing in regard to global economic governance. The EU and the United States have agreed on the basic contours of liberal economic orders in the transatlantic area and on a global scale, and the EU member states have accepted US economic leadership in the global order while cooperating more equally with America in the transatlantic area.

In conclusion, Europeans have bandwagoned consistently with the United States in regard to the global economic order and only balanced softly on particular aspects of the global security order. This very limited use of balancing strategies is not necessarily characteristic of issue areas with less impact on the security and survival of states. Thus, in regard to global politics on human rights and the environment, European states have balanced the American position in a number of high-profile cases. One of the most controversial was the negotiations on the International Criminal Court, where

> differences of opinion arose between the United States and most EU member states in several areas: the crimes and penalties that would be included in the statute, the court's jurisdiction, the court's rules and proce-dures, the ability of the prosecutor to initiate cases, the role of the [United Nations Security Council], and most critically, specific protections for American military personnel.
>
> (Mowle 2004: 90)

In the final negotiations in 1998, most EU member states participated in the group of 'like-minded' states favouring a court with universal jurisdiction and an independent prosecutor, leaving the United States isolated with only six other states to oppose the court. In regard to the environment, as regards the Kyoto Protocol on the emission of greenhouse gases, the Europeans took a strong stand against the American position and profiled themselves as the protectors of the environment (cf. 2004: 70–77). After prolonged negotiations, the United States eventually signed the protocol in 1998, but announced in 2001 that they would not ratify it. This resulted in a strong reaction from the EU stressing the import-ance of the protocol and the European commitment to its goals (2004: 75).[12] Nonetheless, the high-profile transatlantic disagreements over the International Criminal Court and the Kyoto Agreement are marginal compared to the wide and strong European support for the American world order.

Explaining European grand strategy

The analysis has thus far yielded the following results:

- Bandwagoning has dominated over balancing in the European strategy. Bandwagoning is the general rule for European behaviour in the American world order; balancing is the exception.
- There is no evidence of hard balancing, but there is evidence of soft balancing by European states. Soft balancing is discernible in regard to the development of European security institutions, military action and global governance.

- Soft balancing has rarely questioned the basic institutional or diplomatic structures in the Euro-Atlantic relationship; it has mainly been confined to issues without direct importance for the security and survival of the states. When soft balancing has touched directly on issues of central importance for security and survival, the balancers have been extremely attentive to American reactions.
- France (in particular) and Germany have been the main soft balancers of American power in Europe.

These results are generally in accordance with the theoretical expectations derived from our realist model for explaining security strategy. This section aims to discuss and explain each of these results by applying the model.

The dominance of bandwagoning over balancing

Balancing is always difficult due to the collective action problem in anarchy: even if all states except the unipole wish for a balancing effort, they all have an incentive to pass the buck and allow someone else to endure the costs of balancing. In a unipolar world, this problem is exacerbated by two factors playing a particularly important role for Europe in the current order. First, in international relations, power and incentive tends to wane with distance (Boulding 1962: Ch. 12). As noted by Wohlforth, '[b]ecause power – especially the power to take and hold territory – is difficult to project over long distances, the most salient threats and opportunities tend to be nearby' (2002a: 102; cf. Mearsheimer 2001; Mouritzen 1998). The current unipole, the United States, is located with the Pacific Ocean to the West, the Atlantic Ocean to the East, Canada to the North and Mexico to the South. The European continent is far away and subject to the 'stopping power of water' (Mearsheimer 2001). Although troops are stationed on the European continent, these numbers have been significantly reduced, and the US government has signalled intention to reduce their number even further. For these reasons, the United States only poses a remote military threat to any state on the European continent. This is particularly true of the states that are not poles, because unlike the poles, they can do little to change their threat environment by military conquest or strategies of political and economic dominance (Mouritzen and Wivel 2005: 17). Thus, many of the states that are not poles will be too concerned with their immediate vicinity to engage in systemic balancing. Second, the relative power of the unipole renders the costs of balancing high and the potential benefits doubtful. This is particularly important in the current era of unipolarity, due to the overwhelming capabilities of the United States. In sum, general difficulties of balancing in international anarchy were exacerbated by the specific characteristics of the American world order and the position of Europe within this order.

In order to explain why European states chose to adapt to the American world order through a bandwagoning strategy, we must consider the effects of relative security. Throughout the post-Cold War period, the United States has continued as Europe's most important 'ally and protector' (Art 2004: 180) – both before and after 9/11 – thereby exercising a significant positive impact on the relative security of Europe. This impact is increased by the role of the United States as the guardian of the present world order, which is much more in accordance with European interests and values than any likely alternative. Even though US foreign policy after the Cold War has gradually become assertive of American national interests in relations with allies, this assertiveness has not jeopardized the role of the United States as the most important guarantor of European relative security. In the first few years after the Cold War, the United States made economic security an important foreign policy concern and applied the zero-sum logic prominent in the military competition in the Cold War to the economic sector. This assertiveness in foreign economic policy was combined with reassurance of allies of continued US commitment to their security (Mastanduno 1999). At the same time, however, the United States gradually asserted its national security interests more vigorously, even when they differed from the interests of its allies. This was evident in the Clinton administration's policy of 'multilateral when you can, unilateral when you must' and more recently Defence Secretary Rumsfeld's statement that it's the mission that determines the coalition and not the coalition that determines the mission.[13] This view of the world is expressed systematically throughout the 2002 NSS. As noted by Wyllie,

> [t]he phrases 'coalitions of the willing' and 'mission-based coalitions' are used almost in passing in the NSS, but from the context the signal is clear. In matters of high national security, the United States will not be denied the utility of coalition support because of the institutional constraints of formal collective defence or security arrangements out of kilter with the realities of contemporary global threats.
>
> (Wyllie 2006: 171)

As shown in the analysis, however, this approach to global security has not basically challenged the continued American commitment to NATO and European security.

The 'relative power' and 'relative security' incentives not to balance in the current order are amplified by 'relative ideology' incentives. The ideological distance between the governing elites of the United States and Europe is short. As noted by Robert Lieber, 'Europe and the United States continue to share basic values, including liberal democracy, open economies (albeit in different variations), the rule of law, the dignity of the individual, and Western notions of morality and rationality' (2005: 92). Thus, in this respect, '[i]t makes sense to speak of a Western *community* precisely because the Atlantic democracies share a political space grounded in common values and a common identity' (Kupchan 1998: 68). These shared values have often been translated into common international action as reflected in the close cooperation of Europe and the United States on economic and security issues. For instance, Europe has been a close

American ally in the IMF, G8 and the WTO and generally supported American-led economic globalization based on the principles of free trade and market economy. Europe and the United States have cooperated closely on the spread of human rights and democracy by institutional means – awarding the EU and NATO membership to states in Central and Eastern Europe complying with these basic liberal values – by economic means – linking foreign aid as well as economic sanctions to the implementation of basic values – and by military means – by bombing the Milosevic regime in Serbia and the Taleban regime in Afghanistan and engaging in a number of acts of humanitarian intervention after the Cold War. Moreover, over the past three decades, the ideological distance between Europe and the United States has been shrinking; not growing. In Central and Eastern Europe, Communist regimes were replaced with liberal democracy as a result of the end of the Cold War. In Western Europe, socialist ideas played an important role in the construction of the welfare state in the 1960s and 1970s, but social democratic parties have since come to embrace the market economy; most vigorously in Britain. Communist parties previously prominent in some western European countries have lost political influence and voter support.

The absence of hard balancing and presence of soft balancing

There is no evidence of hard balancing by European states. In regard to external balancing, EU member states have made significant progress in developing a European Security and Defence Policy, but this development has been closely coupled to the development of NATO and mostly focused on developing 'soft' capabilities. The emphasis has been on institutional and diplomatic capabilities, not military capabilities. Therefore, it is not an alternative alliance. In regard to internal balancing, European defence spending has been stable after the Cold War, even falling recently in Western Europe. Thus, there is also little evidence of internal balancing. This is in accordance with our expectations, as long as the United States continues as the main provider of hard security to the major European states.

Although the particular incentives for Europeans to balance hard against the United States in the current world order are weak, unipolarity generally creates strong incentives for states to balance the unipole. The highly asymmetric distribution of power provides strong incentive for states to pursue balancing strategies, because no pole is potentially more dangerous than a unipole. The most fundamental reason for this is the anarchic structure of the international system, which means that states in international anarchy face a '911 problem' in the sense that there is nowhere they can turn for help if threatened (Mearsheimer 2001: 32). The fear of dominance and the dependence created by lack of alternatives (cf. Hansen 2000a) creates an incentive to balance; for the Europeans, however, this incentive is lacking in the military sector, where the Americans guarantee their continued security through NATO, the stationing of troops, and the most technologically advanced military in the world. Moreover, the gap between American and European military balancing would render the military balancing of the United States highly risky and would most likely fail.

This incentive to balance – but not to balance 'hard' – is amplified by the increased visibility of ideological distance between the United States and Europe, even though this distance remains modest compared to the ideological distance between the United States and Europe on one side, and most third world countries on the other. The increased visibility of ideological distance creates an incentive for the European states to balance, but only as long as balancing does not affect the US provision of European security. As noted by Robert Art,

> [t]he summary rejection of the Kyoto Treaty, the tearing up of the Anti-Ballistic Missile Treaty, the attack on the International Criminal Court, the proclivity of the Bush administration to inform its allies of its policies rather than to consult them, its apparent intolerance for those who disagree with it, and its willingness to punish those who cross it politically

have illustrated to the Europeans 'their inability to restrain Washington's growing unilateralist impulses as have the conflicts in Kosovo and Iraq' (2004: 200). Thus, the power disparity in relation to the United States renders it impossible for the Europeans to influence American security policy unless acting through diplomatic and institutional channels.

The ideological intensity of American foreign policy discourse amplifies the incentive to soft balancing. Cold War rhetoric against the Soviet Union was often hard, but it was directed against a specific enemy. Post-Cold War foreign policy has been directed at shaping international relations in general. Even though the Europeans share a set of basic values with the United States, their relative weakness leaves them unable to influence the specifics of this reshaping. At the same time, as long as soft balancing does not touch on vital security interests, the shared ideological substance of liberalism makes conflict an intrinsic and non-threatening aspect of transatlantic relations. Critique and competition are fundamental aspects of all liberal societies, and these values are influencing the interaction between Europe and America.

The ideological substance of the American world order provides a third amplifier to the incentives to soft balancing. The pluralist nature of the liberal unipole allows for differences among allies and means that all of the states in the transatlantic area, including the unipole, are constantly negotiating how their power position ought to be translated into influence, prestige etc. Thus

> [t]ransatlantic relations are embedded in a dense network of multilateral links, including annual meetings of the Group of Eight major industrialized nations, semiannual consultations among top officials, and shared membership in the Organization for Economic Cooperation and Development (OECD). The transatlantic relationship's central organization, NATO, holds biennial summits, frequent meetings of foreign and defence ministers, and

regular consultations among permanent national delegations based in Brussels. The partnership is supplemented by extensive cooperation among U.S. and European law enforcement agencies for combating money laundering, drug trafficking, and illegal-refugee smuggling.

(Wallace 2001: 17)

In some sectors, the European and American societies consequently 'have become so closely knit in a "quasi-domestic" relationship that disputes penetrate far beyond the shallow level of the old trade wars and "affect such fundamental domestic issues as the ways Americans and Europeans are taxed, how societies are governed, or how economies are regulated"' (Daniel Hamilton quoted in: Pond 2003: xii). Europe and the United States share a set of fundamental values, and the spread of these values does not threaten Europe. This reduces the European incentive to hard balancing against the United States. At the same time, however, the ideological substance of liberalism makes competition and conflict an intrinsic aspect of the transatlantic relationship. This does not create an incentive to hard balancing, but it allows the Europeans to seek to maximize their interests through soft balancing without punishment that could threaten their security and survival.

The focus of soft balancing

European soft balancing against the United States appeared in relation to multilateralism, European security institutions, military actions in Bosnia and Iraq, and on marginal issues of global governance.

Europeans have only rarely attempted to balance the United States on the central aspects of the European security order, and they have backed down on these issues every time a conflict with the United States appeared inevitable; sometimes with humiliating implications. Our theoretical model offers a simple explanation: Europeans are stuck in dependence. They continue primarily as consumers of security and stability produced by the United States. The end of the Cold War created a perception among European leaders that they could reduce their dependence on the United States, but a lack of resources combined with disagreements amongst the Europeans revealed to them that they could not. The initial attempts at marginalizing NATO and solving the security problems related to the break-up of Yugoslavia failed. Thus, the European states' lack of power, military power in particular, explains why soft balancing has mainly assumed three forms after the initial period of optimism: 1) a general – and sometimes rather abstract and therefore non-threatening – focus on multilateralism (e.g. the ESS); 2) a focus on security issues with no direct impact on Euro-Atlantic security structures (e.g. Iraq); and 3) a focus on issues that are either very specific (e.g. genetically modified foods) or at the margins of the American world order (e.g. global warming).

The balancers

All EU member states have supported the ESS call for increased emphasis on multilateralism, and Europeans have generally followed a grand strategy with greater emphasis on international institutions than the United States. Working diplomatically inside and outside international institutions, Europeans have attempted to create an international order with greater emphasis on multilateralism. Aside from multilateralism, however, Europeans have demonstrated little agreement in relation to soft balancing.

Germany and France are the main European soft balancers in the post-Cold War period. They have been supported by smaller states, most notably Belgium and Luxembourg, and more recently Sweden and Finland. The United Kingdom is the leader of the opposite camp, advocating a strong and continued transatlantic relationship with little room for competing European initiatives.

Why are Germany and France the primary European soft balancers? An answer consistent with our realist model for explaining security strategy is that the costs and benefits of unipolarity are unequally distributed, even within Europe. Britain is the closest American ally and the most prominent exponent of 'Atlantic Europe', the group of European NATO member states who tend to support US initiatives (Forsberg and Herd 2006: 37). Even though all states seek to avoid dependence, the UK has sought to preserve as much security and influence as possible as a declining power through its special relationship with the United States (cf. Ash 2004: 64–65). As noted by Johnston, 'Britain's "special relationship" is special because no other European country [...] has a relationship with the United States that deliver the same benefits' (2005: 45). These benefits are mainly found in nuclear, military and intelligence policy (Forsberg and Herd 2006: 39). Since 9/11 and the conflict over Iraq, this cooperation has been strengthened in order to protect both countries against terrorist attacks. Thus,

> [a] working group on Homeland Security was created between the two sides and the focus has been upon sharing best practice in domestic counter-terror preparations, joint training exercises, cyber- and physical infrastructure protection, and border transportation security.
>
> (Rees 2006: 33)

The US-UK relationship is highly asymmetrical and unipolarity has made it even more so, as documented in the beginning of this chapter. However, since British security, including the exclusive benefits following from the special US-UK relationship, depends on the continued relative strength of the unipole, Britain is highly unlikely to engage in balancing against the United States, whether hard or soft.

Although France and Germany are both consumers of American security provision to Europe – and as argued above, they take care not to challenge the central aspects of the Euro-Atlantic security order – unipolarity entails different costs and benefits for them than for the UK. On the one hand, the American unipole continues to guarantee a low probability of conflict in Europe. On the other hand, unipolarity challenges the relative power and influence of both France and Germany. Whereas Britain has used American power as a hedge against the consequences of decline, unipolarity accentuates French decline by challenging its leadership over Europe and its vision of a multipolar world as the best long-term guarantee of continued security and stability. Thus, 'France does remain a strong ally, but wishes at times to embody an alternative to the unipole, and is therefore ready to contest its dominance and to assume the costs associated with this policy' (Tardy 2003/04: 3). Thus, it is hardly surprising that this country 'happily took on the role of leader of the opposition' in the Iraq war (Sloan 2005: 220) as well as in the post-Cold War period more generally. In the Cold War era, 'France consistently sought to create independent roles for itself as a hub of opposition to US leadership within Europe and across the developing world', including the acquisition of nuclear weapons and withdrawal from NATO military command (Pauly 2005: 13). Initially, after the end of the Cold War, France appeared to redirect its opposition to American power from critique on hard security issues to the creation of a strong EU capable of acting independently of the Americans in most issue areas. As argued by Rynning, French opposition to the United States in the post-Cold War period is a conflict over the leadership of Europe:

> [t]he French leadership knew that their claim to primacy could not be realized in NATO where the United States naturally dominated; they therefore hoped to relegate NATO to a background security guarantee and propel the EU onto center stage.
>
> (2005: 171)

With the general stalemate of the European project since the early 1990s and the British opposition against European independence in the single area where it has moved forward considerably – security affairs – France returned to direct opposition to the United States. However, the lack of French military capabilities meant that France could only balance through diplomatic means, particularly through the use of its UN Security Council membership (cf. Pauly 2005).[14]

Germany is perhaps more puzzling, because it has been explicitly dependent on American security provision since 1945. Germany is also the main beneficiary of US supported Euro-Atlantic and global institutions, because these institutions have allowed Germany to pursue an active foreign policy despite its history, capabilities and geopolitical location without facing a balancing coalition. However, it is exactly for these reasons that German power and influence is challenged by unipolarity and why Germany seeks to balance the United States and its recent attempts to change the regional and global order. This is also why Germany reacted particularly strongly in the case of the Iraq war. Since 1945, Germany has had a strong tradition of non-intervention grounded in its constitution. Participating in or even politically supporting intervention in Iraq was different from the many peacemaking and peacekeeping operations of the post-Cold War period, because it meant taking sides in a conflict without a UN mandate (or stopping genocide, as in the case of Bosnia). It was not an action of the international society, but of a particular coalition within that society. Germany had developed its foreign and security policy solidly within NATO, the EU and the UN, and could only play an active security policy role within strong international institutions due to its relatively weak military capabilities and its history of aggression in the first half of the twentieth century.[15]

In essence, both France and Germany had much to lose if the multilateralism of the Cold War was to be replaced by a new, more flexible multilateralism reflecting the power political realities of the American world order. In contrast, for the UK, increased US relative power in combination with more flexible multilateralism rendered its benefits from cooperating with the United States potentially more exclusive and solidified the relationship, as it is typically the extension of these benefits to other countries that has been seen by the British as a threat to their special relationship with the United States (Johnston 2005: 45).

Two factors reinforce these effects. First, Britain experienced a shorter ideological distance to the United States than the continental welfare states, a tendency which was accentuated in the last years of bipolarity and during unipolarity, when 'both Thatcher and Blair embraced a type of liberalism that broke with deep-seated and relatively collectivist party traditions' (Lieber 1999: 57). This factor may have intensified the differences between the UK, on one side, and France and Germany on the other, but there is little evidence that it has been decisive. Small European states with extensive welfare states such as the Netherlands and Denmark have continued, and to some extent accentuated, their Atlanticist security policies after the Cold War by generally supporting the American world order as well as many specific aspects of American security policy. Second, experiences from earlier power configurations may have played a role for all three countries. For Germany, the historical experience of being a great power and conducting traditional power politics was closely linked to the two world wars in the first half of the twentieth century. Moreover, as noted by Timothy Garton Ash, '[i]n the French case as in the British, an overall approach to international relations was inextricably bound up with a national diplomatic strategy to preserve as much as possible of a former world power's status and influence' (2004: 64).

Conclusion

This chapter has answered two questions: What characterizes European strategic behaviour in the unipolar world order? And how is this strategic behaviour explained? The answer to the first question is that European strategic behaviour is best characterized as hard bandwagoning with soft balancing at the margins. The European states have accepted American pre-eminence in security affairs and adapted their overall security strategies in accordance with American preferences. In accordance with our model, they can expect less support from the

United States than in the past, and they can expect the United States to be less interested in modifying its own position to accommodate the views of its allies. Thus, it becomes more important for Europe to increase its security capabilities, but to do so in a manner that cannot be perceived as hard balancing by the unipole. This helps explain why the ESS shares its basic goals and values with the NSS, and European states continue their strong commitment to NATO while European cooperation on security and defence policy is intensified and Europeans voice their dissatisfaction with American behaviour on marginal issues.

The results of the empirical analysis were in line with the expectations for European behaviour deduced from our theoretical model. Thus, the answer to the second question is that strategic European behaviour is explained by a combination of relative power, relative security and relative ideology. The model predicted strong incentives for the European states to bandwagon with the unipole and balancing only to be soft to the extent that it happened. This was also the case. Only one expectation from the model seems not to be borne out by the evidence. We expected the incentive to hard bandwagoning to be dampened over time due to the growing visibility of an ideological gap between the United States and Europe on specific issues. In fact, the analysis revealed that soft balancing was more characteristic of the early post-Cold War period than later. This behaviour points to the importance of relative power and relative security over relative ideology: despite the growing visibility of an ideological gap between Europe and the United States, the European states did not choose a strategy that could risk their security interests. Thus, as argued in Chapter 2, relative ideology mainly played a role as an 'amplifier' of incentives following from unipolarity and relative security.

To sum up, the general conclusion of the chapter is shown in Figure 4.1: the combination of a low probability of conflict and a short ideological distance in the unipolar world order resulted in strategic behaviour characterized mainly by hard bandwagoning as expected from our model.

Relative security/ relative ideology	Long ideological distance	Short ideological distance
Low probability of conflict	Soft bandwagoning	Hard bandwagoning **Europe**
High probability of conflict	Hard balancing	Soft balancing

Figure 4.1 The model and European strategic behaviour.

5   The Middle East

The states in the Middle East and North Africa (MENA)[1] were profoundly affected by the end of the Cold War and the challenges of adapting to the new, unipolar world order. Various expectations regarding the MENA region were promptly forwarded. To some, the focus was on the promise of democratization, as in the former Eastern Europe (Sadowski 1993; Hudson 1991). Democracy did not materialize, prompting others to examine the particularities of the region. Authors such as Samuel Huntington warned against the clash of civilizations between the Islamic civilization and the West (Huntington 1996). The US administration focused on the 'rogue' character of some MENA states and after 9-11, political attention to the democratic deficit and Islamism grew.

On the one hand, the so-called 'third wave' of democratization (Huntington 1991) following the collapse of the Soviet Union by-passed the region; the MENA states did not appear to follow the path of other states in this regard. On the other hand, the 'Islamic' dimension did not materialize as a driving conflict factor, and the region in its entirety did not clash with the West. Instead, we witnessed a variety of security strategies: in the adaptation process 1989–2007, different and shifting strategies for coping with the new challenges were pursued.

Many states in the region suffered a relative loss following the end of the Cold War. The losers of relative power and influence were mainly to be found among the former Soviet allies. The 1956 Suez Conflict was a turning point in the penetration of the Cold War dynamics into the MENA region. From that point on, the superpowers intensified their efforts to gain and maintain allies in the region, and the MENA increasingly became part of the bipolar rivalry. Superpower alignments and affiliations were not completely stable in the MENA; neither by degree nor by partners. Egypt replaced its previous Soviet alignment with a US alignment following the outcome of the War in October 1973. Iraq received substantial support from the US and other Western and Arab countries in addition to Soviet support during the war against Iran until the ceasefire was agreed upon in 1988. In addition to their primary alignment to either superpower, the Yemens both received some support from the rivalling superpowers. Iran (as the only state) remained outside of the alignment game after it broke its alliance with the US during the 1979 Islamization of the revolution. Lebanon was engulfed in civil war, in which groups affiliated with both pro-US and pro-Soviet states fought one another.

Despite these changes, 'doubles' and internal in-fights, however, the general picture by the end of the Cold War was one of two clear camps.[2] When the Cold War came to an end, the MENA region in general suffered a loss in terms of reduced strategic importance. Nevertheless, the previous Soviet-affiliated states suffered the greatest relative loss: they lost their superpower guardian.

The former Soviet-allied states in the MENA comprised – to different degrees – Algeria, Libya, Syria, Iraq, Afghanistan and South Yemen. Two more actors deserve mention: the Palestine Liberation Organization (PLO), and the Polisario, though they were not state actors. For this reason, they fall outside of the purview of our state-centred analysis. South Yemen merged with North Yemen in 1990, and Algeria and Afghanistan disintegrated in civil war during the 1990s. Unifying with another state is a state strategy (although not a fre-quently used strategy) for coping with external challenges including changes in external pressure. Breaking down in civil war is a (relatively common) outcome of international systemic change following shifting positions of strength. The implication of civil war is often the actual abandonment of conventional external state strategy. Iraq, Libya and Syria were thus the obvious choice of case coun-tries, as they all 'survived' the 1989 systemic change and were able to pursue coherent security strategies as state actors.

In addition, MENA was politically fragmented. In Chapter 4 on Europe, it was stated that 'Europe' should definitely not be analysed as a unitary actor. However, the European states have committed themselves to coordinating a range of pol-icies, and their EU membership reflects intense cooperation. This was not the case in MENA in 1989–2007. Furthermore, the MENA states remained reluctant to commit to intense regional cooperation after the Cold War in contrast to the Euro-pean states, which intensified their mutual cooperation within the EU and initiated a gradual enlargement process that granted membership to the former Communist states in eastern and central Europe. In contrast to Russia, the MENA states are small. Their small size has limited their room for manoeuvre in the adaptation process, but it has also provided them with some freedom of action.

Presenting individual analyses of all of the MENA states is beyond our scope. Instead, we intend to scrutinize regional variations regarding the process of adaptation. We have singled out three MENA states for examination: Iraq, Libya and Syria. These three states were all among the major losers in the region due to their previous alignments and beneficial relationships with the Soviet Union, thereby already matching our fundamental condition for lost power. Further-more, they were all formerly 'radical nationalist or Islamic' states (Hinnebusch and Ehteshami 2002: 347), and two of them were under Ba'athist rule, indicat-ing considerable ideological distance to the American world order. To what extent would such states address their losses by countering the world order, aligning against the US and pursuing balancing policies? And would they behave according to general expectations or according to their specific domestic attributes?[3]

Our model would generally lead us to expect the emergence of the American world order to be met with reluctance. The three states fell short of superpower support and lost out in terms of a weakened bargaining position. Furthermore, the American world order presented them with severe political challenges by promoting an international free market space coupled with demands for democratization.

However, we should initially enquire as to whether the model is applicable to the MENA states. States in the MENA region are often described as having specific features or being exceptional: prolonged debate has taken place within the academic community as to whether dynamics in the region should be analysed by means of general explanatory models or analysed *sui generis* and attributed to particular domestic factors.[4] The particular features are attributed to a variety of factors, including Islam, authoritarian rule, post-colonial status, traditional economic structures, specific historical circumstances and heterogeneous populations; or combinations of these factors. In accordance with the lack of their importance in the MENA states, institutions, however, which in the case of Europe assumingly have affected the cost-benefit analyses carried out by the states, have not been assigned any substantial impact. The Arab League, which in the 1989–2007 period of analysis was the major institution in the region, has typically been analysed in terms of the member state interests and perceived as a denominator of shared positions at the rhetorical level.

Nonetheless, the MENA states have been forced to undergo a process of adaptation like other states, and our basic assumption (cf. Waltz 1979) is that states must adapt to a similar structural self-help condition, although not necessarily in identical ways. For this, our general model should, in principle, be applicable. On the other hand, given the particular features of the MENA states, their strategies will tell us about the usefulness of a general model. Should we limit the scope of the model to only some groups of states? Or is it useful in general regarding the post-Cold War processes of adaptation? Our findings will contribute to this debate.

From our (neo)realist point of view, we therefore anticipate differences as well as similarities in the findings when analysing the three apparently non-conformist MENA states. We also anticipate that it is possible to relate these finding to our theoretical expectations. The aim of this chapter is to answer our research questions in the case of Syria, Iraq and Libya: which security strategies did the three states choose, and why? As we will see, the variations regarding their strategic choices were considerable.

The baseline: the losses and challenges

The shifts in Soviet foreign policy from the middle of the 1980s reduced the competition between the superpowers in the MENA region. The Soviet allied states in particular were confronted by a different situation, and policy changes were carried out. Nevertheless, the end of the Cold War in 1989 seriously challenged the states and the region in general.

We assume that the loss of a superpower ally is in principle the most import-ant loss to a state that is comparatively weak in relative capabilities, such as the MENA states. Losing a major security ally that guarantees one's security should be regarded as decisive as compared to a specific loss in one or more cap-abilities. The loss of a superpower ally typically also implies specific losses in terms of the loss of favourable arms deals, economic agreements, training for military officers and/or civil servants, political leverage in low politics, and ideological support.

In particular, the former Soviet MENA clients (Algeria, Libya, Syria, Iraq, Afghanistan[5] and South Yemen/YAR) were particularly subject to relative losses in at least three respects:

- They lost their major ally and a series of specific assets and benefits.
- They had to cope with new and different international conditions. The con-ditions favoured democratization and capitalist economies tuned to compet-ing in the world market (the two nodal points of the political project of the remaining superpower, the US).
- They had to cope with an altered regional balance of power, as the US allied states retained their superpower ally.[6]

In addition to the previously Soviet-affiliated MENA states, North Yemen and Iran were also subjected to losses, although both to a minor extent. US support to North Yemen was reduced, even if North Yemen had been a US Cold War ally. With no bipolar rivalry and no risk of North Yemen falling into the hands of the Soviet Union, support for either of the Yemens began to appear superflu-ous from the American perspective. In the case of Iran, the loss was minor and unrelated to superpower protection or material support, since Iran had remained aloof from both superpower camps since 1979. Instead, it was related to its *room for manoeuvre*. In the absence of the bipolar rivalry, Iranian security policy was no longer something on the sideline towards which the US deliberately pursued a policy of restraint for the sake of avoiding bipolar escalation. Iran thus reap-peared as a subject of potential superpower pressure.

As already mentioned, major non-state actors were also strongly affected. Most notably, the PLO lost out, as did the Polisario. Moreover, we could include the al-Qaida terrorist network in the group of losers. It had not come into exist-ence before the end of the Cold War, first emerging in the early 1990s (Gunaratna 2002), when the network's members began to respond to what they perceived to be an undesirable political situation. Actually, the undesirable dimension was related to an anticipated loss of social and ideological positions. This loss was related to the expansion of the US presence in the region follow-ing the Operations *Desert Shield* and *Desert Storm* together with the prolifera-tion of the US world order. The new world order not only made those who became the al-Qaida-originals redundant regarding their previous militant struggle against the Soviet occupation of Afghanistan, but it challenged religious and economically traditional segments as well, and among these segments mobilization took place. Al-Qaida thus represents the collective action of angry losers at the sub-state level; losers, who were opposed to their own states as well as the American unipole.

The end of the Cold War also affected the status of the MENA region in general. The American MENA policy during the Cold War had largely been shaped by the bipolar competition with the Soviet Union (resulting in strategic interests and an emphasis on regime stability among the American allies); secondly, by oil interests, and in the second half of the Cold War by concern for Israeli security (Quandt 1993). However, the American strategic interests changed in the new world order with the Soviet Union no longer a peer competitor and rival for influence and allies. The region became subject to unipolar management considerations rather than bipolar competition for allies. Consequently, regime stability became a less important priority.

The US agenda and political project also began to broaden and define the new order. This favoured states suited to competing and socializing on the new terms comprising democratization and market economy. For different reasons, the MENA states in general were poorly suited for that, and the region thus suffered general losses in comparison with most other regions (Henry and Springborg 2001). In addition to the losses they shared in common, the pre-conditions of our three case countries, Iraq, Libya and Syria, differed in numerous ways. In the first place, the states had not been equally dependent on the Soviet Union, and neither had they received the same amount of specific support. Consequently, they were subject to various degrees of loss. In the second place, their security situations diverged in terms of their own state of vulnerability, including their capabilities and geopolitical surroundings. In the third place, the end of the Cold War resulted in a series of rapid changes in the region, which made up a *process* in which new alignments became possible.

Iraq

Iraq, an oil-rich country in the Gulf area with roughly 27 million people, had been under Saddam Hussein's authoritarian rule since 1979; the most brutal regime in the MENA region.

Saddam Hussein's Iraq was subjected to a double loss in the years prior to and following the end of the Cold War (Hansen 2000a). In the first place, its 1980–88 war against Iran left Iraq with substantial war-related losses, and Iraq had lost out in respect to updating its society in terms of material and human infrastructure and capital. The war had drained the state's resources, with the exception of its military resources. During the war, Iraq had received support from the oil-rich conservative Arab states and the West, which had feared a spread of the Iranian revolution. This support ended together with the war, however, thereby weakening Iraq economically and socially. Nevertheless, it had a comparatively strong army and modern military equipment at the end of the Cold War.

In the second place, the end of the Cold War left Iraq in a neighbourhood dominated by US allies after it had lost its own superpower ally and a series of benefits. The trade and arms deals with the Soviet Union disappeared with the superpower ally (although the alignment had been 'thin'). In the meantime, Egypt and Israel, two of Iraq's regional rivals, experienced a relative strengthening as they remained close US allies, as was the case with Saudi Arabia. Furthermore, Iraq was part of the general regional decline, as it had neglected developmental reforms during the 1980s and was particularly poorly suited to compete on the new market economic conditions.

Regionally, Iraq was virtually isolated. It had political rivalries with Syria and Egypt, tense and conflict-prone relationships with Iran and Israel, and the Southern Gulf States feared a re-constructed and powerful Iraq.

In short, Iraq entered the new order as a major loser, although a loser with oil and military strength. Its first strategic move of invading Kuwait further added to its losses and affected Iraqi strategy for many years. Furthermore, the years of sanctions further weakened Iraq and produced severe social problems (Anderson and Stansfield 2005).

Libya

In terms of relative power position, Libya was already affected negatively by President Gorbachev's policy changes in the mid-1980s, which aimed to save the Soviet Union but in effect spelled the beginning of its end. During the 1980s, the balance in the Libyan-Soviet relationship had changed because of lower oil prices and shifting Soviet priorities (Arnold 1996: 129–131): on the one hand, the Soviet Union became less dependent on Libyan oil. On the other hand, Soviet priorities to improve relations with the US and Western Europe made it less willing to cooperate with Libya, as Tripoli had antagonized the US and major West European powers. Instead, Moscow aimed at converting previous political, economic and cultural agreements into a 'simple arms-for-cash relationship' (El-Kikhia 1997: 136). An indication of the Soviet downgrading of Libya was the lack of Soviet response to the US bomb raids on Tripoli in 1986. Libya thus suffered the loss of its superpower ally and advantageous arrangements.

Like Iraq, Libya is an oil-rich country but with a small population (approximately six million). During the 1980s, Libya benefited from high oil prices and spent some of its oil-related surplus on societal investment. The loss in terms of specific benefits was thus less important to Libya than was the case in Iraq and Syria. The loss of its superpower ally was also of less importance regarding immediate Libyan security needs, but it challenged the previously radical Libyan foreign policy.

Libya was also ill-suited to deal with the new, competitive order. Apart from its oil-wealth (almost all of Libya's export revenues stemmed from the oil industry), Libya only had agriculture and raw material processing to add, and its economic infrastructure was unsuited to the brunt of international competition (Henry and Springborg 2001).

Regarding the regional balance of power, Libya had engaged in a fierce political rivalry with Egypt during the Cold War (despite attempts to form unions between the two states in phases of 'deténte' and common interests). In 1977, a three-day long 'border war' broke out over the Arab-Israeli issue, but the tensions eased. Aside from the rivalry with Egypt and political conflict in the Arab League regarding policy towards Israel, Libya was not engaged in serious regional conflicts. Its political role in the Maghrib, however, was weakened by the end of the Cold War, relative to Egypt, Morocco and Tunisia. Internationally, Libya was facing huge problems by 1990 due to its role in the Lockerbie bombing and US accusations of supporting international terrorism.

In short, Libya was bereaved of its security alliance, and its room for manoeuvre consequently decreased. It was isolated and at odds with the remaining superpower, and the country war ill-suited for coping with the challenges of the post-Cold War order. It had its oil wealth to rely on for domestic as well as international purposes; at least temporarily, however, the oil prices were decreasing.

Syria

Syria, with roughly 19 million people and very modest oil reserves, was as deeply affected by the Soviet disintegration as Iraq, although differently. The economy was generally poor, and the military depended on advisors, support and equipment from the Soviet Union. Syria began to lose superpower support in the late 1980s during the political re-orientation undertaken by Mikhail Gorbachev. Syria had thus far officially aimed to achieve strategic parity with Israel with Soviet aid, but was told by the USSR that this was no longer a realistic option (Karsh 1993), as the economic and military support from the Soviet Union was reduced. The loss of the Soviet alignment was of great significance, and a Syrian diplomat put it this way: 'we regret the Soviet collapse more than the Russians do'.[7]

Syria was also in trouble regionally. Damascus was at odds with Iraq to the East; to its West it was engaged in the Lebanese civil war and later entangled in Lebanese politics (while the civil war ended after agreement on the Ta'if Accords of October 1989, Syria maintained its presence); and it had not made peace with Israel to the South, struggling instead to re-gain the Golan Heights, which Israel had occupied since the 1967 War. Internationally, Syria's relations with the US were hampered by American accusations of Syrian support for international terrorism, by Syrian hostility towards Israel, and by Syrian intervention in Lebanese affairs.

In short, Syria's prospects for coping well with the competitive conditions of the new world order were unfavourable: like Iraq and Libya, its institutional economic basis was poor; unlike Iraq and Libya, however, Syria did not possess vast oil reserves.

The model and the MENA region: theoretical expectations

A range of security strategies was available to the losers. As seen in Chapter 2, we have divided the strategies available into four broad types for analytical reasons: soft and hard bandwagoning and soft and hard balancing.[8] We are aware that states do not necessarily pursue coherent strategies and possibly choose to mix elements from different strategies. Consequently, we consider the strategies as bunches of strategic elements and add up the use of elements and make a judgement as to which strategies dominated.

We argued in Chapter 2 that the structural incentives – our condition variable – relating to a unipolar distribution of power and the specific alliance dynamics are indeterminate, but that hard balancing is extremely costly in the case of unipolarity. Conversely, bandwagoning strategies offer short-term benefits and protection while at the same time involving long-term dangers such as subjugation. The MENA states were thus facing a difficult dilemma. Our independent variable, relative security, leads us to expect balancing behaviour, while our intervening variable, relative ideology leads us to expect *hard* balancing by the three states.

According to Chapter 2, a high level of relative security provides bandwagoning incentives, while a low level disposes for balancing. Ideological distance arguably amplifies the incentive to pursue either hard or soft strategies. Considerable ideological distance coupled with low relative security favours the choice of hard balancing strategies over soft strategies, while a short ideological distance coupled with high relative security favours hard bandwagoning over soft bandwagoning.

The three case countries could all be described as being caught in a cross-fire of incentives when having to adapt to the unipolar world order. Their loss and lack of relative power created a dilemma. Basically, they had a strong incentive to balance the US and counter the effects of the emerging world order, but their weakness also appeared to produce incentives for the case countries to pursue bandwagoning strategies, as it would be costly to balance the US and the benefits would be doubtful.

However, our independent variable – relative security – points to a balancing incentive. Their exposure to a low degree of relative security was favouring the choice of balancing strategies. A corresponding relatively high probability of conflict assumingly matches the high costs of balancing and may appear worthwhile. The unipole may lower the probability of conflict by means of an alignment or other forms of close cooperation or increase the probability in the event of hostility. An important dimension in this regard is thus the role played by the unipole. The unipole may lower the probability of conflict by guarding the security of a state or a group of states, thus enhancing the incentive to bandwagon, or it may increase the probability of conflict, which in turn enhances the balancing incentive. The unipole's commitment to a state or group of states is therefore important. In 1989–90, American engagement in the MENA region was limited, owing to a preoccupation with the developments in the collapsing Soviet Union (Hansen 2000a), which left the MENA states with a considerable room for manoeuvre when choosing strategies. Following the Iraqi invasion of Kuwait in 1990, the US increased its presence in the region considerably (Cordesman 1997) and engaged in the peace process until the mid-1990s. During the second half of the 1990s, the US granted priority to other issues, once again opening the door for the MENA states' room for manoeuvre regarding their security strategies. Following 9/11, the US strategic interest and engagement in the region dramatically increased, providing some states with enhanced opportunities to bandwagon and a few with enhanced incentives to balance; and several states to reconsider their options.

Iraq and Syria were facing a relatively high probability of conflict. In the case of Syria, the degree of relative security was further challenged by the fact that Syria found itself at odds with the US. Iraq was initially relatively at ease with the US, though this already changed to a course of confrontation in 1990. Libya was also facing a high probability of conflict regionally, although not as high as Iraq and Syria. Like Syria and Iraq, however, Libya was at odds with the sole remaining superpower, the US. The low degree of relative security in the case countries and the absence of alternative security arrangements thus provided them with incentives to pursue balancing strategies.

The value on our intervening variable, ideological distance to the US and the current unipolar world order, encouraged hard balancing strategies because of disagreement on core issues and due to the risk of being forced to surrender core values. In Chapter 1 we pointed out a number of general ideological features of the US political project and the current world order: promotion of democracy, human rights, market economy and the non-proliferation of weapons of mass destruction (WMDs). While Iraq, Libya and Syria are certainly very different societies, they all resisted these specific American goals (albeit differently) when the new world order emerged. None of the states were democracies (not even close), and they had poor human rights records. Their economies were characterized as those of 'bunker' states. According to Henry and Springborg (2001), the 'bunker' states displayed the 'least institutional capacity of any of the MENA states to manage their economies' (2001: 100). The bunker states comprised Algeria, Iraq, Libya, Sudan, Syria and Yemen. The bunker states shared in common the largest informal economies, low tax revenues outside of the petroleum sector, major proportions of such revenues were allocated to ruling factions, low political influence (ruling clans distorted information), and difficulties faced by private entrepreneurs regarding the accumulation of capital (2001). Finally, the three states were suspected for or known to possess chemical weapons and suspected of also having ambitions to achieve nuclear capabilities. The considerable ideological distance thus provided them with incentives to pursue hard balancing strategies.

Summing up these different and partly contrasting incentives, we are able to put forward the following initial expectations regarding the behaviour of Iraq, Libya and Syria:

• The three case countries in the MENA region all faced a dilemma: on the one hand, they had a structural incentive to pursue balancing strategies due to their loss of relative power; on the other hand, their weaknesses favoured bandwagoning strategies because of the costs and doubtful benefits.

- They had an incentive to pursue balancing strategies because of the independent impact of relative security. Regionally, they were all facing a relatively high probability of conflict; most notably Iraq and Syria. Regarding the unipole, Libya and Syria were at odds with the US from the beginning, and Iraq quickly followed.
- In principle, they all had an incentive to pursue hard strategies in the case of balancing due to the amplifying effect of ideological distance, which endangered their core values.
- We expect to find mixed strategies because of the basic dilemma.

Since we have been dealing with a time span of nearly 20 years, we have had to look for changes in the conditions that assumingly affect the incentives of the states. Although the unipolar distribution of aggregate strength remained throughout the period of analysis, we are well aware that the world orders are subjected to fluctuations (Copeland 2000). As there are no strong counter-balancers present in unipolarity, fluctuations in the policies of the sole remaining superpower become a particularly decisive factor (Hansen ftc.). Furthermore, the variables of relative security and relative ideology are prone to fluctuations. In order to explain variation in our dependent variable (state security strategy and behaviour), we must therefore look for variations in 1) relative security, and 2) ideological affinity – regionally as well as in relation to the role of the unipole. Such variations are expected to affect the incentives of the three states.

We must then categorize the behaviour of the case countries according to the four ideal types established in Chapter 2: hard bandwagoning, soft bandwagoning, soft balancing and hard balancing.

In order to assess and categorize the strategies, we have chosen to analyse how the three states related to the following main issues in the MENA region as well as the main issues regarding the use of military force in the international arena in the 1989–2007 period using these events as our strategy indicators. They were high on the unipolar agenda; they were all defining security issues in the region; and they all had an international dimension, implying that the MENA states had to show their proverbial hands. We have analysed the case country positions and identified the trends. We specifically examined the following indicator events:

- Military action and security issues
  The international coalition and the Gulf conflict (1990–91)
  The Arab–Israeli–Palestinian peace process
  The War on Terrorism and the invasion of Afghanistan (2001)
  The War against Iraq (2003)
- Global governance, the reliance on WMD and on support for international terrorism
- Strategy and alignments

Some comments should be added to the issues, which have served as indicators for assessing the respective state strategies.

In the first place, we look at issues regarding military action (in three cases including US involvement) and security (in terms of the Arab–Israeli–Palestinian peace process). The peace process also involves the US, but regionally positions towards the Arab–Israeli–Palestinian conflict have served as a defining element in the respective foreign policies of the MENA states throughout the period in question.

In the second place, we examine the reliance of the states on WMD strategies and support for international terrorism. Such reliance has been at the top of the international agenda since the termination of the Cold War; it has been part of MENA regional politics since the 1960s; and counter measures have been crucial to US management efforts in the new world order. Reliance on WMDs and support for terrorism have been connecting the involvement of the states with the American attempts at global management, and although the reliance reflects opposition to the world order, it nonetheless interacts with 'global governance'.

In the third place, we consider the direction of the 'grand' strategies of the states, with special emphasis on the military dimension; military strategies reflect goals and signal intentions. The analysis has been based on the specific security and foreign policy priorities and strategies of each state, as these are important elements in the processes of adaptation; not least regarding the compatibility of the respective strategies with the US world order. There is no 'EU' in the MENA region, and international cooperation has thus far played a minor role, except in the case of alignments, which have been an important aspect of state policies in the regional and international political game.

The issues addressed are integrated in the three sections dealing with the three case countries in the following.

Games to be lost?

While the Cold War-related losses thus affected the three countries in different ways and to different degrees, they all suffered substantially. In terms of relative security, the case countries all had a low score. Particularly Iraq and Syria were facing a high regional probability of conflict, and this condition was aggravated by the fact that they were at odds with the unipole, whereas most of their adversaries were US allies. They disagreed with the world order and the region rose to the top of the US agenda on two occasions: after the Iraqi invasion of Kuwait and after 9/11. Furthermore, they were all ideologically remote from the 'the new world order' and poorly suited to embrace it. They were authoritarian regimes: Syria and Iraq with Arab socialist Ba'ath-parties, Libya with Islamic-nationalist rule.

The strategies of adaptation: Iraq, Syria and Libya

Iraq

The initial Iraqi moves in the new world order reflected the choice of a highly risky strategy. In the spring of 1990, Iraq began confronting Kuwait following a continuing slump in oil prices. Iraq accused Kuwait of deliberate over-production, pushing oil prices down and reducing revenues, thereby hampering Iraqi reconstruction plans after the war against Iran. Iraq also raised territorial questions regarding two minor islands, Warba and Bubiyan, and the Rumaila oil field. When tensions grew, a meeting took place towards the end of July between President Saddam Hussein and April Glaspie, US ambassador to Iraq. Glaspie's message was that the US did not have an 'opinion' on the border dispute (Freedman and Karsh 1993: 53). The Iraqi regime took this to support their evolving perception of the post-Cold War MENA region as a superpower-free region (Hansen 2000a), and subsequently attempted to compensate itself for its losses by attempting to gain control over the Kuwaiti oil wealth in order to relieve Iraqi financial problems and debts; but also to 'make Iraq the leading power in the Arab world' (Freedman and Karsh 1993: 62).

The comprehensive invasion took place in the early hours on 2 August, and Iraq annexed Kuwait as it 19th Province on 8 August. The invasion was met by overwhelming international condemnation (Malone 2007). After the Iraqi invasion, a broad coalition[9] was assembled leading to the launch of Operation Desert Storm, resulting in the liberation of Kuwait in February, 1991, following a massive air campaign and brief ground war.

Despite the massive international pressure and US military build-up, Iraq did not initiate a voluntary withdrawal from Kuwait. During the autumn of 1990, Iraq responded with a series of counter-measures aimed at weakening the international pressure and breaking up the coalition. The first step was to offer Iran concessions in order to formally end the Iraq–Iran war (since 1988, a ceasefire had been in place). Iraq offered to accept the 1975 Algiers agreement (the status of which Iraq had tried to alter when invading Iran) and exchange prisoners of war (Freeman and Karsh 1993:108). While Iran accepted the offer and Iraq thus partly closed one front, Iran did not withdraw its opposition to the occupation of Kuwait. The second step was to take Western nationals hostage in order to provide a human shield, to achieve negotiation opportunities, and to split the coalition members. The third step was taken in the beginning of January, 1991, when the international military build-up had been completed. Saddam Hussein threatened to invoke 'The Mother of All Battles', *Umm al-M'aarik* in Arabic. The Iraqi references to what this battle would actually imply were limited to rhetoric. Saddam Hussein did not apparently dare to threaten the US and the coalition with the use of WMDs, which would have resulted in a devastating response. Instead, he relied on hints and vague apocalyptic references in order to scare the adversaries from acting. Saddam Hussein indicated that Iraq was prepared to suffer great losses but that the West (and on other occasions, Israel) would not be ready to bear such losses. The threat, however, did not deter the coalition forces, which began their air campaign against Iraq on 16 January 1991. Against the abortive deterrence of military action, Iraq took a fourth – and very dramatic – step on 18 January: a Scud Missile attack on Israel. The Scud campaign aimed at provoking Israel to counterattack. Israel had otherwise remained outside of the coalition. Were Israel to join the coalition, the Arab members might leave it, or at least to change their policy in order to prevent domestic popular unrest. Israel was able to refrain from retaliating, however, the coalition remained intact despite the missile attacks, and the air campaign continued. On 24 February, a brief ground war resulted in defeat for Iraq and drove the Iraqi forces from Kuwait. The coalition imposed a ceasefire.

Despite the efforts to break the coalition and offer concessions to Iran, Iraq failed to form alliances with other states during the conflict. Not even traditional American adversaries such as Iran or Libya had accepted the invasion or taken practical steps to attempt to prevent the liberation of Kuwait. Only Jordan, the weak Iraqi neighbour, attempted to pursue a 'neutral' stance. One non-state actor, the PLO, sided with Iraq, but possessed no means to make a difference. Iraq attempted to use the 'Palestinian card' in order to stir up demonstrations in Arab coalition states, but failed to achieve its aim in terms of producing Arab policy changes.

Iraq had to rely on its own means, e.g. attempting to compromise US policy, to mobilize its military resources, and to attack a US-allied state. The attempt to occupy Kuwait ended in an outright hard balancing act against the US order, but it did not begin as such: apparently Iraq had counted on a post-Cold War 'regional autonomy' in light of the limited US engagement in the MENA region during the Soviet disintegration; however, this was not the case. When the US recognized that the Iraqi military build-up along the Kuwaiti border represented more than an attempt at intimidating Kuwait and putting weight behind Iraqi demands, the US signals became stronger, but Iraq did not back down. Although Iraq possibly counted on creating a *fait accompli*, and therefore invaded despite the warnings, the formation of the coalition and the military build-up in the autumn of 1990 was an overwhelming signal; nevertheless, Iraq chose to maintain its policy.

The Iraqi defeat resulted in losses of military manpower and conventional weaponry. The opportunities to replace military equipment were now limited. The defeat also incurred war-related damages on the rest of Iraqi society, and Iraq lost control over parts of its territory in the north and south in the first two years after the invasion of Kuwait. The Shi'ites in the south and the Kurds in the north rebelled in the aftermath of the defeat. The Republican Guard and the regime responded by crushing these uprisings. A Kurdish safe haven north of the 36th parallel was imposed in 1991, and the US, UK and France imposed a no-fly zone along the 32nd parallel in August 1992.

Despite losing control over parts of its territory, the safe haven in the North relieved the Iraqi regime of the task of maintaining control and dealing with unrest and secessionist attempts, thereby facilitating its own reorganization and hold on power. Nonetheless, the loss of sovereignty was a major blow to the regime. Furthermore, the harsh reactions to the rebellions in the aftermath of the 1990–91 conflict increased the international spotlight on Iraq, and the international society deemed the regime's reactions unacceptable.

Iraq was also subjected to a range of UN regulations, demands and sanctions following the defeat over Kuwait (Malone 2007). The most important demand was the destruction of Iraqi WMDs. In the first years after the 1991-defeat, Iraq reluctantly cooperated with the UN. In particular, the Iraqi stockpiles of biological weapons,[10] which had been underestimated, were destroyed. While the Iraqi-UN relations had been troubled from the outset over the question of compliance with the Security Council Resolutions, they rapidly deteriorated even further (Butler 2001; Trevan 1999). In 1993–94, the Iraqi post-defeat strategy resumed a hard edge with open provocations, including military actions within Iraq and troop movements along the Kuwaiti border. In 1993, the US fired cruise missiles against intelligence facilities around Baghdad after accusations of Iraqi missile transfers to the south and revelation of an assassination plot against President George W. Bush, Sr., while he was visiting Kuwait in April. In the course of 1993, Iraq was also criticized for challenging the northern no-fly zone; of not complying with the UN demands; of intimidating the Kurds; and of continuing to harass the Marsh Arabs in the southern part of the country, forcing many into exile.

In September–October 1994, a serious confrontation was close. The Iraqi regime moved troops to the Kuwaiti border. The troops were removed after heavy US deployments in the Persian Gulf area, and Iraq ultimately recognized Kuwaiti sovereignty.

After winning re-election on 15 January 1995, with a reported 99.96 per cent of the vote, Saddam Hussein took Iraq into the second half of the 1990s with a series of confrontations. By the end of August 1996, Iraqi armoured divisions invaded Irbil in the Kurdish safe haven. The US extended the southern no-fly zone in response, and the US further strengthened its presence in the Persian Gulf area in 1996.

These events – together with numerous minor events – preceded a major crisis in November 1997 after Iraq expelled American experts in the United Nations Special Commission (UNSCOM) team following an UNSCOM report and the adoption of UN Security Council Resolution 1134. The resolution stated that Iraq was not fully complying and therefore no date was set for ending the sanctions. The sanctions, imposed in the aftermath of the liberation of Kuwait, had had a considerable negative impact on the Iraqi economy and social conditions in Iraq. The sanctions had also become a symbol of the conflict between Iraq and the international society. Iraq demanded an end to the sanctions, while the international society insisted on maintaining them until full Iraqi compliance with the demands were secured and verifications had taken place.

The expulsion of the experts led to a series of protests, warnings, UN Security Council meetings, other diplomatic activity and further US military build-up in the area. The situation developed into a test of strength among the parties involved. The UN sought to avoid a military conflict, while the US stood firm regarding the question of Iraqi WMDs. Iraq attempted to limit the inspections and drive a wedge between the major states in order to reduce the political pressure.

The outcome of the test was an Iraqi retreat. Iraq allowed the American experts to return by the end of November, but Iraq also raised a new issue and demanded that Saddam Hussein's palaces should be exempted from inspections.

While Iraq had to drop its initial demands, it still achieved at least three things: it had gained time during the crisis; it had challenged the UN agreement on the policy of sanctions; and it had attracted attention to humanitarian problems in Iraq.

Tensions again grew and another confrontation erupted towards the end of October 1998. Iraq declared that it would suspend cooperation with the UN weapons inspectors unless a series of demands were met. This move met condemnation from the Security Council. Shortly thereafter, an UNSCOM report of 15 December stated that UNSCOM was unable to carry out its obligations due to a lack of cooperation from the Iraqi side. This lack of Iraqi compliance with the UN demands once again led to military action being taken. Operation Desert Fox was carried out on 16–19 December 1998 by the US and UK. The operation targeted Iraqi military installations.

Following the bombardments, Iraq decided to end all cooperation with the UN in January 1999 until the sanctions were lifted. This was a dramatic move and left Iraq totally isolated. While isolation was the result, one could ask whether the background of the Iraqi move was one of brinkmanship and actually a continuation of the testing of unity and resolve. After Operation Desert Storm and the continuing skirmishes with the UN, however, there was hardly any hope for openings without concessions, which Iraq was unwilling to give.

Iraq remained isolated in the years to come and Saddam's regime began to incorporate a new element in its strategy: highlighting the negative effects of the sanctions and focusing on its status as 'victim'. This articulation of weakness and need for protection stood in sharp contrast to previous discourses, all of which had emphasized Iraqi strength, even in times of trouble, e.g. the Iraqi signals prior to the coalition attack in 1991, when Iraq persistently referred to its strength and capabilities. In the spring of 2003, however, the US Administration stated that the only effective way forward would be a regime change in Iraq.

The isolation and general weakening of Iraq disabled the regime from compensating for the economic decline and sufferings it caused to the Iraqi population. At the same time, concern over these effects grew within the international community, and 'smart' sanctions and other measures were discussed. However, the issue of inspections and WMDs remained unsolved. The 2003 invasion brought an end to the Saddam Hussein regime and left Iraq under foreign occupation.

In the spring of 2003, US pressure on Iraq was growing. The US had become much more engaged in the MENA region after 9/11, and the US Administration advocated a new regime in Baghdad and began seeking support for an offensive coalition while completing a military build-up. Although the US was unable to obtain UN endorsement of military action, the preparations for war might have caused Saddam's regime to change its position and surrender its limitations regarding the UN weapons inspections. Instead, the regime sought confrontation anew. Five means were invoked prior to the US-led invasion: 1) mobilizing the Iraqi military; 2) issuing threats against Israel; 3) working the UN; 4) attempting to reconcile with Arab neighbours; and 5) a media strategy based on appeals issued to the world public portraying Iraq as the victim.

The means were quite similar to those resorted to by Iraq prior to the coalition counterattack in 1991. One difference was the regime's articulation of Iraq as victim and the greater emphasis on appeals to the world public; particularly to Western publics.

Iraq also attempted to appease its neighbours. As Charles Tripp wrote, '[r]ather belatedly, Iraq tried to cultivate its neighbours' (2007: 272). However, the 2002 Iraqi initiatives towards Saudi Arabia and Iran resulted in nothing beyond symbolic gestures. Instead, the Iraqi military was defeated by immensely superior coalition forces in only six weeks.

Saddam Hussein's military was, in the words of Tripp, poorly 'skilled at countering the challenge of direct military intervention' (2007: 272). Given the later findings that Iraq possessed no WMDs at the time of the invasion, the Iraqi defeat can hardly be explained in terms of its military performance, as the capability gap was too great; the only possibility for avoiding defeat when war became imminent would have been a different political strategy.

Iraq obviously pursued a strategy of hard balancing prior to and during the war: Iraq rejected the international demands for full inspection of Iraqi sites, carried out a military build-up, escalated its rhetoric, and issued threats of using chemical weapons if attacked. The only hard balancing element not included was the formation of a counter-alliance. This was not an option, however, as there were no available alliance partners at the time.

The Iraqi policy prior to 2003 tells a story about reliance on WMDs in the sense that Iraq kept the international society guessing about its capacity (Hansen 2003: Ch. 13; Tripp 2007: 273). The investigations following the 2003 war revealed that Iraq had no active nuclear programme and had not succeeded in rebuilding its chemical and biological stockpiles, which were destroyed in the aftermath of Operation Desert Storm. Over the years, Saddam's regime nevertheless insisted first on limited cooperation with the inspections teams – then on no cooperation at all – thereby deliberately attempting to raise doubts about its capacity. The Iraqi actions should be viewed against its previous record: Iraq had used chemical weapons during the Iraq–Iran war (Haselkorn 1999); stockpiles and programmes were revealed after Operation Desert Storm; chemical weapons had been used in Halabja; and a mock chemical attack had been carried out in Southern Iraq (Baram 2003). These actions lent some credibility to the Iraqi WMD-policy.

States considered nuclear threshold states may occasionally want to give the impression that they have already achieved a capacity or that they are so close that it is impossible to prevent them from crossing the threshold. If the adversaries believe or fear that the state in question has already crossed the threshold, they are likely deterred from attacking. On the other hand, a threshold state may also be careful not to overstate its efforts in order to avoid invoking condemnation or pre-emptive strikes (Hansen 2003). The Iraqi WMD-policy between 1993 and 2003 reflected both concerns. In particular, the blocking of UN inspections between 1998 and 2002 represented a dangerous policy, even though Iraq attempted to accompany the policy with public statements that they did not possess WMDs. Against the background of general Iraqi weakness, the WMD-policy of ambiguity came to play a major role in the Iraqi attempts to carry out hard balancing. The American emphasis on non-proliferation policy highlighted this element of the Iraqi strategy.

The US also emphasized the question of international terrorism. There were only two indications of active Iraqi support for terrorism. The first was providing shelter to Abu Nidal, the famous Palestinian terrorist and leader of the Abu Nidal Organization, which had a long record of international attacks. Abu Nidal, however, was already reported dead in August 2002. He was found shot in his apartment in Baghdad, and it is likely (although the circumstances remain somewhat unclear) that he was murdered on orders from Saddam's regime in order to remove a legitimate 'excuse' for the international community to pursue further pressure on Iraq in the light of 9/11. The second indication was the Iraqi support for Palestinian suicide bombers attacking Israeli targets; some of the bombers' families were offered rewards.

After 9/11, Iraq was the only Arab state to fail to condemn the terrorist attacks. In the light of the worldwide condemnation of the terrorist attacks and the UN agreement on further measures, the Iraqi position sent a strong signal. Nevertheless, there was no evidence of active support beyond this kind of moral and political support for the terrorists. Nor was there any evidence that Iraq supported the Taliban regime in Afghanistan. Consequently, it seems appropriate to designate the Iraqi policy until 2003 regarding reliance on international terrorism as only soft balancing.

The Arab–Israeli–Palestinian peace process, launched in 1991, did not receive support from Iraq. After the 1991 Madrid peace conference initiative, Iraq sharpened its rhetoric. Baghdad generally advocated the Palestinian cause and criticized Israel. Saddam's son, Uday, published twelve articles questioning Israel's right to exist, and Arafat was called a 'traitor' after the signing of the Declaration of Principles in 1993. It was insinuated that Arafat deserved the fate of Egyptian President Anwar Sadat (Bengio 1998), who was assassinated in 1981 after entering the Camp David Accords, the peace agreements signed with Israel in 1978. The Iraqi position was somewhat moderated in the 1990s, possibly an attempt at achieving a lifting of the sanctions (1998). However, Iraq continued to criticize the peace process and oppose this cornerstone in US Middle East policy.

The 2003 War forced Iraq to alter its strategy dramatically. However, Iraq was under coalition occupation the first year after the invasion, and Iraq was struggling with an internal insurgency in the years that followed.

Iraq's post-Cold War strategy was one of persistent hard balancing, although its means after the defeat in Kuwait in February 1991 were rather limited. The story of the Iraqi efforts became a tale of an authoritarian state attempting to compensate for losses of relative power by invasion and continuously trying to keep its opponents at bay by means of a strategy of ambiguity. These ('discount') balancing efforts were severely punished, however, as they eventually resulted in the 2003 invasion and ensuing occupation by the US-led coalition and the downfall of the Saddam Hussein regime.

Libya

When the Cold War ended, Libyan–US relations were hostile. In the course of the 1980s, Libyan foreign policy became increasingly anti-Western, and 'Libya was lodged in a confrontational posture vis-à-vis much of the international system' (Niblock 2002: 227). At the same time, the US sharpened its policy towards Libya (2002: 227).

The main conflict regarded Libyan support for international terrorism, which was 'intended in the first place to eliminate the internal and external enemies of the Libyan Revolution' (Martinez 2007: 55). The Libyan activities resulted in US bombings of targets in Tripoli and Benghazi in 1986 following a terrorist attack in a Berlin discotheque killing two US soldiers and the establishment of the US blacklist of terrorist states. In addition to the Libyan state-sponsoring of terrorism, Libya had pursued a radical stance towards the Arab-Israeli conflict.

However, the Libyan response to the Iraqi invasion of Iraq in 1990 was rather moderate compared to the previous Libyan rhetoric and 'anti-imperialist' policy. To begin with, Libya denounced the Iraqi invasion of another Arab state, secondly, Libya strongly argued against foreign intervention.

At the Arab League Cairo summit on 10 August 1990, Libya was one of only three Arab League members (together with Iraq and the PLO) to vote against sending Arab forces to protect Saudi Arabia. In a description of the summit, Mohamed Heikal wrote that 'Muammar Gadaffi proposed a secret meeting restricted to kings and presidents, because there were too many outsiders following the discussions' (1993: 296). This proposal was dismissed in favour of voting on the resolution. Without exaggerating the importance of the proposal, it indicates a possibility that Libya might have taken a softer position if it could have been done secretly. Initially, Libya accepted UN measures against the Iraqi occupation, but its position was later aggravated after demonstrations in Libya in support of Iraq (Niblock 2002: 229). In December, 1990, Muammar Gadaffi himself led such a demonstration in Tripoli (Heikal 1993: 23).

Still, Libya did not turn to measures such as attempting to create counter-alliances (this is hardly surprising, of course, as the possibilities were meagre) or to offer military support to Iraq. Nor did Libya promote terrorism in order to force the US-led coalition forces to leave. In a discussion of why the Iraqi regime was not supported by acts of terrorism sponsored by other Arab states, Freedman and Karsh argued that Syria was a member of the coalition against

Iraq, Iran had no interest in assisting Iraq, and Libya had been warned by the US not to promote terrorism (Freedman and Karsh 1993: 344).

The Iraqi invasion had led to an international embargo on oil from Iraq and Kuwait. In August, 1990, on Saudi Arabian initiative, OPEC decided to suspend oil quotas in order to increase production. Libya (and Iraq) did not attend the session (Freedman and Karsh 1993: 183). The Libyan absence was perceived as an act of solidarity with Iraq. Apart from this, however, Libya did not take any measures in support of Iraq. Furthermore, Libya criticized the Iraqi hostage-taking of Western nationals (Freedman and Karsh 1993: 156).

The Libyan policy during the 1990–91 Gulf Conflict was conceived against the background of the loss of its superpower ally and broken Arab unity. The Iraqi invasion of Kuwait and resulting split of the Arab League also confirmed the limits of Arab radicalism. The Libyan policy regarding the conflict is characterized as soft balancing: Libya neither supported the US initiatives nor accepted sending Arab forces in defence of Saudi Arabia. It criticized the US policy but refrained from taking any substantial measures to counter this policy. Furthermore, the Libyan rhetoric appeared harsh, but not as harsh as could have been expected in the light of previous Libyan rhetoric.

One of the cornerstones in the policy of Gadaffi's Libya was the Palestinian cause and struggle against Zionism. Libya occasionally assumed a more radical position than the Palestinian leaders: in January, 1980 a conflict between Muammar Gadaffi and Yasir Arafat resulted in the breaking off of Libyan support for al Fatah after accusations that Arafat was abandoning the armed struggle (Arnold 1996). Prior to this, however, Gaddaffi had proposed the hanging of Jordan's King Hussein following the Jordanian clamp-down on Palestinian militants in September 1972; and in 1972, Libya received the bodies of the slain terrorists from the terrorist attack during the Summer Olympics in Munich and provided them with ceremonial funerals (Arnold 1996: Ch. 7).

The agreement of the Declaration of Principles in September 1993 sidelined Gadaffi on the Palestinian issue. During the 1990s, however, Libya criticized the PLO's pursuit of a two-state strategy and supported militant Palestinian groups. Libya criticized the Madrid Process and the Oslo Accords, but 'despite rhetorical fulminations [it] has not disturbed the implementation of the Oslo Accords' (Takeyh 1998: 164).

US–Libyan relations were deeply troubled at the time of the Madrid process. In a speech about the Madrid multilateral track following the 1993 Israeli-Palestinian breakthrough in the process, US Assistant Secretary for Near Eastern Affairs Edward P. Djerejian stated, 'we extended invitations to all regional states, save those – like Libya and Iraq – whose policies had put them outside of the community of nations' (Djerejian 1993).

By the end of the 1990s, however, Libyan policy towards the peace process took a new turn. In 1999, Libya expelled the Abu Nidal Organization and uprooted its infrastructure; it withdrew its support for other Palestinian terrorist organizations such as the PFLP-GC and Palestinian Islamic Jihad, and accepted Yasir Arafat's strategy.

When the second Palestinian Intifada broke out in 2000, Libya once again resorted to harsh rhetoric but did not stray from its new policy. Many reasons have been given for doing so against Libya's radical background; reasons which appear to reinforce one another. At least four factors seem to have influenced the Libyan change in direction regarding the peace process.

First, 'Libya had been searching since the suspension of the sanctions in 1999 for a way to reinstate itself fully in the international community' (Martinez 2007: 48), and it seemed realistic to Muammar Gadaffi also to anticipate an end of US bilateral sanctions. Second, the sanctions had affected living standards and given rise a sense of isolation in Libya (2007: 24–25), which encouraged consequential political action that avoided antagonizing the US. Third, Libya was facing an ever-growing domestic challenge from Islamist groups, which 'crowded-out' the Palestinian cause. Fourth, the Islamist challenge interacted with the growing Islamization of Palestinian politics. Finally, Libyan policy after the end of the Cold War had increasingly been directed towards the African continent (Hansen 2000a), as the North African states constituted the core interest of Libya.[11] This priority rendered support for the Palestinian cause less important than it had previously been.

Nevertheless, Libya did not re-formulate its policy towards the Israeli-Palestinian peace process in accordance with US objectives, and Libya did not send a delegation to the US Annapolis conference to revive the process in November 2007. By the end of the 1990s, however, Libya abandoned its policy of 'rejectionism' and appeared to accept the development. The most important indication of change was the end of Libyan support for militant (terrorist) Palestinian organizations and recognition of the authority of the PLO.

While the previous support for terrorist Palestinian organizations constituted one dimension of Libyan support for international terrorism, 9/11 highlighted the standoff between Libya, the US and the international society on the Lockerbie case.

After the Berlin discotheque bombing in 1986, two major incidents of international terrorism ostracized Libya from the international society. On 21 December 1988, Pan Am Flight 103 from London was bombed over Lockerbie in Scotland, killing 270 people. Among the 259 persons on board, 189 were American. On 19 September 1989, a UTA flight was bombed over Niger, killing 171. Following a report, Scottish authorities issued warrants on two Libyans in the Lockerbie case in 1990, and French authorities had issued warrants for four Libyans. The UN imposed an embargo on arms sales and flights and demanded that Libya extradite the two suspects. The US had already imposed bilateral sanctions in 1986 following the Berlin discotheque bombing, and the sanctions were further expanded twice, in 1992 and 1996.

During the 1990s, Libya refused to comply with the demands. Instead, Tripoli took a series of alternative steps, offering to carry out its own investigation (1991) and proposed cooperation with French investigators regarding the UTA-case (1993). Libya suggested extraditing the two suspects in the Lockerbie case in return for US and UK diplomatic relations (1993). Finally, Libya accepted a trial in Switzerland (1993); however, none of these offers were accepted by the international community. It was first when Libya extradited the two suspects for a trial by the International Court in the Hague in April 1999 that the sanctions were suspended. This was the first turning point.

Finally, in August 2003, Libya settled the long-standing dispute on Lockerbie by accepting responsibility for the bombing. The country agreed to pay US$2.7 billion in a compensation settlement and now denounced international terrorism. The UN Security Council lifted the sanctions in September. About three years later, the US restored diplomatic relations and removed Libya from the blacklist of states sponsoring terrorism. The US ended bilateral sanctions in May–June of 2006. The Lockerbie case thus stretched over 15 years.

The next turning point was the 9/11 terrorist attacks. In contrast to the 1980s, Libya now strongly condemned the terrorist attacks and announced its support for the War on Terrorism. Gadaffi stated on his official website that 9/11 was a 'horrifying' act and that America and other states have the right to self-defence.[12]

The new Libyan approach to international terrorism, its position regarding the terrorist attacks on 11 September 2001, and its willingness to join the global struggle against terrorism was the result of several factors, which all affected the cost and benefits of the Libyan security strategy.

In the first place, the embargo, sanctions and isolation were a costly affair for Libya. As Luis Martinez wrote about the social consequences of the sanctions, '[b]etween 1992 and 1999, the population of Libya faced many new problems', and the feeling of isolation and negative impact on the standards of living led to frustration and dissatisfaction with the regime (2007: 25). Libya thus came under heavy socio-economic pressure from its radical foreign policy, via the sanctions at the time of falling oil prices and 'the cumulative effect of years of economic mismanagement' (Pargeter 2006: 220). The sanctions were part of the high price Libya had paid for confronting the US and pursuing its balancing strategy. The price was beginning to appear excessive given the domestic costs.

In the second place, another result derived from the socio-economic decline was a strengthening of the political opposition within Libya in the 1990s. According to Martinez, there was no significant 'opposition of any kind within Libya between 1969 and 1993' (Martinez 2007: 97). During the 1990s, this changed by a 'swelling of the ranks of opposition' (Takeyh 1998: 165), including the middle class and students. Furthermore, the tribes regained power (Martinez 2007: 100). In 1993–94, Libya saw severe dissatisfaction, which led to an abortive coup d'état, unrest in the military, violent demonstrations and waves of arrests (Arnold 1996: Ch. 4). The dissatisfaction was predominantly caused by the economic decline resulting from the sanctions. One of the results was the rise of militant Islamism, which led to a major challenge for the Gadafi regime. In addition to posing a threat to the regime, the rise of militant Islamism also created a common interest with the US and other actors attempting to fight militant Islamists.

In the third place, the impact of the end-of-the-Cold War developments began to take full effect in Libyan politics. The Israeli–Palestinian Declaration of Principles had undermined Libya's radical policy, and the Iraqi invasion of Kuwait and Syrian participation in the Desert Operations had weakened 'the Arab cause'. In combination with its conflict with the international community, these developments undermined the previous foundations and viability for the previous Libyan policy and resulted in increasing political marginalization.

International terrorism, 9/11 and the Lockerbie settlement reflected a dramatic change in Libyan strategy; at least rhetorically and politically. The preconditions for this new strategy were factors affecting the Libyan cost–benefit analysis by steadily and dramatically increasing the price of a (hard) balancing strategy.

In December 2003,[13] Libya took the most significant step yet in its post-Cold War foreign policy reorientation by officially abandoning its WMD programme. Shortly after, tonnes of equipment were flown and shipped to the US and later displayed at Oak Ridge, Tennessee. In an interview with CNN, International Atomic Energy Agency Chief Mohamed ElBaradei said that the Libyan programme had been at an early stage, and Libya was now working fully with the Agency in order to neutralize all activities that could have led to a nuclear weapon (CNN 29 December 2003).

Libya had sought to obtain WMDs since the 1970s (Sinai 1997: 92). Chemical and biological weapons were initially given priority, but Libya also initiated a nuclear programme. The Libyan efforts began at a time when chemical programmes in particular had become a 'spiral' in the MENA region; and Libya was part of that spiral. Furthermore, WMDs were a useful tool in the region (chemical weapons had been used in Chad in 1987 (Haselkorn 1999)), and the WMD capacity was also aimed at off-setting Israeli nuclear weapons (Sinai 1997: 92). The Libyan WMD arsenal thus served as a bid for influence in the Arab world as well as promoting ambitions regarding the leadership of the radical Arab states.

During the 1980s and 1990s, Libya pursued a strategy of ambiguity, as often seen among threshold states. Libya assured that its nuclear programme was intended for peaceful purposes, while at the same time, Libya 'imported nuclear material and conducted a wide variety of nuclear activities' (IAEA – see NTI). Libya repeatedly refused to join the Chemical Weapons Convention, arguing that this would require a comprehensive agreement in the Middle East, including a ban on Israeli nuclear weapons.

The Soviet Union was Libya's 'main partner in the nuclear field' (Globalsecurity.org 2004), though a number of other foreign suppliers were also necessary to assist these efforts due to Libya's relatively low technical level.[14]

Soviet disintegration represented a set-back for the Libyan nuclear programme. Even worse, however, was the lack of equipment and economic decline resulting from the international sanctions. Despite efforts and some cooperation with Russia, Pakistani scientists and a range of minor suppliers, the Libyan programme continued to lack progress.

Against this troublesome background, the invasion of Iraq in 2003 in all likelihood decisively affected the Libyan cost-benefit calculations. According to Martinez, the Iraq War 'seemed a demonstration of American invincibility' to the Libyans (Martinez 2007: 45), and 'it now became evident to the Libyan regime that if France, Russia and Germany had been unable to prevent the invasion of Iraq, then this meant the unilateral power of the United States was without limit' (2007: 45). Libya certainly feared that it could become the next target in a US campaign to alter power relations and regimes in the region, and that WMD programs as well as support for terrorism were becoming too dangerous.

Immediately prior to the US-led invasion of Iraq, Libya made contact with the US through British brokerage in order to discuss a dismantling of the Libyan WMD capacity.[15] Talks were arranged and British and US inspectors went to Libya. In October, the issue was accentuated by the interception of a German cargo ship carrying centrifuge parts to Libya. In December, Libya agreed to eliminate its entire WMD arsenal and allow UN inspections of key sites.

In an interview with CNN, Muammar Gadaffi stated that although the programmes would have been for peaceful purposes, the 'Iraq War may have influenced' the Libyan decision to 'get rid of them completely' (CNN, 22 December 2003).

The WMD programmes, of which the nuclear programme appeared to have been underestimated by the US and other intelligence agencies (CNN 19 December 2003), had been part of the Libyan balancing strategy throughout the 1990s and became the centre-piece in its new strategy in the beginning of the twenty-first Millennium. Libya maintained its chemical and biological programmes and renewed efforts to further its nuclear programme during the 1990s – in spite of its withering ability to do so as a result of the Soviet disintegration and sanctions, which rendered it difficult for Libya to obtain spare parts and additional equipment. These efforts were also limited by the consequential economic decline. During those years, Libya deemed it necessary to secure itself by means of a nuclear programme. It was weakened by the loss of its Soviet ally, and its relationship with the US was clearly confrontational. Libya pursued a strategy of ambiguity, but it was a less offensive version than the Iraqi strategy and virtually restricted its signals to assurances that any nuclear programmes were exclusively intended for peaceful purposes.

By the turn of the Millennium, Libya's cost–benefit analysis had changed. In the first place, the developments in the Lockerbie case held promise that Libya would reap important benefits by escaping sanctions and become re-integrated into international political life. In the second place, the 2003 War against Iraq sent a message that Libya could be the next target for an overwhelming invasion. Instead of devoting resources to a programme that was far from completion and extremely dangerous to pursue because it could invite invasion, Libya chose to abandon it and reap the benefits from becoming internationally re-integrated. Another gain to the Gadaffi regime was its survival, which was endangered by external threats, including US policy to promote regime changes, as well as internal threats, including the domestic rise in militant Islamism in the context of social decline and a general Islamist ideological wave.

In the course of a few years, Libya thus changed course from hard balancing to soft bandwagoning with respect to international terrorism as well as the pursuit of WMDs. It had challenged the world order and the US by building up its non-conventional military arsenal and by means of sub-national violent operations. This hard-balancing strategy was replaced by soft bandwagoning after Libya changed course and complied with crucial US demands regarding those two key issues in the US world order. Regarding the peace process, Libya also changed its policy from support for militant Palestinian groups and rejection of the results of the process to criticism – but acceptance – of the Palestinian authorities.

Libyan strategy from the end of the Cold War to 2007 was thus one of slow but continuous adaptation from a strategy of hard balancing, via a trend towards soft balancing from 1999, towards soft bandwagoning from 2003, which became possible politically due to the regime's firm grip on Libyan politics.

Syria

When Iraq invaded Kuwait in August 1990, Syria had to balance a series of concerns. American influence was on the rise in the region, and the close US-Israel alliance complicated matters for Syria. Siding with the coalition would turn previous Syrian policy towards the US upside down and hamper its image as a radical Arab state. On the other hand, joining the coalition might lead to an improvement in Syrian-American relations, thereby facilitating peace negotiations with Israel. As Raymond Hinnebusch wrote, the end of the Cold War implied that 'Syria was exposed to a power-imbalance in Israel's favour and left without the military option' (2003: 213). To Syria, US brokerage had therefore become a potentially necessary path forward (2003: 113). Joining the coalition would also further weaken its Iraqi rival (2003: 213; Dawn 2003: 175). The Syrian-Iraqi rivalry had lasted for a generation, and the Syrian presence in Lebanon was challenged by General Aoun's militia, which was supported by Iraq (Freedman and Karsh 1993: 96).

As Drysdale has pointed out, the Syrian regime had always 'recognized the need for superpower backing to overcome Syria's fundamental weakness, particularly in relation to Israel' (1993: 278). On this background, Syria opted for joining the international coalition that the US had began assembling immediately after the invasion. Syria contributed 14,500 troops to Operations Desert Shield and Desert Storm, and it remained part of the coalition right to the end, despite Iraqi attempts to promote the 'Arab cause' and split the coalition.

The only proposed alternative was the notion of 'an Arab approach', which at the time symbolized the attempt to create an alternative to the international coalition and use military means to liberate Kuwait. However, 'the Arab approach' was not endorsed by the oil-rich Gulf states, from whom Syria was hoping for financial assistance, and '[t]hese states were quick to reward Syria for its participation in Desert Storm' (Shad and Boucher 1995: 84). Indeed, the

Syrian participation in the coalition produced political rewards and financial benefits, and the Syrian–US relations were much improved.

The Syrian participation in the coalition, its military contribution and its policy changes clearly qualify as hard bandwagoning.

The next major issue was the Madrid Conference and the initiation of the Arab–Israeli peace process. In the late spring of 1991, The US formally invited the parties involved in the Arab–Israeli–Palestinian conflict to Madrid to kick-start the peace process. While the preparations for Operation Desert Shield took place, the US had stated that it would invest greater effort in the peace process when the Iraqi problem was solved. The Madrid Conference became a corner-stone in these efforts and in the initial US post-Cold War Middle East strategy.

In contrast to Israel, Syria quickly joined the efforts, even though the set-up for the peace process differed from previous Syrian approaches: Syria now accepted engaging in direct bilateral talks with Israel, to engage in talks based on Palestinian conditions less favourable than hitherto demanded, and without the role of the UN, which had previously been a Syrian demand (Drysdale 1993: 284). The Syrian approach to the bilateral peace talks with Israel called for a full and un-interrupted Israeli withdrawal from the Golan Heights (Leveret 2005: 46, 48). Until the mid-1990s, Syrian/Israeli talks took place, and 'left both sides with a clearer understanding of each other's position' (Perthes 2004: 52); but the process failed to bring about a peace agreement or other accords.

After three rounds of negotiations in Aspen between 1994 and 1996, the Syrian–Israeli talks stalemated (Leverett 2005: 47). President Hafiz al-Asad referred to an Israeli demand for a surveillance station on Mount Hermon (Hinnebusch 2002: 161) as a breach to the proposal for a full withdrawal. Attempts at reviving the process were carried out twice. New attempts made by President Clinton in 1999–2000 ended unsuccessfully at meetings in Geneva (Perthes 2004: 53). The next initiative to revive the process was the so-called Roadmap initiative,[16] which was launched under the auspices of the US, EU, UN and Russia in April 2003. The Syrian approach was to neither endorse nor resist the initiative (Perthes 2004: 59).

When Bashar al-Asad took over the Syrian presidency from his father in June 2000, he did not rule out peace with Israel but made it a strategic priority in his inauguration speech (Baidatz 2001: 30); however, Syrian rhetoric regarding Israel soon became very harsh (2001: 30; Perthes 2004: 54). Syria continuously stressed its demand for a full Israeli retreat to the June 1967 Golan boundaries, its commitment to the Palestinian cause and the need for the US to grant higher priority to Syrian and Lebanese tracks in the peace process.

Syria also supported the Palestinian uprising, which began in September 2000. According to Israeli sources, Syria funded Hamas and Islamic Jihad, which enabled them to establish an infrastructure and carry out terrorist operations from Jenin.

The peace process was generally in a stalemate during the first years of the new millennium. The Israeli–Syrian track had already reached an impasse; the breakdown of the US-initiated 2000 negotiations in Camp David halted the

Israeli–Palestinian track when Yassir Arafat turned down the final offer (Rubin and Rubin 2003); the Palestinian uprising renewed Israeli–Palestinian actual conflict; and the US decided to shelve the peace process until the parties them-selves would demonstrate greater effort. Soon thereafter, 9/11 triggered a re-direction of US efforts in the region.

In the autumn of 2007, the US resumed its commitment to playing an active official role in the peace process and invited the parties to a major peace confer-ence in Annapolis. The conference did not aim to result in any accords but merely to revive the peace process, and 40 countries – including the Roadmap Quartet and 16 Arab countries – participated. Right up until the start of the con-ference, there was doubt as to whether Syria would participate or not. Syria ulti-mately sent its deputy foreign minister, which was considered a low rank choice. Syria did not want to be isolated and miss opportunity for dealing with the Golan Heights, but at the same time, Damascus did not want to fully endorse the initiative.

One of the controversial Syrian positions regarding the peace process throughout the period was its support for Hezbollah in southern Lebanon. Hezbollah's armed struggle against Israel appeared to be Syrian proxy activity to destabilize Israel's northern frontier, thereby pressuring the Israeli position. The attacks continued after the May 2000 Israeli unilateral retreat from its posi-tions in Lebanon, but they did not escalate. In October 2003, Israel carried out air strikes against a target in Syria after a suicide terrorist attack in Haifa. Islamic Jihad claimed responsibility for the attack, and Israel claimed that the target camp in Syria had been used by Islamic Jihad for training.[17]

In addition to the Syrian support for Hezbollah, its military presence and political influence in Lebanon was also of concern to the other parties in the peace process. Prior to the 2005 Lebanese elections and following a series of popular protests in Lebanon against the Syrian presence, the UN Security Council adopted a resolution calling for a free and fair electoral process in the upcoming Lebanese presidential elections, i.e. demanding respect for Lebanese sovereignty. Although a Syrian spokeswoman dismissed the resolution,[18] Syria began to act accordingly, and preparations for a withdrawal from Lebanon were made. The last Syrian troops withdrew from Lebanon in the end of April 2005,[19] though this hardly brought an end to Syrian efforts to influence Lebanese poli-tics. In February, 2005, former Lebanese Prime Minister Rafik al-Hariri was killed in a Beirut bombing, and this led to a prolonged political controversy. Four pro-Syrian security chiefs were detained and accused of planning the assas-sination.[20] Hariri was anti-Syrian, and the UN Security Council adopted Resolu-tion 1595, which called for an investigation of the murder. The Mehlis Report was released in October 2005 (and a later second report), which implicated Syrian and Lebanese officials in the assassination. Syria denounced the report and opposed an international inquiry, proposing instead to undertake its own.

Other problems related to the issue of international terrorism: Syrian support to Hezbollah and Hamas. On the one hand, the so-called HISH alliance, Hezbol-lah, Iran, Syria and Hamas (Rubin 2006), worried the US; on the other hand, it represented Syria's available allies. The HISH alliance came onto the agenda in the summer of 2006 following the conflict in Lebanon. The conflict began when Lebanese Hezbollah abducted two Israeli soldiers in July in an attack in Israel. The Israeli Prime Minister called the abductions 'an act of war', and Israel launched an offensive. Syria supported Hezbollah.

The Syrian approach to the peace process saw significant changes over the years in question. Between 1991 and the mid-1990s, the approach reflected a bandwagoning strategy. Syria joined the US-initiative and adjusted its policy considerably, although it did not abandon its fundamental claim of a return of the Golan Heights. After a stalemate phase at the end of the 1990s, Syrian policy turned into balancing. From 2000 to 2007, the Syrian approach consisted of its traditional demand for a full return of the Golan; increased weight on the Palestinian issue after the inauguration of Bashar al-Asad; and non-endorsement of the Roadmap but openness towards future negotiations with Israel although with demands for improved pre-conditions. Hezbollah, which the US considered to be a terrorist organization, remained a political card in the hands of Syria, which on the other hand withdrew its military forces from Lebanon. Nevertheless, Syria cooperated with Iran via Hezbollah and continued to attempt to influence Lebanese politics.

Syrian support for Hezbollah and attacks into northern Israel interfered with at least three other terrorist-related issues: the 1990s skirmish with Turkey over Syrian support for Kurdistan Workers' Party (PKK) groups, the war against the Afghan Taliban regime at the end of 2001, and the skirmish with the US over continued Syrian support to militant Palestinian groups.

The Syria/Turkey relationship had been sour for years, particularly due to four issues: Syrian support for the PKK, including protecting then-leader Abdallah Öcelan, water disputes, the Syrian position on WMDs, and Syrian claims to the Turkish Hatay province. In the spring of 1998, it appeared as though the Syrian–Turkish relationship was improving, with a focus on commerce (Kirisci 2000: 47); however, a PKK-related crisis developed in the autumn. Turkish accusations and military build-up on the border forced Syria to sign the Adana Agreement on 20 October 1998 to end support for the PKK and expel Öcelan (Larrabee and Lesser 2003: 145).

Already in November[21] and December 1998, however, Turkey called for Syria to take the implementation of the Adana Agreement seriously.[22] Nevertheless, the Syrian–Turkish relationship was substantially improved, and Syria had officially agreed to end support for the PKK.

After the 9/11 terrorist attacks in the US in 2001, Syria had to cope with the fact that terrorism was at the top of the American and international political agendas. An attack on the Taliban regime was imminent. The Syrian position on the War of Terrorism was to denounce the 9/11 attacks and offer assistance to the US (it contributed to the arrest of at least one suspected terrorist and provided intelligence information). On the other hand, Syria did not seriously address its own sheltering of terrorists (Zisser 2003). These measures took place parallel to Syrian support for Hezbollah and Hamas and, after 2003, Syrian approval of militants entering Iraq across their shared border. The US was harsh as regards the Syrian 'border problem', as the militants entered Iraq to join the insurgency and fight the Coalition forces.

Syrian policy on international terrorism was thus mixed. Despite condemning 9/11 and (modest) assistance to the US in the immediate aftermath, we label the Syrian strategy regarding the issue of international terrorism as hard balancing: Syria built alliances with terrorist organizations and supported them.

The next defining moment occurred in conjunction with the war against Iraq. In 2002, during the prelude to the war, Syria voted in favour of UN Security Council Resolution 1441, which stated that Iraq was in violation of the ceasefire terms laid down in Resolution 687; nevertheless. Syria talked against military action. Prior to the war, Syria provided Iraq with rhetorical support, accepted the smuggling of weapons into Iraq, and allowed Arab volunteers to cross the border (Zisser 2003).

Syria later effectively accepted Resolution 1483 on the rebuilding of Iraq, Damascus also voted in favour of Security Council Resolution 1511 on international involvement, and later restored diplomatic relations with Iraq. In the meantime, however, the Syrian rhetoric against the war was strong, and President Bashir Asad expressed support for Iraqi resistance against the 'invaders' (Podeh 2005).

Like Libya, Syria had few allies available after the end of the Cold War; only Iran presented an option. The Syrian–Iranian relations had developed during the Iraq–Iran War 1980–88, when Syria supported Iran. Since then, Syria and Iran had supported the Hezbollah and Hamas due to shared interests, and some measures of direct cooperation had been initiated after the Iraq War in 2003, including Iranian offer to support Syria against 'challenges and threats' (BBC News, 16 February 2005). Apart from such initiatives and cooperation on support for the Hezbollah and Hamas, there was no evidence of any substantial alliance activity.

After the new regime in Iraq brought about by the war, Syria displayed an element of bandwagoning by withdrawing its troops from Lebanon in April 2005; however, Syria also displayed elements of balancing by allowing militants to cross its border into the Iraqi upheaval, continuing its support for Hezbollah and the Hamas, and by apparently attempting to influence Lebanese politics by means of violent intimidation.

The Syrian story was thus one of a substantial loss of relative power directly related to the end of the Cold War and the disappearance of its Soviet superpower ally. The Syrian strategy for coping with the new order has been changing as well as mixed. It has been labelled a 'dual' strategy by several authors (e.g. Perthes 2004; Heurlin 2006). Syria's foreign policy initially took a U-turn and became one of bandwagoning in the realm of security politics. Since the mid-1990s, however, the general picture has been that of opposition, i.e. pursuing a balancing and opposing strategy, but a strategy carefully designed to avoid direct confrontation with the US. In summary, the Syrian strategy is labelled one of hard bandwagoning in the beginning of the 1990s and soft balancing in the following years.

Regional comparison and explanation

The three cases of Iraq, Syria and Libya tell something about alternative ways of coping with losses and the challenges emerging from shifting to the unipolar international order. In comparison, all of the Cold War US-allied states in the MENA region chose some form of bandwagoning behaviour. They did not oppose or seriously balance the US, nor did they seriously object to the issues on the unipolar agenda. Disputes with the US mainly erupted in relation to the 2003 War against Iraq. However, none of the US-allied Arab states took their reservations further than criticism or rejection of US proposals for cooperation. The predominant strategy in the MENA region between 1989 and 2007 was thus bandwagoning. This type of strategy was often pursued discreetly or without exhilaration, but was nonetheless preferred by the Cold War US allies.

The Iraqi invasion of Kuwait served as the proverbial moment of truth for some Arab states; this was certainly the case in the Gulf states. Prior to the invasion, as Joseph Kostiner wrote, 'the United States was already regarded as the main defender of the Gulf', but yet 'the Arab Gulf states themselves were not eager to institutionalize a US military role' (2001: 136). In addition to participating in the Desert Operations, the Gulf states subsequently accepted – and to some extent assisted – the build-up of US military presence.

Turkey compensated for the loss of strategic value after the disappearance of the Soviet threat by intensifying its bonds with the EU. These efforts were strongly supported by the US, and US/Turkey cooperation continued in NATO and beyond. Prior to the War against Iraq in 2003, Turkey refused to allow the US to open an additional front against Iraq from Turkish territory, but allowed the US to use its airspace. This skirmish aside, Turkey displayed hard bandwagoning throughout the period in question.

North Yemen (YAR) merged with South Yemen (PDRY) in 1990. The unified Republic of Yemen turned to bandwagoning after soft balancing during the Gulf Conflict 1990–91. Following some years of struggle for power in the new republic resulting in the outbreak of a minor civil war in May–June 1994, Yemen chose to pursue a bandwagoning strategy and later joined the global War on Terrorism.

It was widely debated whether the special US–Israeli relationship would survive the changes following the end of the Cold War (Steinberg 2001). The US dilemma was highlighted by the formation of the Coalition after the Iraqi invasion of Kuwait. The coalition was sensitive owing to the participation of eight Arab states, all of which faced domestic criticism because of this action. In full understanding with the US, Israel therefore remained outside of the coalition but was provided with Patriot missiles during the Iraqi Scud campaign in the beginning of 1991. When the US called for the Madrid Peace Conference after the war, Israel chose to join the process after a series of procedural manoeuvres (Hansen 2000a). The special relationship survived, and Israel displayed hard bandwagoning throughout the period in question.

Egypt displayed hard bandwagoning during the 1990–91 conflict. For the rest of the period, Egypt pursued a soft bandwagoning strategy (although with criticism of the 2003 Iraq War).

While the US-allied Arab states pursued bandwagoning strategies within the realm of security, they were less inclined to opt for domestic political change, i.e. democratization. Democratic reforms began almost only to appear after the fall of the Saddam Hussein regime in 2003. Bandwagoning strategies by these states are no big surprise, because, ceteris paribus, they all enjoyed a high degree of relative security due to their security ties to the US.

Regarding the former Soviet-allied states, the picture differs considerably. Iraq, Syria and Libya chose balancing strategies at some point, though the Syrian strategy was initially one of hard bandwagoning, and the Libyan strategy ended up as one of hard bandwagoning.[23]

Two of the other Cold War Soviet allies suffered from internal conflict and thus refrained from pursuing coherent external strategies. Algeria was subjected to a low-intensity but bloody civil war during the 1990s and had a low-profile foreign policy. Afghanistan was subject to civil warfare until the Taliban gained control over major parts of the country in 1996. After the Taliban regime took over, the Afghan strategy became a balancing strategy. Afghanistan provided safe haven for al-Qaida and refused to extradite Osama bin Laden after 9/11. A US-led airborne invasion in October 2001 resulted, which eventually brought about the fall of the Taliban regime.

Another previous Soviet ally, the PLO, later the Palestinian Authority, suffered a devastating blow after losing its superpower ally. This loss was aggravated by the initial post-Cold War strategic move by the PLO, namely support for Iraq and the invasion of Kuwait. This caused additional losses in terms of an end to support from the conservative Gulf States. The PLO subsequently changed to a bandwagoning strategy and engaged in the Madrid (later the Oslo) Peace Process. By the mid-1990s, however, the Palestinian Authority again changed strategies, now embracing a strategy of soft balancing. In June 2007, the Palestinians split. Hamas took control over the Gaza Strip, and civil war-like struggles took place. President Mahmoud Abbas and Fatah, which remained in control in the West Bank, opted for soft bandwagoning, while the Hamas resorted to a hard balancing strategy.

Iran, one of the major MENA players, suffered no direct losses in terms of superpower support due to the end of the Cold War, as it had remained outside the bipolar camps since the revolution in 1979. Instead, it suffered losses regarding its political room to manoeuvre, because it was no longer protected (in the eye of the storm) from superpower interference by the bipolar fear of escalation. In the first half of the years in question, 1989–2007, Iran pursued a soft balancing strategy, which tilted towards hard balancing by the end of the 1990s. The full step was taken in the years after 9/11 and 2003, when Iran confronted the US and the international community by accelerating its nuclear programme. Iran insisted on uranium enrichment, which led to sanctions. Iran also continued to support the Hamas and Hezbollah, thereby countering the peace process initiatives.

In sum, the previously pro-US states all chose (different degrees of) bandwagoning strategies, while the previously Soviet-allied states chose very different strategies, ranging from hard balancing to hard bandwagoning, and typically adopted a new strategy along the way.

The model and state strategies in the MENA region

The states in the MENA region that were exposed to serious losses tended to pursue strategies of soft or hard balancing between 1989 and 2007. In contrast, the states on the 'winning' side tended to pursue bandwagoning strategies.

The losers chose different strategies, however, and their strategies varied considerably in terms of degree of opposition, consistency and stability. Libya pursued a balancing strategy for quite some time but shifted to a soft bandwagoning strategy; Iraq persistently pursued a strategy of hard balancing until being forced to change to hard bandwagoning in 2003; and Syria initially pursued a strategy of hard bandwagoning but changed to soft balancing in the second half of the 1990s. None of the case countries or other major losers voluntarily launched serious domestic democratic or economic reforms during the 1989–2007 period, but Iraq was forced to do so after the 2003 invasion.

Iraq had suffered losses that were aggravated by its post-Iraq–Iran War position. It was regionally isolated, and although its relationship to the US was tolerable in the beginning of 1990, its strategic move towards Kuwait brought it into a deep confrontation with the sole remaining superpower. Its ideological distance to the US was also very long, being the most authoritarian regime in the MENA region.

The Iraqi policy of hard balancing after invading Kuwait and initially allowing UN inspection is fully consistent with our expectations. The serious loss of power as the basic condition provided a balancing incentive and the impact from a high degree of relative insecurity – regionally as well as in relation to the unipole – in combination with great distance provided an incentive to hard balancing.

However, the massive US pressure beginning in the late 1990s could have forced Iraq to change its cost-benefit analysis. This pressure meant that Iraq's 'relative security' further deteriorated, pointing to the choice of balancing. However, the meagre prospects for a successful outcome could have changed the Iraqi calculations to favour bandwagoning in the sense of 'strategic surrender', as in the case of Libya. Our model cannot explain why this did not happen and Iraq was ultimately invaded. The regime was probably convinced that any concessions or openings would backfire and produce domestic vulnerability, and it would probably become subject to violent revenge. An additional factor might have been the Iraqi capability profile: while Iraq was weakened in most respects, it had a robust military capacity, disposing Iraq to a military response to external challenges.

In contrast, after the end of the Cold War, there was a rapid shift in strategy in the Syrian case, which altered previous Syrian positions towards the US and the peace process. By joining the US-led international coalition against Iraq and contributing with troops, as well as actively participating in the US-initiated Madrid Peace Process, Syria displayed a hard bandwagoning strategy. This is difficult for our model to explain. The initial Syrian strategy-shift to hard bandwagoning took place against the background of a substantial loss of power (and although Syria did not suffer from Iraq's double loss, it was even more vulnerable due to its lack of oil wealth). Syria also faced a low degree of relative security and considerable ideological distance to the US and the new world order. Our model would therefore expect Syria to have pursued a strategy of hard balancing. Only one element may count for the Syrian hard bandwagoning: the strong US engagement in the region beginning in August 1990. We expected that when the unipole engaged in lowering the probability of conflict for a state, which was the case in regional terms in the early 1990s, the state is provided with strong incentive to maintain its security benefits by means of a bandwagoning strategy. This seems to have affected the Syrian choice of strategy, though without the expected gains.

However, this hard bandwagoning strategy lasted only about five years. The Syrian strategy then turned to balancing, as expected in our model. The Syrian weakness had promoted strategic change to bandwagoning, but what promoted the subsequent shift to balancing?

In terms of relative power, Syria was subjected to a continuous weakening during the 1990s and onwards, though the 1991 Iraqi defeat at the hands of the coalition improved Syrian relative security to some extent, as one of Syria's two major rivals was further weakened and contained. The US–Syrian rapprochement also improved Syria's security. The peace process did not bring about the anticipated security gains for Syria, however, as it failed to re-gain the Golan Heights from Israel. Syrian participation in the peace talks became even more formal than real, and its overall strategy gradually turned into balancing. In short, Syria experienced a slight regional improvement in the first half of the 1990s and improvement in its relations with the US, which triggered the bandwagoning strategy. The loss of relative security following the fall in American engagement in the MENA region in the mid-1990s (in terms of relative ideology, the considerable distance remained unchanged), counts for the return to balancing. This raises the question as to why Syria did not resort to hard balancing.

Libya experienced a loss of relative power, as did Iraq and Syria; however, the Libyan oil wealth and limited population reduced the impact of this loss to some extent. In terms of relative security, Libya was regionally better off than Iraq and Syria, but it had been on a collision course with the US since 1986 and became subject to an international embargo in 1992. Ideologically, the distance to the US and the world order was great. We would therefore expect hard balancing from Libya. In the first years of the post-Cold War era, Libya pursued a hard balancing policy by means of increasing its WMD capacity. Libya sought alliances with militant Palestinian organizations that carried out terrorist activities, and Tripoli assumed a high rhetorical profile in a series of MENA issues.

By the end of the 1990s, however, the Libyan strategy began to shift to band-wagoning. Between 1999 and 2005, Libya complied with UN and US demands regarding the Lockerbie affair, ended support for Palestinian terrorist groups, accepted the Declaration of Principles, and officially abandoned its WMD programmes.

Libya's initial strategy was a balancing strategy. Its score on all three variables in the model pointed towards choosing balancing. The strategy was one of hard rather than soft balancing, which is compatible with the expectations arising from the model in the sense that considerable ideological distance and low relative security (which, in the Libyan case predominantly concerned its relationship with the US) point towards choosing hard balancing strategies.

The Libyan shift in strategy to bandwagoning took place on the background of further relative losses: the embargo and US sanctions seriously weakened Libyan society and impeded its attempts to obtain WMD capacity. Regarding relative ideology, there was no change. As to relative security, the invasion of Iraq was the defining event, proving that non-conformist states risked invasion and the Libyan regime could fall. Declines in power and relative security thus appeared to influence the Libyan choice in strategy in favour of bandwagoning over balancing; in the sense of virtual surrender.

Figure 5.1 provides a survey of the states' strategic choices between 1989 and 2007 according to the analysis:

In summary, then, the analysis of the three MENA states in the above selected from amongst those suffering substantial losses of power as of the end of the Cold War produced the following results:

- Balancing became the prevalent strategy in Iraq, Syria and Libya between 1989 and 2007, but we also found bandwagoning strategies.
- Dramatic changes of strategy took place – from bandwagoning to balancing and from balancing to bandwagoning. Furthermore, the strategies were characterized by including different elements.
- Hard balancing was only a stable strategy in one case, namely in Iraq until 2003. Except for this, soft versions of the strategies dominated.

When comparing these findings to the expectations derived from the model, we find a number of matches and shortcomings.

Iraq	Hard balancing 1990–2003
	Hard bandwagoning 2003–07
Libya	Hard balancing in the early 1990s
	Soft balancing from the mid-1990s to 2003
	Soft bandwagoning 2003–07
Syria	Hard bandwagoning from 1990 to the mid-1990s
	Soft balancing from the mid-1990s to 2007

Figure 5.1 State strategies 1989–2007 – Iraq, Syria and Libya.

In the first place, the findings highlight the unipolar dilemma of states *losing relative power*. On the one hand, they have an incentive to balance the unipole, i.e. the dominant concentration of power. On the other hand, they have an incentive to bandwagon, as their ability to balance is limited and the potential gains are doubtful. This dilemma was reflected in the change in strategies: Libya's from balancing to bandwagoning and Syria's from bandwagoning to balancing. Iraq's strategy was forcefully changed from balancing to bandwagoning by the war in 2003.

In the second place, we ought to expect the states to pursue balancing strategies due to the intervening variable *relative security*: the states were all located in a region, which in the period in question was characterized by a low level of relative security. At first glance, we saw one full-fledged example of hard balancing: the Iraqi strategy from 1990 to 2003. We also observed some hard balancing pursued by Libya in the beginning of the 1990s and a preponderance of soft balancing. When examining variations in 'relative security', it appears as though the relationship with the US plays the major role: in the case of prospects of a major confrontation (and certain defeat) with the US, the states appear to abandon hard balancing – with the important exception of Iraq until 2003. When Syria replaced its bandwagoning strategy with balancing in the mid-1990s, it chose a soft version. It backed down in a series of cases when risking further confrontation with the US. When political pressure on Libya mounted in the 1990s, it began replacing hard balancing with soft balancing. The pressure on Iraq was substantial throughout the 1990s and even increased after 2001, when the US included the option of 'regime change' in its strategy towards Iraq. Iraq, however, took a gamble and continued its hard balancing policy and was ultimately invaded.

In the third place, we should expect the three states to pursue 'hard' balancing strategies due to the *considerable ideological distance*. We expected that ideological distance would amplify the incentive to pursue hard versions of balancing and bandwagoning. The three case countries were all ideologically distant to the world order and the unipole; during the period of investigation, there was no significant variation except for the case of Iraq, which saw fundamental changes imposed after the war in 2003. The post-2003 change in policy in Iraq was largely promoted by the US-led coalition, and the changes in strategy, ideology and relative security occurred simultaneously.

In the fourth place, the model leads us to expect strategic behaviour to be produced not only by the individual variables but, given the loss of relative power, by the *combination* of relative security and relative ideology. We assumed above that the MENA states were subjected to mixed incentives, which ought to lead us to expect greater strategic variation than in the two other regions in this study. Furthermore, we should expect to see a comparatively high degree of balancing in the MENA region. This was also the case.

Finally, even minor changes in the mixed incentives should count for changes, which was the case to some extent. Iraq, which pursued the most coherent hard balancing strategy until 2003, was lacking in relative security as well as power and ideology, while Libya changed strategy twice in contrast to Iraq, Libya was relatively secure regionally, but ultimately proved sensitive to US pressure. Syria, which changed its strategy initially but also 'changed back again' later, was regionally less secure than Libya and seemed to have acted mainly in accordance with low regional security in the case of limited US engagement.

Conclusion

Our study asked which strategies were pursued, in the cases of Iraq, Syria and Libya, between 1989 and 2007, and whether we could explain the choice of strategies by means of the model presented in Chapter 2.

We discovered that the three states had pursued a variety of strategies with a comparative prevalence of hard balancing, which is significant compared to the two other regions. The three losing MENA states had difficulties accepting the US-dominated post-Cold War world order and relations of strength. They were deprived of their major ally in the regional games as well as countering the US, and the US world order challenged their political and economic systems. Furthermore, they lost bargaining power in the sense that the US did not have to act to prevent a nuclear confrontation with the Soviet Union. When dealing with these challenges, the three states would have to surrender fundamental political aims and values or attempt to counter the US pressure. They all tried the hard way in one way or another. By 2007, however, Iraq had been forced to change its policy. Libya had – after substantial pressure – chosen to adapt in a conformist manner in several respects. Syria was still fighting on, but had continuously done so within limits: it had not seriously confronted the US. Nevertheless, none of the three states had reformed their domestic systems in accordance with the US unipolar demands but the authoritarian, Ba'athist Iraqi system was overthrown and was replaced by the Parliamentarian Republic.

The results of the empirical analysis generally matched the expectations derived from our model. Consequently, we explain much of the strategies of the three MENA states on the basis of realist logic and a combination of relative power, relative security and relative ideology – including the mixed incentives. Our findings indicate that, in the case of the MENA, the relative security variable regarding the US policy was particularly important. Moreover, it would appear as though one other factor in particular influenced the strategic choices of the case countries: the degree of authoritarian rule. Saddam Hussein's regime in Iraq was the most brutal of the region's authoritarian regimes; in the case of a downfall, it could therefore anticipate revenge as well as a lack of refuge options. This might contribute to explain why the regime clung to power and did not abandon its policy of hard balancing, even under ultimate US pressure, in which case it was most likely bound to lose.

Three other factors ought to be mentioned in respect to the pursuit of nonconformist strategies. The first factor is the capability profile of the three states, which in all cases – most notably in the Iraqi case – was characterized by a high degree of asymmetry between the general level of capabilities and military capabilities. When choosing a strategy, states must consider the means available. In the three cases, military means was at their disposal. This possibly favoured balancing strategies, either by means of aggression, military build-up or support for sub-state terrorist groups. The second factor was the states' engagement in the development of WMDs. Iraq had previously had a record of granting high priority to the development of WMDs, and although there was no evidence at all of a continuation or revival of such development to be found after the 2003 war, Iraq had pursued a policy of ambiguity until the defeat. In contrast, the Libyan nuclear programme turned out to be more advanced than estimated when Libya decided to give it up towards the end of 2003. The Syrian efforts are still to be revealed, but the 'threshold' status (genuine or not) of the three states might have encouraged them to choose more non-conformist strategies than otherwise would have been the case. The third factor is the authoritarian character of the states' regimes. As Steven David has shown, authoritarian regimes tend to act differently, even in the case of alignments and the choice of security strategies. The regimes fear what will happen to them in the case of a new regime, making them act differently to some extent compared to non-authoritarian elites by granting priority to their own security over state interests (1991; Garnham 1991).

Regarding the change in strategies, US military intervention or the threat of intervention endangering relative security by means of the unipole's policy appears to have been the most important factor. Syria opted for a change to bandwagoning in light of the US 1990 build-up; Libya changed its strategy to bandwagoning after the invasion of Iraq, and Iraq was forced to change by the 2003 War. This observation of the production of change tells us that the MENA states had much at stake and were comparatively less inclined to follow suit voluntarily. This means that the unipole is able to scare weak states to adopt bandwagoning strategies. As we saw in Chapter 3, however, this is not an option in regard to stronger states with nuclear weapons such as Russia.

In summary, the three MENA states pursued mixed strategies and displayed a relatively considerable amount of balancing – as expected by our model. The combination of incentives, particularly the unipole's management and the crossfire of the incentives largely accounted for their choice of strategies.

6 Conclusions

The aim of *Security Strategies and American World Order: Lost Power* was to describe and explain the security strategies of the states that lost out as a result of the end of the Cold War.

We wanted to explain *how* and *why* they adapted their strategies to the unipolar world order. In order to explain how they adapted their strategies, we distinguished between hard balancing, soft balancing, hard bandwagoning and soft bandwagoning. This allowed us to draw on some of the most recent developments of realist IR theory in order to systematically characterize the strategies of the states under scrutiny. In order to explain why they adopted the strategies they did, we developed a theoretical model consistent with this type of theory. Our explanatory variables were relative power, relative security and relative ideology. Relative power was virtually constant throughout the period 1989–2007 and between the cases: all shared the same basic and constant condition of unipolarity. Relative security and relative ideology varied within and between the cases. The analysis revealed that relative security had the greatest explanatory value of these two variables, whereas relative ideology mainly played the role of an 'amplifier' of the effects of relative power and relative security.

The book offered a general explanation for the strategy choices of otherwise very different state losers: Russia (the remains of the Soviet Union), Europe (EU member states), and the Middle East (Iraq, Syria and Libya). All three were an integral part of the Cold War superpower confrontation (Zakaria 1990) and therefore strongly affected by its conclusion in 1989. The Soviet-Russian Empire was the main loser: the protagonist, which lost out in the Cold War rivalry and subsequently dissolved and shrank to the imperial core of Russia. Europe was the centrepiece of the Cold War superpower confrontation, and it was the main battle theatre in the war plans of the bipolar superpowers. After the end of the Cold War, the political importance and relative power of Europe was reduced. Over time, the Middle East became increasingly sucked into the central arena of the Cold War, and it became subject to proxy conflicts as the nuclear race intensified and froze the bipolar rivalry in Europe. When the Cold War came to an end, actors in the Middle East lost out in terms of international relative position, strategic importance and specific assistance.

The nature of our investigation encouraged us to carry out case studies rather than quantitative surveys; consequently, we focused on the most important losers. As we also wanted to investigate the causes of variations in the strategies for adaptation, we analysed the three very different groups that all lost out from the end of the Cold War but chose different strategies for adaptation. In the case of the Middle East, we had a very large and heterogeneous group of states, and we therefore also decided to carry out case studies *within* this group of states.

In this final chapter, we outline and compare the main findings in our three case studies and conclude the analysis in order to reflect on the analysis and the theoretical and empirical implications of our findings.

Which strategies did the losers choose?

Russia

The Soviet disintegration towards the end of 1991 left its Russian successor state in a position of substantial loss measured in terms of most capabilities. The loss of territory was severe, and this loss was further aggravated by the accompanying loss of industrial bases as well as human and economic resources.

Facing the massive challenge of adapting to the new world order from a position of a dramatic loss of position, Russia faced a spectrum of strategic choices spanning from hard balancing to hard bandwagoning. The classic structural realist expectation would be that Russia would seek to balance American power. From our modified realist model, however, we inferred two specific hypotheses regarding Russia. The first hypothesis expected Russia to abstain from balancing against the US world order, initially choosing a bandwagoning strategy thanks to its relatively high level of security as a result of its nuclear deterrent and few geopolitical rivals in the early 1990s. However, we expected Russia to edge towards balancing in the latter half of the 1990s as its relative security declined. Russia's bandwagoning and balancing strategies were expected to be soft, however. In the early 1990s, ideological distance to the US world order remained high, leading us to expect that Russian bandwagoning would only be soft – not hard. Russia's balancing strategy was also expected to remain soft – not hard. This is because Russia democratized and moved closer to the US world order.

The empirical findings showed us that Russia initially chose a soft bandwagoning strategy, which by the mid-1990s was replaced by soft balancing (interrupted by a short period of bandwagoning following 9/11). The findings were based on an analysis of the Russian strategy toward the US, other major powers, and its borderlands. From 1991 to 2007, the Russian strategy was characterized by a basic acceptance of the American world order and its rules of play; at least in the sense that Russia did not take any steps in terms of military build-up or the forging of serious counter-alliances in order to challenge the world order.

In the first five years after 1991, the Russian strategy was one of soft bandwagoning; however, changes in relative security contributed to changes in

Russia's strategy towards one of soft balancing in the mid-1990s, when Russia distanced itself from the US, improved its relations with other major powers, particularly China, and began seeking the re-integration of other CIS-states by means of carrots as well as sticks (in the form of blackmail and divide-and-rule-policy). The changes in relative security resulted mainly from the deterioration of the state of the Russian nuclear capacity, NATO expansion (which brought US influence very close to Russian territory) and the 2003 Iraq War (which represented a conflict of interest).

Why was there no hard balancing in the case of Russia despite the basic incentive to balance the unipole? The overwhelming relative power of the United States made hard balancing virtually impossible and extremely costly and therefore favoured softer approaches (until the opportunity to form a strategic coalition arises). The initial high level of Russian relative security also strongly discouraged balancing. Even though Russian relative security declined during the 1990s the inclination for hard balancing became even smaller as a result of the growing ideological proximity to the American world order as Russia democratized – and became a semi-democracy – as this move reduced the potential for ideologically generated conflict.

Europe

In contrast to the Cold War defeat of the Soviet Union and the consequential weakening of Russia, Europe appeared to emerge from the Cold War in a winning position: its main enemy had withered away, and the emerging world order seemed much more in line with European interests than the bipolar rivalry.

However, it soon became evident that Europe was subject to relative loss, as the US came to enjoy a previously unseen asymmetrical edge of power as a result of the end of bipolarity. In the post-Cold War period, American relative power continued to grow, making the United States a superpower of unprecedented strength in the history of the state system. In particular, American military power left the United States undisputed and Europe dependent. Europe was falling behind in terms of military expenditures and its importance for US security was dramatically reduced as it was no longer the primary focus of US attention. 9/11 demonstrated that US security concerns were primarily focused on other regions, and furthered European fears of US disentanglement. Furthermore, the United States shifted its priorities towards its relationship with China and to the Pacific area in general. Still, throughout the period 1989–2007, the United States continued its commitment to European security through NATO enlargement and reform and by stationing a large number of troops in the region.

Our theoretical model allowed us to make a number of predictions about European strategy in the American world order. First, we argued that the asymmetric distribution of power in a unipolar world order creates both a strong incentive to balance and, at the same time, important obstacles, making balancing even more difficult than in bi- or multipolar systems. Second, we argued that relative security was likely to have three separate effects on European strategy.

First, after the Cold War, Europe has generally been characterized by a low probability of conflict creating an incentive for the European states to bandwagon in order to focus on obtaining values, which may be used for protecting security in the future. Second, the United States continues as Europe's primary provider of hard security, thereby creating an incentive for European states to bandwagon. Third, the possession of nuclear weapons allows the Europeans greater independence from the United States than they would otherwise have. Independence dampens the incentive for bandwagoning. However, at the same time nuclear weapons increase relative security and therefore dampens the incentive to balance. As regards relative ideology, we expected the short ideological distance between Europe and the United States to create an incentive for hard bandwagoning. Starting from these assumptions, we analysed whether Europe's strategic behaviour during 1989–2007 was best characterized as balancing or bandwagoning when considered in relation to four dimensions: institutions, strategy, military action and global governance.

Regarding the development of European institutions, the first post-Cold War step was the creation of the Common Foreign and Security Policy (CFSP). This led to strong US opposition, which brought about cautious end formulations presenting the CFSP as support for – as opposed to a challenge to – NATO. In 1992, France and Germany initiated the creation of a Franco-German corps in order to address the gap between European ambitions and the lack of military capabilities. Shortly thereafter, the EU adopted the Petersberg Declaration aimed at enhancing the operational role of the WEU. With a British addition, it was stated that the WEU should not create its own command structures. The declaration thus ended up as an expression of a more limited European approach aimed at supplementing the US security order rather than challenging it. The ESDP comprised the specification of military capabilities allocated for European defence for each country (except Denmark). This move was interpreted very differently by the individual European countries. The US supported the move but signalled that it would not want it to duplicate NATO. Regarding the integration of the European defence industry, on the one hand we witnessed an increase in intra-EU cooperation compared to the cooperation with US firms that was the norm in the Cold War. In 2003, the European Defence Agency (EDA) was set up (supported by the US). On the other hand, the EDA mainly comprised a series of practical initiatives rather than balancing initiatives. In this area, we found no evidence of hard balancing, though a number of examples of soft balancing, particularly the ESDP.

In regard to strategy, the EU member states only agreed on common strategies on a very limited number of issues during the first decade after the creation of the CFSP in 1993. Following the transatlantic and intra-European disagreement on the 2003 War on Iraq, the European Security Strategy (ESS) was agreed upon by the end of 2003. However, the ESS did not allow the EU to act independently of the US in military affairs, nor did it provide the capability to do so. Furthermore, the content of the ESS was generally in line with the US National Security Strategy. Consequently, the ESS was categorized as soft bandwagoning.

We examined five cases of military action. The first four of these all qualified as hard bandwagoning: the Gulf conflict 1990–91, Bosnia 1991, Kosovo 1998, and Afghanistan 2001, although the action taken in Bosnia began with a soft balancing approach but ended up with hard bandwagoning. However, the fifth case, the 2003 Iraq War, represented an entire array of strategies – and massive intra-European disagreements.

Regarding global governance, two areas were examined. The first was the global security order, in which the findings revealed European cooperation with the United States but disagreement on multilateralism and the War on Terror. No hard balancing or full soft balancing was found – but a few examples of the soft balancing of particular aspects of the American order aiming to modify US policy. The second area examined was the global economic order. In the post-Cold War era, the EU and the US continued to be main trade partners and developed a highly institutionalized economic relationship. This area was generally characterized by European bandwagoning behaviour as well as examples of soft balancing of particular aspects of US policy.

In the case of Europe, the balance sheet thus showed no evidence of hard balancing, some evidence of soft balancing (in non-vital areas and regarding particular aspects of US policy). The main instigators of the soft-balancing strategies were France and Germany. In general, however, bandwagoning was the dominant European strategy – predominantly and in vital areas, even hard bandwagoning with soft balancing only at the margins.

How did we explain the dominance of bandwagoning over balancing strategies in the case of Europe? Relative power, relative security and relative ideology all help explain this strategic pattern. The relative power of the unipole made the costs of balancing high and the potential benefits doubtful. The continued US commitment to NATO and European security meant that Europe was relatively secure and the United States remained the most important guarantee that it would stay relatively secure. These effects of relative security were amplified by the ideological proximity between Europe and the United States. In short, the distribution of relative power, which made hard balancing a very costly affair with doubtful benefits; the high degree of relative security in Europe, which was primarily supplied by the US; and the basically consistent ideological approach of the EU and the US all came together to create strong incentives against hard balancing.

How did we explain the presence of soft balancing? The strong basic structural balancing incentives originating from the unipolar distribution of relative power in favour of the US provided incentives for soft balancing on abstract multilateralism, non-security low-cost issues, and very specific or marginal issues. Europeans only balanced on non-vital issues because of their continued dependence on US security provision. They continued primarily as consumers of security and stability produced by the United States. Moreover, the short ideological distance between the United States and Europe discouraged hard balancing. At the same time, the ideological intensity of American foreign policy discourse sometimes underlined the differences between Europeans and

Americans. This amplified the incentive to soft balancing. Also, the pluralist nature of the liberal American order allowed for disagreement among allies without punishment. France and Germany were the main instigators of soft balancing because of their risk of losing from the post-Cold War flexible US multilateralism.

The Middle East

The Middle East as a region lost substantially from the end of the Cold War. In the first place, the former Soviet allies lost position in terms of losing their superpower ally as well as specific benefits. Among the major losers were Syria, Libya and Iraq. Iraq was particularly affected, because it was already struggling with a loss of position related to its 1980–88 war against Iran. None of the former Soviet allies experienced compensatory reforms (like those in Eastern Europe), which could enable them to benefit from the global political changes.

In the second place, almost the entire region suffered decline in terms of being poorly suited for coping with the competitive dimensions of the new market-oriented economic world order. In addition, the region generally lost interest to the remaining superpower in terms of security.

According to our specific hypotheses on the Middle East, the states in the region should be prone to pursue a variety of strategies. Although the region as such has a low score on relative security, the individual states were subject to very different degrees. The states allied to the US enjoyed a much higher degree of relative security than those which were not. Likewise, the degree of relative power loss was comparatively high regarding the entire region. For the individual states, however, the degree differed substantially – the former Soviet allies suffered substantial relative losses as did the states which had benefited from the bipolar rivalry by means of obtaining 'shelter' (the Yemens and Iran). The ideological distance to the world order suggested dispositions for balancing strategies. While the internal organization of the respective states differ in many ways, they are similar (except for Israel and Turkey) in the sense that they are non-democratic. We thus expected the strategies to be particularly diversified, as the states were different according to our variables. We focused on how Syria, Libya and Iraq adapted on five major security issues in the region during the 1989–2007 period: the 1990–91 Gulf Conflict, the Arab–Israeli peace process, the 2001 invasion of Afghanistan, the 2003 invasion of Iraq, and the approach to WMDs and terrorism.

The findings revealed mixed strategies as well as changes of strategies. In the 1990–91 Gulf Conflict, Iraq was the incarnated hard balancer seeking to conquer oil-rich Kuwait to rebuff its relative loss of capabilities, thus heading for an armed confrontation with the US and the international coalition; Libya chose a strategy of soft balancing; and Syria chose hard bandwagoning by participating in the coalition against Iraq. Regarding the Arab–Israeli peace process, Saddam Hussein-Iraq chose hard balancing; Libya chose soft balancing initially but tilted to soft bandwagoning; and Syria replaced its initial hard bandwagoning with hard balancing. The invasion of Afghanistan was accompanied by an Iraqi strategy of continuous balancing, a Libyan strategy of soft bandwagoning, and a Syrian strategy of soft bandwagoning. The 2003 invasion of Iraq evidently reflected an Iraqi strategy of hard balancing; Libya pursued a strategy of soft balancing; and Syria opted for soft balancing in the aftermath of the invasion. Regarding the issues of WMDs and terrorism, the picture becomes even more complex. Iraq displayed soft balancing until 2003 – although against a background of low capacity; so did Libya until it began to change its strategy into elements of hard bandwagoning after 2001 (fully unfolded in 2005), and Syria maintained a low-profile soft-balancing strategy regarding the issues.

In addition to these issues, we examined the general strategies of the three states and specific issues of special interest to their relationship with the US. The findings generally supported the findings of the five security issues. In the case of Libya, however, a slow but continuous softening of its position to the new world order took place alongside its balancing strategies and change of strategy of the early years, while the opposite was the case in the case of Syria – except for the 2005 Syrian withdrawal from Lebanon. In the case of Iraq, the 2003 invasion and regime change led to a dramatic change of strategy (initially in the light of the occupation, and following that by the new government's dependence on coalition forces), which, however, was overlaid by the outbreak of violence in Iraq.

The findings show us that Iraq maintained a strategy of hard balancing until 2003. Libya initially pursued a strategy of hard balancing in the beginning of the 1990s. This was replaced with soft balancing from the mid-1990s until 2003, when soft bandwagoning became the Libyan strategy. Syria initially opted for hard bandwagoning but changed its strategy to one of soft balancing as of the mid-1990s.

When asking why the Middle Eastern states adapted in the way they did, we conclude that the high frequency of balancing strategies is mainly explained by a combination of severe loss of relative power and a relatively high level of conflict (i.e. a low level of relative security) amplified by ideological distance to the American world order.

The states in question had strong incentives to limit the impact of the world order in order to preserve their own models of society in combination with their limited capacity to benefit from the competitive market conditions of the new order, and they all had to operate in a context of tense local relations, which prompted them to choose sides.

Iraq involuntarily changed its strategy after 2003, because its balancing strategy led to nothing but the ultimate cost: invasion. Syria and Libya also changed their strategies dramatically. Syria changed from its initial hard bandwagoning to soft balancing. This change occurred after a lack of benefits in terms of regaining the Golan Heights or economic progress to the Syrian regime in combination with internal pressure. Libya changed from balancing to bandwagoning after years of pressure and negotiations, but the triggering factor seemed to be the invasion of Iraq, which illuminated the costs of a balancing strategy from a weak position. Finally, another similarity was present in the case of the states pursuing balancing strategies of adaptation: authoritarian regimes. This signalled a significant ideological distance to the liberal norms of the American world order.

Why did the losers choose different strategies?

The empirical analyses showed that even though we analysed three very different regions – Russia, Europe and the Middle East – relative power, relative security and relative ideology played an important role in determining strategies in all three cases. However, the analyses also revealed that there were major differences among the losers and their strategies for adaptation. Russia moved towards soft balancing after a few initial years of soft bandwagoning; the European strategy was predominantly one of (hard) bandwagoning; and several examples of soft and hard balancing were found in the Middle East. In this section, we compare the different strategies and relate them to the expectations deduced from our model in order to explain the variations.

Relative power

Relative power tells us where to look for external influence on state strategy. Unipolarity creates a strong incentive to balance; at the same time, however, it also embodies important obstacles to successful balancing.

This book has examined the adaptation strategies of states in the unipolar world order, which had all been subject to a loss of relative power. Does a substantial loss promote balancing behaviour? We are well aware of the difficulties related to distinguishing between various kinds of loss. Russia had to act against the background of losing a superpower position as well as a substantial amount of relative capabilities. The EU lost strategic position and relative power compared to the US over a longer time period rather than in an instant stroke, and Iraq, Syria and Libya lost their superpower ally and specific benefits.

Despite these differences, the case studies provide information concerning the impact of the different degrees of loss. Despite its substantial relative loss, Russia managed to limit its losses enough to maintain a position as a major player in world politics. The EU comprised the group of states suffering the least relative loss by the end of the Cold War among those analysed in this book. Consequently, the EU member states faced comparatively modest challenges in their adaptation processes. Nevertheless, Europe lacked unity and the capability gap to the United States remained vast. This also discouraged high-cost balancing strategies. In the Middle East, the losses related to the termination of the Cold War were most severe in the cases of Syria and Iraq. Syria still had considerable military forces together with a bargaining asset in relation to Israel. When the gains did not materialize, Syria turned to a low-scale balancing strategy. Iraq was hit hard, as it was already weakened. After the 1991 defeat, it was close to being cornered. By refusing to give up its WMD-ambitions, the resulting confrontation with the unipole resulted in another defeat. Conversely, while losing the support of the Soviet Union, the loss was less devastating for Libya, being an oil rich country with a modest population situated in a less conflict-prone part of the Middle East. Among the Middle East case countries, Iraq was thus the state to suffer the greatest losses while pursuing the 'hardest' strategy of balancing.

Relative security

A low probability of conflict encourages bandwagoning strategies, because they are low-cost strategies. And bandwagoning does not place state survival at unnecessary risk when relative security is high. We argued that the role of the unipole was decisive for the level of relative security for individual states: the more the unipole contributes to lower the probability of conflict in respect to a given state, the greater the inclination to pursue a bandwagoning strategy will be, and vice versa.

The EU preference for (often hard) bandwagoning strategies fully matched our expectations regarding the impact of relative security. The EU area is characterized by a high degree of relative security. This is primarily due to the US military presence and its commitment to preserve NATO. Even though Europe did see the outbreak of armed conflict in its periphery following the dissolution of Yugoslavia, these conflicts were contained and eventually stopped, partly due to US intervention.

Russia's degree of relative security was lower than that experienced by the European states. However, Russia initially still possessed its nuclear second strike capability. This factor provided Russia with a basic level of security, which not only allowed scarce resources to be diverted away from armaments to economic and societal reconstruction but also affected Russia's cost-benefit analysis regarding international strategies. The nuclear arsenal limited the amount of pressure the victorious unipole could muster against Russia, on the one hand, and it dampened the Russian incentive to pursue high-cost balancing strategies on the other. The important shift in Russia's strategy from soft bandwagoning to soft balancing by the mid-1990s appeared to be related to rising conflicts of geopolitical interests with the unipole, especially the enlargements of NATO. The unipole's decision to push for NATO expansion into the previous Soviet sphere – even despite previous alleged promises to Russia of not doing so – caused deep security concerns in Moscow and changed the Russian cost-benefit analysis. Later, the Russian incentive was enhanced in the same way by the issues of allegiance related to Ukraine, the southern Caucasus, and Central Asia – and importantly the erosion of Russia's nuclear capacity (although Russia maintained its basic deterrence capacity).

The Middle East suffered from a low degree of relative security. Unsurprisingly, it comprised examples of hard balancing. In the case of Iraq, the hard balancing strategies mainly related to its confrontation with the US unipole, but also to its need for reconstruction after its war against Iran, which was a major factor behind its invasion of Kuwait. Syria initially opted for hard bandwagoning when the United States attempted to re-establish a new regional order after the Iraqi invasion in 1990 and continued when the United States initiated Arab–Israeli peace talks. Later, when the peace talks from a Syrian perspective did not result in gains or increased Syrian security (such as the return of the Golan Heights) while the US simultaneously confronted Syria with other contentious issues (such as pressure on Syria's Lebanon policy), the Syrian cost-benefit analysis changed and Syria resorted to a mixture of elements of soft and hard balancing. However, Syria also displayed a single element of hard bandwagoning (following serious pressure) when withdrawing its troops from Lebanon. Libya followed a strategy of hard balancing in the beginning of the 1990s before turning to soft balancing in the mid-1990s and eventually soft bandwagoning as of 2003. The US engagement in the Middle East (the 2001 invasion of Afghanistan and the 2003 invasion of Iraq) appeared to deeply affect Libya's strategic considerations and choices. Libya attempted to escape the group of states at risk of US confrontation and to join the group of states enjoying US protection or indifference. The notion of relative security thus appears to hold quite some explanatory power regarding the strategies for adaptation. This contributes to explaining why Syria, Libya and Saddam Hussein-Iraq all resorted to balancing strategies.

In conclusion, relative security played an important role for strategic choice in Russia, Europe and the Middle East.

Relative ideology

Power tells us where to look for external influence on state strategy. Relative security tells us about state incentives to balance or bandwagon. Relative ideology tells us which means security policy decision makers are likely to use to respond to this influence, i.e. their willingness to employ hard and soft security strategies. In this manner, ideology serves to amplify the effects of relative security. Relative security provides the main incentives for choosing either balancing or bandwagoning strategies, but ideology provides the major incentives for whether balancing or bandwagoning is hard or soft. Most importantly, we expect states to be more likely to employ a strategy of hard balancing against a unipole with a rival ideology than a unipole with an ideology similar to its own and, conversely, we expect states to be more willing to employ a strategy of hard bandwagoning vis-à-vis a pole with an ideology similar to its own than with a pole with a rival ideology.

In Europe, relative ideology amplified the bandwagoning incentives created by relative power and relative security, creating strong incentives for the Europeans to pursue hard bandwagoning strategies. Russia stuck to soft strategies, shifting from soft bandwagoning in the early years to soft balancing following NATO expansion. In line with our expectations, ideological affinity may thus contribute to explain Russian preferences for soft strategies but not its shift from bandwagoning to balancing strategy. In this regard, it is noteworthy that Russia pursued a soft bandwagoning strategy in the early years after the Soviet disintegration until about 1994 and that Russia, alongside the consolidation of democratic rule and market economy, began to pursue a soft balancing strategy. Comparatively, the ideological gap between the Middle East and the United States was by far the most important. Generally speaking, the findings of several cases of hard balancing in the Middle East thus match our expectations: we should find a number of hard balancing strategies in the Middle East, and we should find more cases of hard balancing in the Middle East than in the EU and Russia, because of ideological distance. The most illuminating example regards Iraqi hard balancing prior to the 2003 invasion. The US had announced a regime change in Baghdad as one of its objectives. However, the ideological factor neither accounts for variations in Middle Eastern strategies nor for shifting strategies. Libya changed its strategy dramatically by the end of 2003 without any preceding ideological changes, as did Syria in the mid-1990s.

However, while the regional ideological difference may appear as independent importance on the surface, closer investigation does not confirm this importance. States such as Kuwait, Saudi Arabia and Egypt were all as ideologically distant from the US as other states in the region; nevertheless, they occasionally pursued strategies of hard bandwagoning. However, they had suffered lesser relative losses of power and they had a higher degree of relative security due to American support than the states pursuing other strategies.

In sum, relative ideology is best seen as an amplifier of the strategic incentives created by relative power and relative security.

In conclusion, relative power, relative security and relative ideology all played a part in explaining the strategies of states that suffered a loss after the end of the Cold War. None of the factors fully explained the strategies or strategic variations, but each of them contributed to delimit the range of strategic outcomes. The analysis showed how each of the three variables played a different role in the explanation:

- Relative power is a condition variable in the analysis, i.e. relative power frames the antecedent condition (cf. Van Evera 1997: 11); it tells us where to look for external influence on state strategy.
- Relative security is the independent variable in the analysis. It is the most important causal factor explaining the balancing and bandwagoning strategies of losers.
- Relative ideology is an intervening variable in the analysis. Relative ideology has little effect of its own on state action, though it amplifies the effects of relative power and relative security.

Combining the three variables allowed us to reach a number of specific conclusions about their effect:

- Unipolarity creates both strong incentives to balance and strong obstacles to successful balancing. Thus, we cannot explain state strategy from unipolarity alone.

- A major loss of relative power favours balancing strategies, whereas a minor loss favours bandwagoning strategies.
- A low degree of relative security favours balancing strategies, whereas a high degree of relative security favours bandwagoning strategies.
- A considerable ideological distance favours hard balancing strategies, whereas minor ideological distance favours hard bandwagoning strategies.

Critical reflections

Our analysis points to the importance of relative power, relative security, and relative ideology, explaining how these variables affect state strategy. However, it does not tell us everything about the adaptation strategies of losers. In particular, the analysis suffers from four limitations.

First, we did not examine the adaptation of all losers or of losers from all regions. This may bias our conclusions. Nevertheless, we chose to examine the adaptation policies of losers from the three most import regions regarding the specific systemic transformation of 1989. The three regions are very different in terms of their score on our variables; furthermore, some of the countries within the regions are also very different. We thereby aimed to utilize a 'most different research design' based on the view that systematic similarities of behaviour and the key variables cannot logically be accounted for by many other potential variables that differ widely.

Second, we only examined a selected range of factors. Relative power and relative security had an important effect on state strategy, and relative ideology amplified the effect of these factors; however, other factors – and combinations – may also be important. For instance, the importance of relative ideology may be more significant than it seemed in our analysis. A revised model could allow us to look for different types of otherwise ideologically similar (e.g. liberal democratic) societies, thereby refining our expectations and our analysis of the effect of relative ideology on state strategy. The analysis of the Middle Eastern case countries suggests that one should also pay attention to the notion of omnibalancing (cf. David 1991; Garnham 1991).

Third, we only examined the politics of adaptation relating to one case of international systemic change. Analysing historical precedents may lead to different results by pointing to the specifics of the 1989 systemic change. Furthermore, international history is not neatly organized in finalized chapters; what happens in one historical era spills over into the next. This is true even if the structure of the international system has a decisive effect on state action. As shown in our cases, Europe may be particularly prone to this kind of spill-over, as the major institutional structures in unipolarity continued from bipolarity and were conditioned on the continued security guarantee of the American superpower.

Fourth, when categorizing strategic behaviour, one could ask whether 'balancing' is an appropriate category with respect to the Middle East. The Middle Eastern states are generally too weak to be able to balance the US; however, they are able to pursue strategies that comprise balancing. A sharper distinction between regional and global balancing as security strategies may be of relevance here, and it may also be of importance for both Russia and the European states.

Perspectives

Our analysis has a number of implications for realism as well as for the policies of and towards losers in international relations.

Theoretical perspectives: the realist framework

Our analysis provided substantial support for some of the key tenets of the realist perspective on international relations: 'the perennial presence of conflict', 'the impossibility of ignoring power', and the continued importance of looking 'beneath the benevolent surface and find selfish motivations beneath' (Clinton 2007: 244, 249, 252). Furthermore, the analysis revealed that even if unipolarity allows the individual states greater manoeuvring room when designing their security strategies than bipolarity did, the strategies of the Cold War losers were predominantly shaped in their interaction with the new unipolar world order rather than being the products of specific unit level attributes. Moreover, our analysis had implications for three contemporary debates on the relevance and utility of a realist perspective on international relations.

First, our analysis shows the utility and relevance of a more fine-grained conceptualization of balancing and bandwagoning than has traditionally been the case in realist analyses.[1] Distinguishing between hard balancing, soft balancing, hard bandwagoning and soft bandwagoning allowed us a more detailed description and explanation of security strategies. Much of the realist debate has focused on the distinction between hard and soft balancing, but an important finding of our analysis is that states may opt for bandwagoning strategies much more frequently than expected in the literature. Thus, one important implication of this book is that bandwagoning is underexplored, both theoretically and empirically. Theoretically, it is important to develop the concept of bandwagoning further in order to gather a more precise understanding of the logic of bandwagoning, when it applies, and how it is related to balancing. Empirically, bandwagoning strategies are likely to be particularly frequently employed in unipolar international systems compared to bi- or multipolar systems due to the costs associated with balancing against a single superpower (cf. Chapter 2). Empirical analyses of bandwagoning are therefore likely to result in important knowledge about our current world order and the strategic challenges and opportunities faced by foreign policy decision makers.

Second, our analysis documented the analytical value of adding relative security and relative ideology to relative power in a realist model. The inclusion of these variables allowed us to narrow down the range of expected outcomes and explain foreign policy strategies. While our analysis did not provide a full explanation of strategies for adaptation, it provided a clear specification compared to explanation that may be deduced from the logic of relative power alone. As noted by Telhami, 'structural realism is first and foremost a theory about outcomes of international interaction'. Even so, 'one can infer some propositions about expected state behaviour', most importantly that states 'seek self-preservation' (Telhami 2003: 106). Fortunately, realist foreign policy analysis is not an either/or choice between rigorous theoretical parsimony and empirically rich case studies. Ideally it proceeds in stages from the parsimonious and highly general starting point to rich case studies allowing us to explain the specific foreign policy of individual countries (Wivel 2005a: 374). By specifying realist theory, *Security Strategies and American World Order: Lost Power* can provide a stepping stone towards a realist foreign policy theory. It does so by providing both a theoretical and conceptual development of realist theory resulting in the model presented in Chapter 2 and by applying this model in a detailed analysis of three cases. However, it leaves one of the main challenges of realist foreign policy theory to future developments: how to integrate the foreign policy maker into a realist foreign policy analysis, i.e. how to account for the way the materialist forces of international relations (most importantly relative power) is perceived and interpreted by the civil servants and politicians making foreign policy (cf. Wivel 2005a: 368–373).

Third, our analysis points to the importance of the transformation of the conditions for competition among states for the strategic challenges and opportunities facing states (Hansen, ftc.): new world orders give rise to new competitive conditions that are more difficult for some states to adapt to than others. The interplay between competitiveness, ideology, security and power could provide a dynamic edge to the explanation of the politics of adaptation: the efforts to rebuff a loss depends not least on the ability of the state in question to cope with the challenges arising from the competitive conditions of the world order. The American world order favours those states able to compete effectively on the condition of democratic rule and market economy. For states short of these abilities, the process of compensating for losses becomes very difficult – and may result in the further loss of position.

Empirical perspectives: the policy of and towards losers

Our analysis pointed to the fact that becoming 'a rogue' or 'an angry loser' is not a matter of coincidence but closely related to the external factors conditioning the challenges and opportunities facing each loser of relative power. However, the analysis also suggested that the transition from bipolarity to unipolarity challenges the power and security of states to an extent that some of them will most likely respond with aggression and possibly violence.

What advice does our analysis have for the losers and winners in the international system? For the losers, the most important piece of advice stemming from our study is that whereas balancing might be the most viable strategy in bi- and multipolar systems, bandwagoning is the most viable strategy in unipolar systems. Because of the overwhelming power of the single superpower and the costs associated with balancing against it, unipolarity leaves all states but the unipole with 'a single option'; they have only one choice in terms of asymmetrical alignment: the superpower (Hansen 2000a: 17–21). Thus, even for states that would benefit from an alternative world order, short-term bandwagoning is often the rational choice. This allows the loser to avoid the costs of balancing and to free-ride on the provision of collective goods by the unipole. This has two important effects: it contributes to the exhaustion of the unipole and allows the loser to quietly maximize relative power in the shadow of the unipolar world order. In the long term, the loser might thus become sufficiently strengthened and the superpower sufficiently weakened by exhaustion for balancing to be viable, most likely by a combination of military build-up and alliance formation against the unipole.

For the winners, the most important piece of advice stemming from our analysis is that the lack of relative power is likely to result in aggressive and violent security policies against the unipolar world order, particularly if the superpower is perceived as both a strategic and ideological threat. Thus, signalling non-aggressive intentions, pragmatic political pluralism and providing generous security guarantees are key components of a successful winner strategy. Moreover, the well-managed horizontal proliferation of nuclear weapons could increase relative security throughout the international system by increasing the potential costs of conflict. However, managed proliferation should be pursued with caution. The very process of proliferation is a dangerous and conflict-prone process that might shift the balance of power. Furthermore, offering relative gains and advantages to off-set the decline of the losers could be important to induce these states towards constructive adaptation rather than defiant balancing strategies. However, this presents a real dilemma for the victorious states, since such gains may be difficult to offer as they may typically be achievable only at the expense of other states, which are highly likely to resist and may be pushed to pursue balancing strategies if their competitors are supported by the winners. Finally, supporting voluntary ideological assimilation to the winning world order could help amplify the effects of strategies focused on relative security and relative power. This may be the most difficult strategy of all, however, as it directly challenges the power and security of the foreign policy makers who have built their careers in existing political structures and on rhetoric challenging the ideology of the winners.

The first 18 years of the unipolar era and the American world order were turbulent in terms of the transformation of the foreign and security policies of most states in the international system, wars (e.g. in the Persian Gulf), civil wars (e.g. in former Yugoslavia and the Middle East), and terrorist attacks of an unprecedented scale. It showed us that strategic adaptation to new conditions is neither a peaceful nor easy process. *Security Strategies and American World Order: Lost Power* describes and explains this adaptation process for actors in three regions central in Cold War bipolarity. By combining relative power with relative security and relative ideology, we provided a bridge between a pure structural theory explaining 'the constraints that confine all states' (Waltz 1979: 122) and a pure foreign policy theory allowing us to explain 'why state X made a certain move last Tuesday' (1979: 121). This middle ground position allowed us to outline the strategic challenges and opportunities of different types of losers and to explain how they responded. The lessons learned from this adaptation process by winners, losers and those of us trying to understand what they do and why, will hopefully provide a better starting point for minimizing the costs of adaptation in the future than has been the case in the past.

Notes

1 Introduction: from loss to strategy

1 This focus reflects the American bias in the study of international relations in general and in the study of unipolarity in particular. An exception, however, is Hansen (2000a), which serves as the theoretical starting point for our conceptualization of unipolar dynamics.

2 See Chapter 2 for an overview of the positions in this debate.

3 For discussions of recent developments of the realist research programme, see Brooks (1997); Hanami (2003); Legro and Moravcsik (1999); Paul et al. (2004); Rose (1998); Rosecrance (2001); Schweller (2003); Vasquez (1997); and Wivel (2002b). Recent comprehensive assessments of the broader realist tradition include Clinton (2007); Donnelly (2000); and Haslam (2002).

4 Hansen (1995, 2000a, 2000b, 2001a, 2001b, 2002). For discussions of its logic and application, see Sheikh (2002) and Toft (2002).

5 For a brief summary of the positions in this debate, see Mearsheimer (2007: 75–78).

6 The most comprehensive statement of the defensive realist position is Waltz (1979). The most comprehensive statement of the offensive realist position is Mearsheimer (2001). For a call for reconciliation between the two positions, see Snyder (2002).

7 See e.g. Elman (1996); Rynning and Guzzini (2001); Rose (1998); and Wivel (2002a, 2002b, 2005a) as well as the contemporary debate on soft balancing discussed in Chapter 2.

8 See also Walt (1989: 6) for a slightly different definition.

9 See e.g. the essays collected in Brown et al. (2000).

10 The model is globalized via the lack of powerful constraints and the active American policy for globalizing its model (Hansen 2000d, 2002); the model thereby makes up the content of what is being globalized, and the current globalization process is facilitated by the lack of competition and constraints. Other realist analyses that couple globalization and unipolarity include Wolfowitz (2000); Kapstein (1999); and Waltz (2000b). For an overview and discussion of how this argument relates to other realist arguments on globalization and regional integration, see Wivel (2004).

11 For a discussion of these concepts, see Hansen (2000a: Chapter 2).

12 The most important modification is that IR scholars (like most other social scientists) do not give the same weight to falsification as Karl Popper did in the original statement of the position (Popper 1959, 1989). For a discussion of falsification and the social sciences, see (Lakatos 1970), who rejects falsification in social science, and King, Keohane and Verba (1994: 100–105). For discussions of contemporary realism and critical rationalism, see Mouritzen (1997) and Wivel (2000: Chapter 1).

13 For general discussions of the nature and use of case studies in political science, see Eckstein (1975); George (1979); George and McKeown (1985); King et al. (1994: 43–46); McKeown (1999); and Van Evera (1997: Chapter 2). The choice of the case

study as a research strategy is in accordance with most contemporary realist analyses of international relations, see e.g. Grieco (1990); Schweller (1998); Snyder (1991); Walt (1987); and Zakaria (1998).

14 For discussions, see Stake (1995: 7–9); Van Evera (1997: Chapter 2); and Yin (1994: Chapter 1).

2 Explaining security strategy: a realist model of analysis

1 These include structural realism (Buzan *et al.* 1993), neoclassical realism (Rose 1998), postclassical realism (Brooks 1997), defensive and aggressive realism (Snyder 1991), human-nature realism (Mearsheimer 2001), motive based realism (Kydd 1997), state centric realism (Zakaria 1998), fine-grained structural realism (Van Evera 1999), Machiavellian fundamentalism, Hobbesian structuralism, and Rousseau'an constitutionalism (Doyle 1997), specific and general realism (Rosecrance 2001), romantic realism (Liska 1998), subordinate realism (Ayoob 1998), periphery realism (Escudé 1998), and contingent and universal realism (Wivel 2000, 2002, 2005a).

2 On soft balancing, see Brooks and Wohlforth (2005); Art *et al.* (2005/2006); Flemes (2007); Oswald (2006); Lieber and Alexander (2005); Paul (2004, 2005); Pape (2003, 2005); Walt (2005).

3 Cf. Brooks and Wohlforth (2005: 104–106), who find it difficult to distinguish soft balancing from bargaining.

4 On the question of balancing in the current world order, see Joffe (1997); Schweller (2004) and the contributions to Paul, Wirtz and Fortmann (2004); and Ikenberry (2002b).

5 These differences are exacerbated in times of crisis when core values are challenged, e.g. the Gulf Conflict 1990–91 and the War on Terror after 11 September 2001. In both cases, the United States argued that the initial attacks (on Kuwait in 1990 and on New York and Washington in 2001) were attacks on the fundamental values of a legitimate international order.

6 The end of the Cold War – and thus the analytical emergence of unipolarity – is dated to 21 September 1989 (Hansen 2000a).

3 Russia

1 On Russian foreign policy after the Cold War see e.g. Aron (1998); Aron and Jensen (2004); Baranovsky (2001); Blacker (1998); De Nevers (1994); Garnett (1998); Goldgeier and Mcfaul (2003); Lambeth (1995); Legvold (2001); Light (2001); Mcfaul (1999); Menon (2001); Pipes (1997); Ra'anan and Martin (1995); Shearman (1995a); Treisman (2002); Valdez (2000); Wohlforth (2002b); Wohlforth (1995).

2 'Shock therapy' to liberalize the Soviet plan economy was launched in 1992. The therapy included swift mass privatization and an abrupt end to government subsidies and price controls. This shock therapy resulted in hyperinflation, mass bankruptcies and mass unemployment (Desai 1995: 105–107; Treisman and Schleifer 2000).

3 A nuclear state obtains a second-strike capability when it is able to absorb a large-scale nuclear attack while retaining the ability to launch a counter-attack in kind.

4 An effective balancing coalition would by definition require that all candidates able to rival the unipole would have to join (Pape 2005). This increases the risks related to defection, because the defection of just one coalition member would leave the rest unable to match the unipole. In the words of Christopher Layne, 'either the second-ranked powers hang together – or they hang separately' (Layne 2006a: 148–149).

5 On the dangers of bandwagoning, see Waltz (1979); and Mearsheimer (2001).

6 A nuclear state obtains a second-strike capability when it is able to absorb a large-scale nuclear attack while retaining the ability to launch a counter-attack of massive retaliation.

7 Nuclear weapons tend to promote peace because they make deterrence extremely robust as the prospects of nuclear war raises the costs of armed conflict to unimaginable proportions (Waltz 1981). To paraphrase John Mearsheimer: 'the more horrible the prospects of war the less likely war is' (1990). Moreover, as observed by Kenneth Waltz, compared to conventional weapons, nuclear weapons are also cheap, although technologically difficult to develop. This adds to the robustness of nuclear deterrence (1981). Seminal statements on the effects of nuclear weapons include Waltz (1981); Waltz and Sagan (2003); Jervis (1990); and Boulding (1988).

8 In 1998, the United States officially announced that it would forge ahead with a national missile defence system. In 2002, the US government unilaterally abrogated the 1972 ABM treaty, which prohibited Russia and the United States from deploying such systems.

9 Russia's 'Monroe' doctrine was reflected in a 1995-presidential decree declaring former Soviet area a Russian 'priority area' because of Russia's 'vital interests' in the area regarding security, economics and cultural ties (Aron 1998: 33–34). A report published by the influential Russian Council of Foreign and Defense Policy that same year, whose recommendations were widely agreed upon in the foreign policy landscape in Russia, similarly emphasized the goals of maintaining the territorial integrity of Russia in addition to preventing other states from dominating the former Soviet Union as well as securing unhindered access to strategic resources in that region; including transportation routes and sea ports (Aron 1998: 34).

10 For an overview of the academic literature on the state of Russian democracy, see (Robinson 2003). See also the Freedom House annual reports.

11 Robert Pape argues that Russia qualifies as democratic by standard definitions, as the Russian population elects the chief executives and legislature in multiparty elections and have seen at least one peaceful transfer of political power (Pape 2003: 349).

12 Parts of this section draw on my previous account of Russia's external behaviour between 1991 and 2004 in Toft (2006: Ch. 4).

13 We have chosen to analyse Russia's behaviour vis-à-vis these two groups of states rather than how Russia related to specific international issues, as we do in Chapter 5 on Europe. This procedure captures how Russia related to key international security issues as well as capturing the interplay between Russia's relations with the major power subsystem and the regional subsystem.

14 As Europe was closely allied with the United States during most of the period under analysis, we discuss the European major power's relations with Russia separately in those relatively few instances in which the European powers did not follow the US.

15 The contact group consisting of France, Britain, Russia, Germany and the United States was formed on 26 April 1994 in an attempt to inject new momentum to the peace process. The group hammered out a new peace plan that assigned 51 per cent of Bosnia-Herzegovina to a newly formed Bosnian–Croat Federation and 49 per cent to the Bosnian Serbs (IISS, 1995: 98).

16 Once the Dayton Peace Plan came into effect, Russia refused to accept the subordination of Russian forces in Bosnia to the NATO Command structure (McFarlaine 1999: 242).

17 By expansionist, we do not understand a strategy of conquest but rather a policy characterized by extending one's presence and diplomatic influence (cf. Zakaria 1998).

18 Since the formation of the alliance in 1949, the Washington Treaty had embodied a pledge of collective defence in the event of a military attack on one of the member states geographically limited to the North Atlantic area north of the Tropic of Cancer. With the adoption of the new strategic concept in 1991, however, NATO received a wider and more vaguely defined 'Euro-Atlantic' area of operation.

19 Nevertheless, the NRC remains a rather weak mechanism. Beyond consultations on defence issues, some intelligence sharing and the coordination of military flights in NATO and Russian aerospace (cf. NATO 2004b), the seat in the NRC does not commit Russia to a high degree nor does it give Russia much influence in NATO.

20 After the opening campaign to topple the Taliban regime in Afghanistan following the 11 September 2001 terrorist attacks, the United States has retained two major military bases in Central Asia: one in Kyrgyzstan and one in Uzbekistan (until 2005). American troops also operate in Tajikistan and Turkmenistan (Blank 2003; *New York Times* 2005).

21 The PCA did not enter into force until 1997 due to a host of subsequent disagreements between Russia and the EU (Lo 2003: 56, 145–146; *Moscow Times* 2004b).

22 Kaliningrad is Russia's only warm-water port in the Baltic and is home to the Russian Baltic fleet (IISS 2001: 123).

23 Alliances vary according to the degree of commitment by the parties to come to each others' defence. Non-aggression pacts may be viewed as the weakest form, while formal defence pacts demonstrate a high degree of commitment. Ententes fall somewhere in between. On defining alliances and a typology of different types, see Toft and Oest (2007); and Oest (2007).

24 During the 1990s and early 2000s, China and Russia issued a series of joint declarations following summits of the two heads of state that contained thinly veiled criticism of US hegemony, see Wilson (2004).

25 For an overview of the debate on the Russo-Chinese partnership, see Wishnik (2001); and Wilson (2004).

26 Besides Russia and China, the initial members were Kyrgyzstan, Kazakhstan and Tajikistan. Uzbekistan joined in 2001.

27 See fn. 21.

28 The full text of the Friendship Treaty is reproduced in Wilson (2004).

29 Both the Chinese and Russian leaders were keen on toning down possible perceptions that the Friendship Treaty was a military pact. For instance, at the signing ceremony, President Putin explained that Russia had no intention of forging a military alliance with China (Wohlforth 2002b: 202).

30 The Russian borderlands were made up of the 14 other former Soviet republics situated to Russia's west and south, i.e. the three Baltic republics, Belarus, Ukraine, Moldova, Azerbaijan, Armenia, Georgia, Uzbekistan, Kazakhstan, Turkmenistan, Tajikistan and Kyrgyzstan.

31 By 21 December 1991 12 of the 15 former Soviet republics had joined the CIS. The three Baltic republics – Lithuania, Latvia and Estonia – remained aloof. Georgia withdrew its membership in 1992.

32 The Russia–Belarus union was only partially implemented. A 1997 treaty designed to accelerate the formation of a formal political union was never fully accomplished, allegedly due to Russian pressure to change the treaty formulations to grant leadership status to Russia (Garnett 1998: 75, 76; *Moscow Times* 2005a). By the early 2000s, the currency and political union remained largely unfulfilled, although plans remained on the table (BBC News 2002; Ria Novosti 2006; Webber and Sakwa 1999: 408). In December 2007, there were unconfirmed media rumours that Russia and Belarus were on the verge of uniting under a common constitution (Christian Science Monitor 2007).

33 Uzbekistan, Moldova and Turkmenistan were ambivalent in their affiliation. Uzbekistan joined the sceptics-group (GUAM) in 1999 but suspended its membership in 2002 to re-join the Russia-loyal camp (Kuzio 2002).

34 Ukraine is strategically important for Russia due to its size and location en route to Western Europe, key gas and oil pipelines cross Ukrainian territory, and the Ukrainian port of Sevastopol hosts the Russian Black Sea Fleet. The Southern Caucasus is strategically important for Russia, because it is a potential alternative for Central Asian oil and gas pipelines bypassing Russia.

35 The ceasefire implied that Azerbaijan relinquished de facto control over Nagorno-Karabakh as well as seven other districts amounting to 15 per cent of Azerbaijan's territory (Menon, 1998: 130).

36 At the Istanbul OSCE summit in 1999, Russia came under pressure from NATO to remove its troops from Georgia in return for NATO accepting Russian requests regarding the revising of the CFE-treaty. Moscow agreed to withdraw some of its military equipment from Georgia and began disbanding the Gudauta and Vaziani military bases in 1 July 2001. Georgia granted Russia the right to temporarily remain in the bases in Batumi and Akhalkalaki (The NATO-Russia Archive 2005). Russia's withdrawal has generally been incredibly slow (Buzan and Wæver 2003: 401). By 2003, Russia had only taken steps to withdraw from two of its four bases. Evacuation plans to abandon the remaining two bases were postponed, as Moscow linked the issue to NATO enlargement in the Baltic area (the Baltic states are not parties to the CFE-treaty) (Blank 2003; Devdariani 2004; *Moscow Times* 2005c). Russia has announced its intention to evacuate the final two bases by 2008 (Ria Novosti 2006).

4 Europe

1 Some analysts have also argued that realism is unfit for the analysis of the foreign policies of and relations between modern industrialized democracies in general (e.g. Mueller 1988). However, realism continues to be one of the major analytical tools to analyse such modern industrialized democracies in general and the most powerful of them – the United States – in particular.

2 See United States Department of Defense: 'News Transcript', Wednesday, 22 January 2003, 1:30 PM EST (www.defenselink.mil/transcripts/2003/t01232003_t0122sdfpc. html).

3 This provided a stark contrast to the situation a decade earlier, when '[t]he 1980s opened with debate on the 'Eurosclerosis', which blocked further integration, tensions within the Atlantic Alliance and a revival of Cold War mentalities' (Stirk 1996: 203).

4 Most recent available figures are from 2004.

5 Of the ten largest American overseas deployments 1950–2003, five were in Europe: Germany (1 – the largest with approximately 250,000 troops), United Kingdom (5), France (6 – even though the number of troops dropped sharply from 50,000 to less than 100 in the mid-1960s as a consequence of France's NATO policy), Italy (8) and Spain (10), see Kane (2004b).

6 For a more detailed discussion of the European initiatives in the 1990s and the American reactions, see Wivel (2000: 297–320).

7 The full text of the letter can be found at www.sipri.org/contents/expcon/ loiintro.html.

8 For a description of the various ESDP operations, see www.iss.europa.eu/esdp/09-dvl-am.pdf.

9 It should be noted that Peterson's assessment of the European performance in regard to Kosovo is more positive and focuses more on independent European actions than we do here. In contrast, Sloan (2005) perceives the US and NATO as decisive with only a negligent role for the Europeans.

10 The biggest European contributors are the UK, Germany, The Netherlands, Italy and France. Contributors outside Europe include – in addition to the United States – Canada, Turkey, Australia, New Zealand and Azerbaijan (see www.nato.int/ issues/isaf/index.html). For the American critique of the European contribution, see 'Gates: Europe Must Pony Up In Afghanistan', *CBS NEWS*, 25 October 2007, www.cbsnews.com/stories/2007/10/25/terror/printable3411319.shtml and 'Gates tries to soothe feelings in Europe by praising NATO role in Afghanistan', *International Herald Tribune*, 17 January 2008, www.iht.com/articles/ap/2008/01/17/america/ Gates.php.

11 For reports, see i.a. 'Chirac blasts EU candidates', BBC News, Tuesday, 18 February 2003; 'New Europe backs EU on Iraq, BBC News, Wednesday, 19 February 2003; 'The World: French Kiss Off', *The New Republic Online*, 25 February 2003;

'Between Bush and Iraq – Jacques Chirac', *Christian Science Monitor*, 21 February 2003; 'New Europe's Iraq Squeeze', *Christian Science Monitor*, 11 March 2003.

12 It should be noted that even though the EU ratified the treaty, EU member states have failed to live up to its goals.

13 Rumsfeld's statement was made in an interview with Larry King on CNN, 6 December 2001, for a transcript see www.defenselink.mil/utility/printitem.aspx?print= www.defenselink.mil/transcripts/transcript.aspx?transcriptid=2603).

14 In addition, in the case of the war in Iraq, France had strong economic ties to Saddam Hussein's regime. Iraq owed France approximately US$8 billion and French oil companies had strong economic interests in developing Iraqi oil resources (Paul 2005: 13). Nevertheless, US$8 billion is a relatively modest sum for a country with France's capabilities, and there is little solid evidence that French companies negotiated contracts with Saddam Hussein's regime.

15 Other factors may have also contributed. The SPD–Green Party government coalition of the time consisted of two political parties with strong pacifist and non-interventionist traditions, in particular the SPD left wing and the Green Party. There was strong public opposition to the war, but this appears to have played only a marginal role in the policy choice of European governments, as opposition to the war was widespread in most countries regardless of the policy on Iraq of the respective governments (Mouritzen 2005).

5 The Middle East

1 We understand the MENA region as stretching from Morocco in the West to Afghanistan in the East and from Turkey in the North to Yemen in the South.

2 For a survey of the US and Soviet alignment efforts in the MENA region during the Cold War, see Taylor (1991).

3 Our intention is clearly not to present a full-fledged analysis of the policies and behaviour of our case countries; we merely intend to examine selected issues. For comprehensive analyses of the security and foreign policies of the MENA countries, see Korany and Dessouki (1991); Freedman (1991, 1993, 1998); Hinnebusch and Ehteshami (2002); Brown (2003); and Halliday (2005).

4 In the academic debate, emphasis on the particularity of the MENA region has also been advocated, e.g. in terms of a clash of civilizations/characteristics by the Islamic civilization (Huntington 1996), lack of democratic tradition (Lewis 2002), or Western 'neo-imperialism' (Said 1995). General approaches have been advocated by e.g. Walt (1987, 1988); and Hansen (2000a).

5 Obviously, the end of the Cold War brought triumph for Afghanistan with respect to another dimension: the process meant the end of Soviet occupation.

6 However, some of the bipolar US-allied MENA states also became subject to losses.

7 Quoted from Zisser (2001: 37).

8 In addition, the states faced the risk of collapse – which would leave little room for the pursuit of an external strategy.

9 For a survey and an analysis of the coalition, see Cooper *et al.* (1991).

10 S/1995/864 – Report of the Secretary-General on the status of the implementation of the Special Commission's plan for the ongoing monitoring and verification of Iraq's compliance with relevant parts of section C of Security Council resolution 687 (1991), 11 October 1995.

11 For a comprehensive analysis of Libyan foreign policy during the Cold War, see Deeb (1991).

12 www.alghatafi.org/terrorism/terrorism.htm.

13 Asian Tribune, 31 December 2003.

14 www.nti.org/e_research/profiles/Libya/print/3939_3940.prt.

15 www.globalsecurity.org/wmd/world/libya/nuclear.htm, NTI.

16 www.state.gov/r/pa/prs/ps/2003/20062.htm.
17 CNN, 5 October 2003.
18 http://news.bbc.co.uk/2/hi/middle_east/3622260.stm.
19 CNN, 27 April 2005.
20 http://news.bbc.co.uk/2/hi/middle_east/4206530.stm, *BBC* 020905.
21 www.hri.org/news/turkey/anadolu/1998/98–11–28.anadolu.html.
22 Foreign Ministry Deputy Spokesman Sermet Atacanli in a press conference according to the Anatolia news agency reports. www.byegm.gov.tr/YAYINLARIMIZ/CHR/ING98/12/98X12X10.HTM#%209.
23 For a different view on the Libyan change in strategy, that 'the Libyan case is not a very convincing example of bandwagoning', see Walt (2005: 186–187).

6 Conclusions

1 For the argument that balancing is the typical strategy of states, see Walt (1987) and Waltz (1979). For an important argument against the dominance of balancing over bandwagoning strategies, see Schweller ([1994] 1995). Most of the recent debate on 'soft' strategies focuses on balancing (cf. Chapter 2).

Bibliography

Anderson, L. and Stansfield, G. (2005) *The Future of Iraq. Dictatorship, Democracy, or Division?* (Updated edn), Basingstoke: Palgrave MacMillan.

Arnold, G. (1996) *The Maverick State – Gaddafi and the New World Order*, London: Cassell.

Aron, L. (1993) 'The Morass in Moscow: Boris Yeltsin and Russia's Four Crises', *Journal of Democracy*, 4 (2): 4–16.

Aron, L. (1998) 'The Foreign Policy Doctrine of Postcommunist Russia and Its Domestic Context', in M. Mandelbaum (ed.) *The New Russian Foreign Policy*, New York: Council on Foreign Relations: 23–63.

Aron, L. and Jensen, K. M. (2004) *The Emergence of Russian Foreign Policy*, Washington D.C.: United States Institute of Peace Press.

Art, R. J. (2004) 'Europe Hedges Its Security Bets', in T. V. Paul, J. J. Wirtz and M. Fortmann (2004) (eds) *Balance of Power: Theory and Practice in the 21st Century*, Stanford: Stanford University Press: 179–213.

Art, R. J., Brooks, S., Wohlforth, W., Lieber, K. A. and Alexander, G. (2005/06) 'Correspondence: Striking the Balance', *International Security*, 30 (3): 177–196.

Ash, T. G. (2004) *Free World*, London: Penguin.

Asmus, R. D. (2006) 'The European Security Strategy: an American view', in R. Dannreuther and J. Peterson (eds) *Security Strategy and Transatlantic Relations*, London: Routledge: 17–29.

Asia Times Online (2003) 'Russia drops an anchor in Central Asia', *Asia Times Online*. Online, available at: www.atimes.com/atimes/Central_Asia/EJ25Ag01.html (accessed 23 October 2003).

Asia Times Online (2005) War games or word games?, *Asia Times Online*. Online, available at: www.atimes.com/atimes/Central_Asia/GH26Ag01.html (accessed 26 August 2005).

Ayoob, M. (1998) 'Subaltern Realism: International Relations Theory Meets the Third World', in Stephanie G. Neuman (ed.) (1998) *International Relations Theory and the Third World*, New York: St. Martins Press: 31–54.

Baidatz, Y. (2001): 'Bashar's First Year. From Ophthalmology to a National Vision', The Washington Institute for Near East Policy, *Policy Focus*, No. 41, July.

Bailes, A. J. K. (2005) *The European Security Strategy: An Evolutionary History*, SIPRI Policy Paper 10, Stockholm: Stockholm Peace Research Institute.

Ballance, E. O. (1995) *Civil War in Bosnia 1992–1994*, London: McMillan Press.

Baram, A. (2003) 'Saddam's Strategy on the Brink of War', *Iraq Memo # 10*, The Brookings Institution, 20 February 2003.

Baranovsky, V. (2001) 'Russia: A Part of Europe or Apart from Europe?', in A. Brown (ed.) *Contemporary Russian Politics: A Reader*, Oxford: Oxford University Press: 429–442.

Bazhanov, E. (1995) 'Russian Policy Toward China', in P. Shearman (ed.) *Russian Foreign Policy Since 1990*, Boulder, San Francisco, Oxford: Westview Press: 159–180.

BBC News (2002) 'Russia, Belarus edge closer', *BBC News online*. Online, available at: http://news.bbc.co.uk/2/hi/europe/2519025.stm (accessed 28 November 2002).

BBC News (2004) 'US Military Will Stay in Georgia', *BBC News online*. Online, available at: www.bbc.co.uk/go/pr/fr/-/2/hi/europe/3406941.stm (accessed 18 January 2004).

BBC News (2005) 'Push to improve Russia-Japan ties', *BBC News online*. Online, available at: www.news.bbc.co.uk/2/hi/asia-pacific/4173319.stm (accessed 1 January 2005).

BBC News (2006a) 'US House backs India nuclear deal', *BBC News online*. Online, available at: http://news.bbc.co.uk/2/hi/south_asia/5219230.stm (accessed 27 July 2006).

BBC News (2006b) 'Europe blames US for WTO Failure', *BBC News online*. Online, available at: http://news.bbc.co.uk/1/hi/business/5209010.stm (accessed 5 February 2008).

BBC News (2007a) 'US and India discuss nuclear deal', *BBC News online*. Online, available at: http://news.bbc.co.uk/2/hi/south_asia/6611541.stm (accessed 2 May 2007).

BBC News (2007b) 'Putin attacks "very dangerous" US', *BBC News online*. Online, available at: http://news.bbc.co.uk/2/hi/europe/6349287.stm (accessed 10 February 2007).

BBC News (2007c) Missile shield 'threatens Russia', *BBC News online*. Online, available at: http://news.bbc.co.uk/2/hi/europe/6286289.stm (accessed 22 January 2007)

Bengio, O. (1998/2002) *Saddam's Word. Political Discourse in Iraq*, Oxford: Oxford University Press.

Bennett, A., Lepgold, J. and Unger, D. (1994) 'Burden-sharing in the Persian Gulf War', *International Organization*, 48 (1): 39–75.

Berlingske Tidende (2004) *Rusland knurrer over NATO-udvidelse* (14 February 2004). Online, available at: www.berlingske.dk (accessed 13 February 2004).

Bjarnason, M. (2001) 'The War and War-games in Bosnia and Herzegovina from 1992 to 1995: The Main Events, Disagreements and Arguments resulting in a "de facto" divided country', published by the author under NATO auspices. Online, available at: www.nato.int/acad/fellow/99–01/bjarnason.pdf (accessed 20 March 2008).

Blacker, C. D. (1998) 'Russia and the West', in M. Mandelbaum (ed.) *The New Russian Foreign Policy*, New York: Council on Foreign Relations: 167–193.

Blank, S. (2003) 'Central Asia's great base race', *Asia Times Online* (19 December 2003). Online, available at: www.atimes.com/atimes/Central_Asia/EL19Ag01.html (accessed 19 December 2003).

Boulding, K. (1962) *Conflict and Defense*, New York: Harper and Brothers.

Boulding, K. (1988) *Conflict and Defense*, Boston: University Press of America.

Bowker, M. (1995) 'Russian Policy towards Central and Eastern Europe', in P. Shearman (ed.) *Russian Foreign Policy since 1900*, Boulder: Westview Press: 71–92.

Brinkley, D. (1997) 'Democratic Enlargement: The Clinton Doctrine', *Foreign Policy*, 106 (Spring): 110–127.

Broadman, H. G. (2004) 'Global Economic Integration: Prospects for WTO Accession and Continued Russian Reforms', *The Washington Quarterly*, 27 (2): 79–98.

Brooks, S. G. (1997) 'Dueling Realisms', *International Organization*, 51 (3): 445–477.

Brooks, S. G. and Wohlforth, W. C. (2000) 'Power, Globalization, and the End of the Cold War', *International Security*, 25 (3): 5–53.

Brooks, S. G. and Wohlforth, W. C. (2005) 'Hard Times for Soft Balancing', *International Security*, 30 (1): 72–108.

Brown, C. L. (ed.) (2003) *Diplomacy in the Middle East. The International relations of Regional and Outside Powers*, London: I. B. Tauris.

Brown, M. E., Cote, O. R., Lynn-Jones, S. M. and Miller, S. M. (2000) *America's Strategic Choices*, Cambridge: The MIT Press.

Brzezinski, Z. and Sullivan, P. (1997) *Russia and the Commonwealth of Independent States: Documents, Data, and Analysis*, Armonk and London: M. E. Sharp.

Butler, R. (2001) *Saddam Defiant* (paperback edn), London: Phoenix.

Buzan, B., Kelstrup, M., Lemaitre, P. and Tromer, E. (1990) *The European Security Order Recast*, London: Pinter Publishers.

Buzan, B., Jones, C. and Little, R. (1993) *The Logic of Anarchy*, New York: Columbia University Press.

Buzan, B. and Wæver, O. (2003) *Regions and Powers*, Cambridge: Cambridge University Press.

Calleo, D. P. (2001) *Rethinking Europe's Future*, Princeton: Princeton University Press.

Cameron, F. (2006) 'Security strategy: what role for institutions?', in R. Dannreuther and J. Peterson (eds) *Security Strategy and Transatlantic Relations*, London: Routledge: 45–60.

Central Asian Gateway (2006) 'The Collective Security Treaty Organization (CSTO)'. Online, available at: www.cagateway.org/index.php?lng=1&topic=23&subtopic=84 (accessed 20 March 2008).

Christensen, T. J. and Snyder, J. (1990) 'Chain gangs and passed bucks: predicting alliance patterns in multipolarity', *International Organization*, 44 (2): 137–168.

Christian Science Monitor (2007) Putin eyes full merger with Belarus, www.csmonitor.com/2007/1210/p01s02-woeu.html (accessed 10 December 2007).

Clinton, W. D. (2007) *The Realist Tradition and Contemporary International Relations*, Baton Rouge: Louisiana State University Press.

CNN (1998) India, Russia to form strategic partnership in 1999, *CNN online*. Online, available at: www.cnn.com/world/asiapcf/9812/22/india.russia/ (accessed 22 December 1998).

Cooper, A. F., Higgot, R. A. and Nossal, K. R. (1991) 'Bound to Follow? Leadership and Followership in the Gulf Conflict', *Political Science Quarterly*, 106 (3): 391–410.

Copeland, D. (2000) *The Origins of Major War*, Ithaca: Cornell University Press.

Cordesman, A. H. (1997) *U.S. Forces in the Middle East. Resources and Capabilities*, Boulder: Westview Press.

Crowe, B. (2003) 'A common European foreign policy after Iraq?', *International Affairs*, 79 (3): 533–546.

Daalder, I. H. and Lindsay, J. M. (2003) *America Unbound: The Bush Revolution in Foreign Policy*, Washington DC: Brookings Institution Press.

Daalder, I. H. and O'Hanlon, M. E. (2000) *Winning Ugly: NATO's War to save Kosovo*, Washington DC: Brookings Institution Press.

Damro, C. (2006) 'Security strategy and the arms industry', in R. Dannreuther and J. Peterson (eds) *Security Strategy and Transatlantic Relations*, London: Routledge: 132–146.

Dannreuther, R. (1999) 'Escaping the Enlargement Trap in NATO-Russian Relations', *Survival*, 41 (4): 145–164.

Dannreuther, R. and Peterson, J. (2006) 'Introduction: Security strategy as doctrine', in R. Dannreuther and J. Peterson (eds) *Security Strategy and Transatlantic Relations*, London: Routledge: 1–16.

David, S. R. (1991): 'Explaining Third World Alignment', *World Politics*, Vol. 43, January: 233–256.

Davies, N. (1996) *Europe – A History*, London: Pimlico.

Dawn, C. E. (2003) 'The Foreign Policy of Syria', in Brown, C. L. (ed.) (2003) *Diplomacy in the Middle East. The International relations of Regional and Outside Powers*, London: I. B. Tauris: 159–178.

Deeb, M.-J. (1991) *Libya's Foreign Policy in North Africa*, Boulder: Westview Press.

De Nevers, R. (1994) 'Russia's Strategic Renovation', *Adelphi Papers*, 289 (July): 5–82.

Desai, P. (1995) 'Beyond Shock Therapy', *Journal of Democracy*, 6 (2): 102–112.

Devdariani, J. (2004) 'Pulling back Troops, Georgia calls for European Help', *Central Asia – Caucasus Analyst* (25 August 2004). Online, available at: www.cacianalyst.org/view_article.php?articleid=2610 (accessed 25 August 2004).

Djerejian (1993) *The multilateral talks in the Arab-Israeli peace process* – Assistant Secretary for Near Eastern Affairs Edward P. Djerejian speech – includes related article on nuclear-testing moratorium. Transcript. Online, available at: http://findarticles.com/p/articles/mi_m1584 (accessed 19 March 2008).

Donnelly, J. (2000) *Realism and International Relations*, Cambridge: Cambridge University Press.

Dorman, A. and Treacher, A. (1995) *European Security*, Aldershot: Dartmouth.

Doyle, M. W. (1983) 'Kant, Liberal Legacies, and Foreign Affairs', *Philosophy and Public Affairs*, 12 (3): 205–230.

Doyle, M. W. (1997) *Ways of War and Peace*, New York and London: W. W. Norton and Company.

Drysdale, A. (1993) 'Syria since 1988: From Crisis to Opportunity', in R. O. Freedman (ed.) (1993) *The Middle East after Iraq's Invasion of Kuwait*, Gainesville: University of Florida Press: 276–296.

Dubinin, I. (2004) 'How Ukraine became a nuclear-free State', *International Affairs*, 50 (2): 197–224.

Duesterberg, T. J. (1995) 'Prospects for an EU-NAFTA Free Trade Agreement', in B. Roberts (ed.) *New Forces in the World Economy*, Cambridge, Massachusetts: 251–262.

Duke, S. (2004) 'The European Security Strategy in a Comparative Framework: Does it Make for Secure Alliances in a Better World?', *European Foreign Affairs Review*, 9 (4): 459–481.

Duncan, P. (1993) 'The democratic transition in Russia: from Coup to Referendum', *Parliamentary Affairs*, 46 (4): 491–505.

Eckstein, H. (1975) 'Case Study and Theory in Political Science', in F. I. Greenstein and N. W. Polsby (eds) (1975) *Handbook of Political Science*, Reading, Massachusetts: Addison-Wesley: 79–137.

El-Kikhia, M. O. (1997) *Libya's Qaddafi: The politics of Contradiction*, Gainesville: University Press of Florida.

Elman, C. (1996) 'Horses for Courses: Why Not a Neorealist Theory of Foreign Policy', *Security Studies*, 6 (1): 7–53.

Encyclopedia Britannica (1993) *Encyclopedia Britannica, 15th edn*, Chicago: University of Chicago.

Escudé, C. (1998) 'An Introduction to Peripheral Realism and Its Implications for the

Interstate System: Argentina and the Cóndor II Missile Project' in S. G. Neuman (ed.) (1998) *International Relations Theory and the Third World*, New York: St. Martins Press: 55–75.

Eurasia Daily Monitor (2007) 'Nord Stream Project: Bilateral Russo-German, not European'. Online, available at: www.jamestown.org/edm/article.php?article_id=2372457 (accessed 27 September 2007).

Eurasia Insight (2007) 'Azerbaijan pursues NATO integration', *Eurasia Insight*, 13 March 2007. Online, available at: www.eurasianet.org/departments/insight/articles/eav031607.shtml (accessed 23 March 2008).

Eurasia Insight (2008) 'US aid budget to Eurasia: a monument to "inter-agency pettiness"', *Eurasia Insight*, 12 February 2008. Online, available at: www.eurasianet.org/departments/insight/articles/eav021208a.shtml (accessed 23 March 2008).

Europa – Internetportalen til EU (2007) 'Oversigt over den europæiske unions aktiviteter' Online, available at: http://europa.eu/pol/comm/overview_da.htm (accessed 5 February 2008).

European Commission (2007) 'Bilateral trade relations: USA'. Online, available at: http://ec.europa.eu/trade/issues/bilateral/countries/usa/index_en.htm (accessed 5 February 2008).

European Council (2003) 'European Security Strategy', Brussels. Online, available at: www.consilium.europa.eu/cms3_fo/showPage.ASP?id=266&lang=EN&mode=g (accessed 5 February 2008).

Evans, G. and Newnham, J. (1998) *Dictionary of International Relations*, London: Penguin.

Falkenrath, R. A. (1995) 'The CFE Flank Dispute Waiting in the Wings', *International Security*, 19 (4): 118–144.

Felgenhauer, T. (1999) *Ukraine, Russia, and the Black Sea Fleet Accords*, Princeton: Woodrow Wilson School of International Diplomacy, Princeton University.

Feshbach, M. and Friendly, A. (1992) *Ecoside in the USSR: Health and Nature under Siege*, New York: Basic Books.

Flemes, D. (2007) 'Emerging Middle Powers' Soft Balancing Strategy: State and Perspectives of the IBSA Dialogue Forum', *GIGA Working Papers*, No. 57, Hamburg: German Institute of Global and Area Studies.

Forsberg, T. and Herd, G. P. (2006) *Divided West*, London: Chatham House.

Freedom House (2002) *Freedom in the World: Russia 2002*. Online, available at: www.freedomhouse.org/template.cfm?page=363&year=2002 (accessed 20 March 2008).

Freedom House (2006) 'Nations in Transit: Russia 2006'. Online, available at: www.freedomhouse.org (accessed 20 March 2008)

Freedom House (2007a) 'Freedom in the World: Russia 2007'. Online, available at: www.freedomhouse.org (accessed 20 March 2008).

Freedom House (2007b) 'Freedom in the World Country Ratings 1972–2007', www.freedomhouse.org (accessed 20 March 2008).

Freedman, L. (2001) 'A Third World War?', *Survival*, 43 (4): 61–88.

Freedman, L. and Karsh, E. (1993) *The Gulf Conflict 1990–1991*, London: Faber and Faber.

Freedman, R. O. (ed.) (1991) *The Middle East from the Iran–Contra Affair to the Intifada*, Syracuse: Syracuse University Press.

Freedman, R. O. (ed.) (1993) *The Middle East after Iraq's Invasion of Kuwait*, Gainesville: University of Florida Press.

Freedman, R. O. (ed.) (1998) *The Middle East and the Peace Process. The Impact of the Oslo Accords*, Gainesville: University Press of Florida.

Garnett, S. (1998) 'Europe's Crossroads: Russia and the West in the New Borderlands', in M. Mandelbaum (ed.) *The New Russian Foreign Policy*, New York: Council on Foreign Relations: 64–99.

Garnham, D. (1991) 'Explaining Middle East Alignments during the Gulf War', *The Jerusalem Journal of International Relations*, Vol. 13, No. 3: 63–83.

George, A. L. (1979) 'Case Studies and Theory Development: The Method of Structured Focused Comparison', in P. G. Lauren (ed.) (1979) *Diplomacy: New Approaches in History, Theory and Policy*, New York: The Free Press: 43–68.

George, A. L. and McKeown, T. J. (1985) 'Case Studies and Theories of Organizational Decision Making', *Advances in Information Processing in Organizations*, Vol. 2: 21–58.

Gilpin, R. (1996): 'No One Loves a Political Realist' in B. Frankel (ed.) (1996) *Realism: Restatements and Renewal*, London: Frank Cass: 3–26.

Glennon, M. J. (2003) 'Why the Security Council Failed', *Foreign Affairs*, 82 (3): 16–35.

Globalsecurity.org (2004) 'Libyan Nuclear Weapons'. Online, available at: www.globalsecurity.org/wmd/world/libya/nuclear.htm (accessed 25 March 2008).

Globalsecurity.org (2007a): 'Georgia Train and Equip program (GTEP)'. Online, available at: www.globalsecurity.org/military/ops/gtep.htm (accessed on 27 December 2007).

Globalsecurity.org (2007b) 'Ukraine Special Weapons'. Online, available at: www.globalsecurity.org/wmd/world/ukraine/index.html (accessed on 28 December 2007).

Goldgeier, J. M. and McFaul, M. (2003) *Power and Purpose: U.S. Policy Toward Russia After the Cold War*, Washington DC: Brookings Institution Press.

Gordon, P. H. and Shapiro, J. (2004) *Allies at War*, New York: McGraw-Hill.

Gordon, M. R. and Trainor, B. E. (2006) *Cobra II: The Inside Story of the Invasion and the Occupation of Iraq*, New York: Pantheon Books.

Grieco, J. M. (1988) 'Anarchy and the limits of cooperation: a realist critique of the newest liberal institutionalism', *International Organization*, Vol. 42, No. 3: 485–507.

Grieco, J. M. (1990) *Cooperation Among Nations*, Ithaca: Cornell University Press.

Grieco, J. M. (1995) 'The Maastricht Treaty, Economic and Monetary Union and the Neorealist Research Programme', *Review of International Studies*, 21 (1): 21–40.

Gunaratna, R. (2002) *Inside Al Qaeda, Global Network of Terror*, New York: Columbia University Press.

Haglund, D. G. (2003) 'Trouble in Pax Atlantica? The United States, Europe, and the Future of Multilateralism', in R. Foot, S. N. MacFarlane and M. Mastanduno (eds) *US Hegemony and International Organizations*, Oxford: Oxford University Press: 215–238.

Halliday, F. (2005) *The Middle East in International Relations. Power, Politics and Ideology*, Cambridge: Cambridge University Press.

Hanami, A. K. (2003) *Perspectives on Structural Realism*, Houndmills: Palgrave.

Hansen, B. (ed.) (1995) *European Security – 2000*, Copenhagen: Copenhagen Political Studies Press.

Hansen, B. (2000a) *Unipolarity and the Middle East*, Richmond: Curzon.

Hansen, B. (2000b): 'The Unipolar World Order' in B. Hansen and B. Heurlin (eds) (2000) *The New World Order*, Houndmills: Macmillan.

Hansen, B. (2000c) 'Afslutningen på den Kolde Krig', *Udenrigs*, 4 (1): 54–60.

Hansen, B. (2000d) 'Globalization, Unipolarity and the States of Europe', *Conference Paper*, University of Bergen, September 2000.

Hansen, B. (2001a) *Terrorisme – de utilfredse og den nye verdensorden*, Copenhagen: Lindhardt & Ringhof.

Hansen, B. (2001b) *Nye Våben i Syd*, Copenhagen: DUPI.

Hansen, B. (2002) 'Globalization and European State Formation', *Cooperation and Conflict*, 37 (3): 303–321.

Hansen, B. (2003) *Overmagt – USA og Europa i det 21. Århundrede*, Copenhagen: Gyldendal.

Hansen, B. (ftc.) *Unipolarity. Theory and World Order*, London: Routledge.

Haselkorn, A. (1999) *The Continuing Storm*, New Haven: Yale University Press.

Haslam, J. (2002) *No Virtue like Necessity: Realist Thought in International Relations since Machiavelli*, New Haven: Yale University Press.

Henry, C. N, and Springborg, R. (2001) *Globalization and the Politics of Development in the Middle East*, Cambridge: Cambridge University Press.

Heikal, M. (1993) *Illusions of Triumph*, Hammersmith: HarperCollins Publishers.

Heurlin, B. (2000) *The NATO of the Future: Intervention and Integration in Europe*, Copenhagen: Danish Institute of Foreign Affairs (DUPI).

Heurlin, B. (2003) 'False Threats to the Survival of NATO or Why NATO will Prosper', in B. Heurlin and M. V. Rasmussen (eds) *Challenges and Capabilities: NATO in the 21st Century*, Copenhagen: Danish Institute for International Studies: 43–56.

Heurlin, B. (2005) *USA som militærmagt*, Copenhagen: Danish Institute for International Affairs.

Heurlin, B. (2006) 'Syria: an International Loser? US-Syrian Relations after 9–11', The Danish Defence College, *COMER Working Paper*, June. Online. Online, available at: http://forsvaret.dk/NR/rdonlyres/0B538CA3-A601–4FA5-B6D0-DFE97259BDEE/0/BH_SYRIA_JUN2006.pdf (accessed 29 February 2008).

Hinnebusch, R. A. (1998) 'Syria and the Transition to Peace'. In *Freedman 1998*, 134–153.

Hinnebusch, R. A. (2002) 'The Foreign Policy of Syria'. in R. A. Hinnebusch and A. Ehteshami (eds) (2002) *The Foreign Policies of Middle East States*, Boulder, London: Lynne Rienner Publishers: 141–166.

Hinnebusch, R. A. (2003) 'Globalization and the Generational change: Syrian Foreign Policy Between Regional Conflict and European Partnership', *The Review of International Affairs*, Vol. 3, No. 2, Winter: 190–208.

Hinnebusch, R. (2003) *The International Politics of the Middle East*, Manchester: Manchester University Press.

Hinnebusch, R. A. and Ehteshami, A. (eds) (2002) *The Foreign Policies of Middle East States*, Boulder/London: Lynne Rienner Publishers.

Hosking, G. (1998) *Russia: People and Empire 1552–1917*, London: Fontana Press.

Howorth, J. (2003) 'Foreign and defence policy cooperation', in J. Peterson and M. A. Pollack (eds) *Europe, America, Bush*, London: Routledge: 13–28.

Hudson, M. C. (1991) 'After the Gulf War: Prospects for Democratization in the Arab World', *The Middle East Journal*, Vol. 45. No. 3.

Huntington, S. P. (1991) *The Third Wave: Democratization in the Late Twentieth Century*, Norman: University of Oklahoma Press.

Huntington, S. P. (1996) *The Clash of Civilizations*, New York: Simon & Schuster

IISS (1993) *Strategic Survey 1992–93*, London: Brassery's.

IISS (1995) *Strategic Survey 1994–95*, London: Brassery's.

IISS (2001) *The Military Balance 2000–01*, London: Brassery's.

Ikenberry, G. J. (2001a) 'Getting Hegemony Right', *The National Interest*, 63: 17–24.

Ikenberry, G. J. (2001b) *After Victory: Institutions, Strategic Restraint, and the Rebuilding of Order after Major Wars*, Princeton: Princeton University Press.

Ikenberry, G. J. (2002a) 'Introduction', in G. J. Ikenberry (ed.) *America Unrivaled*, Ithaca and London: Cornell University Press: 1–26.

Ikenberry, G. J. (2002b) (ed.) *America Unrivaled*, Ithaca and London: Cornell University Press.

INF Treaty (1987) 'Treaty between the United States of America and the Union of Soviet Socialist Republics on the Elimination of Their Intermediate-range and shorter-range missiles', *U.S. State Department*. Online, available at: www.state.gov/www/global/arms/treaties/inf1.html (accessed 23 March 2008).

International Herald Tribune (2003) 'A Conflict that can be resolved in Time: Ngorno-Karabach', *International Herald Tribune*. Online, available at: www.iht.com/articles/119526.html (accessed 29 November 2003).

International Herald Tribune (2004) 'Powell says U.S. Force won't encircle Russia', *International Herald Tribune*.

Ismailova, G. (2005) 'Chilly Diplomatic Relations between Azerbaijan and Russia', *Central Asia – Caucasus Analyst* (5 October 2005). Online, available at: www.cacianalyst.org/view_article.php?articleid=3704 (accessed 20 March 2008).

Jane's Defence Industry (2005) (14 October 2005) Surrey: Jane's.

Jensen, K. M. S. (2003) 'Ruslands Baltikum-politik 1997–2001', *Master Dissertation*, Department of Political Science, University of Copenhagen.

Jervis, R. (1990) *The Meaning of the Nuclear Revolution: Statecraft and the Prospect of Armageddon*, Ithaca: Cornell University Press.

Jervis, R. (1999) 'Realism, Neoliberalism, and Cooperation: Understanding the Debate', *International Security*, 24 (1): 42–63.

Jervis, R. (2005) *American Foreign Policy in a New Era*, London: Routledge.

Joffe, J. (1984) 'Europe's American Pacifier', *Foreign Policy*, 54: 64–82.

Joffe, J. (1997) 'How America Does It', *Foreign Affairs*, 76 (5): 13–27.

Johnston, M. T. (2005) 'Britain and Transatlantic Security: Negotiating Two Bridges Far Apart', in T. Lansford and B. Tashev (eds) *Old Europe, New Europe and the US*, Aldershot: Ashgate: 41–56.

Jones, S. G. (2006a) 'The Rise of a European Defense', *Political Science Quarterly*, 121 (2): 241–267.

Jones, S. G. (2006b) 'Averting Failure in Afghanistan', *Survival*, 48 (1): 111–128.

Jones, S. G. and Larrabee, F. S. (2005/2006) 'Arming Europe', *The National Interest*, 82: 62–68.

Jonson, L. (2001) 'Russia and Central Asia', in L. Jonson and R. Allison (eds) *Central Asian Security*, Washington DC: Brookings Institution: 95–126.

Kabila, S. (2004) 'Russia Rekindles Strategic Partnership with India', *South Asia Analysis Group*. Online, available at: www.saag.org/papers12/paper1180.html (accessed 20 March 2008).

Kagan, R. (2003) *Paradise and Power*, London: Atlantic Books.

Kane, T. (2004a) *Global U.S. Troop Deployment, 1950–2003*, Washington: The Heritage Foundation.

Kane, T. (2004b) *Troop Deployment Dataset, 1950–2003*, Washington: The Heritage Foundation.

Kapstein, E. B. (1999) 'Does Unipolarity Have a Future?', in E. B. Kapstein and M. Mastanduno (eds) (1999) *Unipolar Politics*, New York: Columbia University Press: 464–490.

Karsh, E. (1993) 'The Troubled Partnership: Moscow and Asad's Syria', in M. Light (ed.) *Troubled Friendships: Moscow's Third World Ventures*, London and New York: British Academic Press: 140–166.

Kay, S. (1998) *NATO and the Future of European Security*, Lanham: Rowman and Little-field.

King, C. (2004) 'A Rose among Thorns', *Foreign Affairs*, 83 (2): 13–18.

King, G., Keohane, R. O. and Verba, S. (1994) *Designing Social Inquiry*, New Jersey: Princeton University Press.

Kirisci, K. (2000) 'Turkey and the Muslim Middle East', in *Makovsky and Sayari* 2000: 39–58.

Kissinger, H. (2001) *Does America Need a Foreign Policy?*, New York: Simon and Schuster.

Kleveman, L. (2004) *The New Great Game: Blood and Oil in Central Asia*, London: Atlantic Books.

Kommersant (2007a) 'Japan Won't Share Islands', *Kommersant*. Online, available at: www.kommersant.com/page.asp?id=-9798 (accessed 5 January 2007).

Kommersant (2007b) 'Some Nuclear Heavy Lifting' *Kommersant*. Online, available at: www.kommersant.com/p769788/r_1/RS-24_ICBM,_Russia,_America,_missile_defense/ (accessed 30 May 2007).

Kommersant (2007c) 'Telephone for Mr. Putin: Russian and US Presidents Mull Over a Joint Missile Defense', *Kommersant*. Online, available at: www.kommersant.com/page.asp?id=754484 (accessed 30 March 2007).

Kommersant (2007d) 'America Hits Russian Policy with Dollar', *Kommersant*. Online, available at: www.kommersant.com/doc.asp?id=838134 (accessed 21 December 2007).

Kommersant (2007e) 'Russia, Belarus to Jointly Oppose U.S. Missile Defense Shield in Europe', *Kommersant*. Online, available at: www.kommersant.com/page.asp?id=-11575 (accessed 25 March 2008).

Korany, B. and Dessouki, A. E. H. (eds) (1991) *The Foreign Policies of Arab States. The Challenge of Change* (2nd edn), Boulder: Westview Press.

Kostiner, J. (2001) 'The United States and the Gulf States: An Alliance in Need', in B. Rubin and T. Keaney (eds) (2001) *US Allies in a Changing World*, London: Frank Cass: 135–144.

Krasner, S. D. (1999) *Sovereignty*, Princeton, New Jersey: Princeton University Press.

Kupchan, C. A. (1998) 'Reconstructing the West: The Case for an Atlantic Union', in C. A. Kupchan (ed.) *Atlantic Security*, New York: Council on Foreign Relations: 64–91.

Kupchan, C. A. (2002) *The End of the American Era*, New York: Alfred A. Knopf.

Kuzio, T. (2000) 'Geopolitical Pluralism in the CIS: The Emergence of GUUAM', *European Security*, 9 (2): 81–114.

Kuzio, T. (2002) 'GUUAM reverts to GUAM as Uzbekistan suspends its Membership prior to Yalta Summit', *Eurasia Insight* (18 July 2002). Online, available at: www.eurasianet.org/departments/insight/articles/eav071802.shtml (accessed 20 March 2008).

Kuzio, T. (2005) 'Ukraine moves closer to NATO Membership', *Eurasia Daily Monitor* (29 April 2005). Online, available at: www.jamestown.org/publications_details.php?volume_id=407&issue_id=3316&article_id=2369682 (accessed 20 March 2008).

Kydd, A. (1997) 'Sheep in Sheep's Clothing: Why Security Seekers Do Not Fight Each Other', *Security Studies*, 7 (1): 114–154.

Laatikainen, K. V. (2003) 'Norden's Eclipse: The Impact of the European Union's

Common Foreign and Security Policy on Nordic Cooperation in the United Nations', *Cooperation and Conflict*, 38 (4): 409–441.

Lakatos, I. (1970): 'Falsification and the Methodology of Scientific Research Programmes' in I. Lakatos and A. Musgrave (eds) (1970) *Criticism and the Growth of Knowledge*, Cambridge: Cambridge University Press: 91–196.

Lambeth, B. S. (1995) 'Russia's Wounded Military', *Foreign Affairs*, 72 (2): 86–98.

Lansford, T. (1999) 'The Triumph of Transatlanticism: NATO and the Evolution of European Security after the Cold War', *Journal of Strategic Studies*, 22 (1): 1–28.

Larsson, R. (2007) Nord Stream, Sweden and Baltic Sea Security, *FOI*. Online, available at: www.foi.se/FOI/templates/PublicationPage_171.aspx?qu=Nord%20Stream&au=&yr=2007&fomr=&sort=ar%20DES (accessed 21 March 2008).

Larrabee, S. F. and Lesser, I. O. (2003) *Turkish Foreign Policy in an Age of Uncertainty*, Santa Monica: RAND.

Layne, C. (1993) 'The Unipolar Illusion: Why New Great Powers Will Rise', in M. E. Brown, S. M. Lynn-Jones and S. E. Miller (eds) (1995) *The Perils of Anarchy – Contemporary Realism and International Security*, Cambridge and Massachusetts: MIT Press: 130–176.

Layne, C. (2006a) *The Peace of Illusions: American Grand Strategy from 1940 to the Present*, Ithaca and London: Cornell University Press.

Layne, C. (2006b) 'The Unipolar Illusion Revisited: The Coming End of the United States' Unipolar Moment', *International Security*, 31 (2): 7–41.

Legvold, R. (2001) 'Russia's Unformed Foreign Policy', *Foreign Affairs*, 80 (5): 62–75.

Legro, J. W. and Moravcsik, A. (1999) 'Is Anybody Still a Realist?', *International Security*, 24 (2): 5–55.

Lemann, N. (2003) 'How it came to War', *The New Yorker* (31 March 2003). Online, available at: http://foi.missouri.edu/evolvingissues/howitcame.html (accessed 20 March 2008).

Leverett, F. (2005) *Inheriting Syria – Basher's Trial by Fire*, Washington DC: Brookings Institution Press.

Levy, J. S. (2004) 'What do Great Powers Balance Against and When?' in T. V. Paul, J. J. Wirtz and M. Fortmann (eds) *Balance of Power: Theory and Practice in the 21st Century*, Stanford: Stanford University Press: 29–51.

Lewis, B. (2002) *What Went Wrong?: Western Impact on Middle Eastern Response*, New York: Oxford University Press.

Lieber, K. and Alexander, G. (2005) 'Waiting for Balancing: Why the World is Not Pushing Back', *International Security*, 30 (1): 109–139.

Lieber, K. and Press, D. G. (2006) 'The Rise of U.S. Nuclear Primacy': Foreign Affairs, March/April 2006.

Lieber, R. J. (1999) 'Great Britain: Decline and Recovery', in R. A. Pastor (ed.) *A Century's Journey: How the Great Powers Shape the World*, New York: Basic Books: 33–62.

Lieber, R. J. (2005) *The American Era: Power and Strategy for the 21st Century*, Cambridge: Cambridge University Press.

Light, M. (2001) 'Post-Soviet Russian Foreign Policy: The First Decade', in A. Brown (ed.) *Contemporary Russian Politics*, Oxford: Oxford University Press: 419–428.

Liska, G. (1998) *In Search of Poetry in the Politics of Power*, Lanham: Lexington Books.

Lo, B. (2003) *Vladimir Putin and the Evolution of Russian Foreign Policy*, London: The Royal Institute of International Affairs.

Lundestad, G. (2003) *The United States and Western Europe since 1945*, Oxford: Oxford University Press.

Malone, D. M. (2003) 'US-UN Relations in the UN Security Council in the Post-Cold War Era', in R. Foot, S. N. MacFarlane and M. Mastanduno (eds) *US Hegemony and International Organizations*, Oxford: Oxford University Press: 73–91.

Malone, D. M. (2007) *The International Struggle over Iraq. Politics in the UN Security Council 1980–2005* (paperback edn), Oxford: Oxford University Press.

Mangott, G. (2000) 'A Giant on its Knees: Structural Constraints on Russia's Global Role, *International Politics*, 37 (December): 479–507.

Martinez, L. (2007) *The Libyan Paradox*, London: Hurst & Company.

Mastanduno, M. (1999) 'Preserving the Unipolar Moment: Realist Theories and U.S. Grand Strategy after the Cold War', in E. B. Kapstein and M. Mastanduno (eds) *Unipolar Politics*, New York: Columbia University Press: 138–181.

McFarlaine, N. (1999) 'Realism and Russian Strategy after the Collapse of the USSR', in E. B. Kapstein and M. Mastanduno (ed.) *Unipolar Politics: Realism and State Strategies after the Cold War*, New York: Columbia University Press: 218–260.

McFaul, M. (1999) 'Russia's many Foreign Policies', *Demokratizatsiya*, 7 (3): 393–412.

McFaul, M. (2002) *Russia's Unfinished Revolution: Political Change from Gorbachev to Putin*, Ithaca: Cornell University Press.

McKeown, T. (1999) 'Case Studies and the Statistical Worldview: Review of King, Keohane and Verba's Designing Social Inquiry: Scientific Inference in Qualitative Research', *International Organization*, 53 (1): 161–190.

Mearsheimer, J. J. (1990) 'Why we will soon miss the Cold War', *TeachingAmericanHistory.org*. Online, available at: http://teachingamericanhistory.org/library/index.asp? document=713 (accessed 23 March 2008).

Mearsheimer, J. J. (1990/91) 'Back to the Future – Instability in Europe After the Cold War', *International Security*, 15 (1): 5–56.

Mearsheimer, J. J. (1994/95) 'The False Promise of International Institutions', *International Security* 19 (3): 5–49.

Mearsheimer, J. J. (2001) *The Tragedy of Great Power Politics*, Norton: New York.

Mearsheimer, J. J. (2007) *Structural Realism*, in T. Dunne, M. Kurki and S. Smith (eds) *International Relations Theories*, Oxford: Oxford University Press: 71–88.

Menon, R. (1998) 'After Empire: Russia and the Southern Near Abroad', in M. Mandelbaum (ed.) *The New Russian Foreign Policy*, New York: Council on Foreign Relations: 100–166.

Menon, R. (2001) 'Russia', *The National Bureau of Asia Research*. Online. Online, available at: www.nbr.org/publications/ (accessed 20 March 2008).

Military Balance (2006) *The Military Balance 2006*, London: The International Institute For Strategic Studies.

Miller, R. F. (1995) 'Russian Policy Toward Japan', in P. Shearman (ed.) *Russian Foreign Policy Since 1990*, Boulder, San Francisco, Oxford: Westview Press: 135–158.

Missiroli, A. (2003) 'Ploughshares into Swords? Euros for European Defence', *European Foreign Affairs Review*, 8 (1): 5–33.

Missiroli, A. (2004) 'Mind the Steps: the Constitutional Treaty and beyond', in N. Gnesotto (ed.) *EU Security and Defence Policy: The first five years (1999–2004)*, Paris: Institute for Security Studies: 145–154.

Molloy, S. (2006) 'Security strategy and the "war on terror"', in R. Dannreuther and J. Peterson (eds) *Security Strategy and Transatlantic Relations*, London: Routledge: 61–77.

Moscow Times (2003a) 'Anti-terror Exercises Only a First Step', *Moscow Times*. Online, available at: www.themoscowtimes.com (accessed 14 August 2003).

Moscow Times (2003b) 'Kremlin hopes for Friendlier Georgia', *Moscow Times.* Online, available at: www.themoscowtimes.com (accessed 25 November 2003).

Moscow Times (2003c) Shanghai Six Talks Nuts and Bolts, *Moscow Times.* Online, available at: www.themoscowtimes.com (accessed 30 May 2005).

Moscow Times (2004a) 'Armenia in Russia's Embrace', *Moscow Times.* Online, available at: www.themoscowtimes.com (accessed 24 March 2004).

Moscow Times (2004b) 'EU wants more WTO Concessions', *Moscow Times* (26 May 2004). Online, available at: www.themoscowtimes.com (accessed 20 March 2008).

Moscow Times (2004c) Russia Warns America over Caspian Sea, *Moscow Times.* Online, available at: www.themoscowtimes.com (accessed 24 March 2004).

Moscow Times (2004d) Saakashvili will meet with Bush, *Moscow Times.* Online, available at: www.themoscowtimes.com (accessed 26 February 2004).

Moscow Times (2005a) 'Borodin: Belarus to get Ruble in '06', *Moscow Times.* Online, available at: www.themoscowtimes.com (accessed 27 January 2005).

Moscow Times (2005b) Georgia, South Ossetia Trade Blame for Shelling, *Moscow Times.* Online, available at: www.themoscowtimes.com (accessed 22 September 2005).

Moscow Times (2005d) Military Set for First War Games With China, *Moscow Times.* Online, available at: www.themoscowtimes.com (accessed 18 August 2005).

Moscow Times (2006a) *Expert Calls for More Missiles.* Online, available at: www.themoscowtimes.com (accessed 4 April 2006).

Moscow Times (2006b) *The Civil Society Paradox.* Online, available at: www.themoscowtimes.com (accessed 13 June 2006).

Moscow Times (2006c) 'What will Russian WTO membership mean for your industry?', *Moscow Times.* Online, available at: www.themoscowtimes.com (accessed 19 April 2006).

Mouritzen, H. (1997) 'Kenneth Waltz: a critical rationalist between international politics and foreign policy', in I. B. Neumann and O. Wæver (eds) (1997) *The Future of International Relations*, London: Routledge: 66–89.

Mouritzen, H. (1998) *Theory and Reality of International Politics*, Aldershot: Ashgate.

Mouritzen, H. (2005) *Europas fremtid – et euro-atlantisk geopolitisk puslespil*, Copenhagen: Danish Institute for International Studies.

Mouritzen, H. and Wivel, A. (eds) (2005) *The Geopolitics of Euro-Atlantic Integration*, London: Routledge.

Mowle, T. S. (2004) *Allies at Odds? The United States and the European Union*, Houndmills: Palgrave.

Mueller, J. (1988) 'The Essential Irrelevance of Nuclear Weapons: Stability in the Postwar World', *International Security*, 13 (2): 55–79.

Mörth, U. (2003) 'Framing an American threat: the European Commission and the technology gap', in M. Knodt and S. Princen (eds) *Understanding the European Union's External Relations*, London: Routledge: 75–92.

Møller, K. J. (2007) 'CSTO: En Russisk domineret forsvarsorganisation I udvikling?', *brief*, Danish Institute for International Studies.

NATO (2001): The NATO Handbook, Brussels, NATO.

NATO (2002): NATO-Ukraine Action Plan, *NATO.* Online, available at: www.nato.int/issues/nato-ukraine/action_plan.html (accessed 15 March 2008).

NATO (2004a) 'Enhancing Security and Extending Stability through NATO Enlargement', *NATO.* Online, available at: www.nato.int/docu/enlargement/html_en/enlargement01.html (accessed 25 March 2008).

NATO (2004b) 'NATO-Russia: Forging Deeper Relations', *NATO*. Online, available at: www.nato.int/docu/nato-russia/nato-russia-r.pdf (accessed 8 March 2008).

New York Times (2003) 'Russian Official Cautions U.S. on use of Central Asian Bases', *New York Times*. Online, available at: http://query.nytimes.com/gst/fullpage.html?res=9900E1D6173FF933A25753C1A9659C8B63&scp=1&sq=Russian+Official+cautions+U.S.+on+use+of+Central+Asian+Bases&st=nyt (accessed 21 February 2008).

New York Times (2005) 'Q&A: U.S. Military Bases in Central Asia', *New York Times*. Online, available at: www.nytimes.com/cfr/international/slot2_072605.html?_r=1&oref=slogin&pagewanted=print (accessed 26 July 2005).

Niblock, T. (2002) 'The Foreign Policy of Libya', in R. A. Hinnebusch and A. Ehteshami (eds) (2002) *The Foreign Policies of Middle East States*, Boulder/London: Lynne Rienner Publishers: 213–234.

Norris, R. S. and Kristensen, H. (2006) 'Global Nuclear Stockpiles 1945–2006', *Bulletin of the Atomic Scientists*, Vol. 62, No. 4 (July/August), 2006. Online, available at: http://thebulletin.metapress.com/content/c4120650912x74k7/fulltext.pdf (accessed 22 March 2008).

Oest, K. N. (2007) 'The End of Alliance Theory?', *working paper*, AP 2007/03, Department of Political Science, University of Copenhagen. Online, available at: www.polsci.ku.dk/forskning/publikationer/2007/AP_2007_03.pdf (accessed 20 March 2008).

Olson, M. (2000) *Power and Prosperity*, New York: Basic Books.

Oswald, F. (2006): 'Soft Balancing Between Friends: Transforming Transatlantic Relations', *Debatte: Journal of Contemporary Central and Eastern Europe*, 14(2): 145–160.

Owen, J. M. (2002) 'Transnational Liberalism and American Primacy; or, Benignity is in the Eye of the Beholder', in G. J. Ikenberry (ed.) *America Unrivaled*, Ithaca: Cornell University Press: 239–259.

Pape, R. A. (2005) 'Soft Balancing against the United States', *International Security*, 30 (1): 7–45.

Pape, R. A. (2003) 'The Strategic Logic of Suicide Terrorism', *American Political Science Review*, 97 (3): 343–361.

Pargeter, A. (2006) 'Libya: Reforming the impossible?', *Review of African Political Economy*, 33 (108), 219–235.

Paul, T. V. (2004) 'Introduction: The Enduring Axioms of Balance of Power Theory and Their Contemporary Relevance', in T. V. Paul, J. J. Wirtz and M. Fortmann (eds) *Balance of Power: Theory and Practice in the 21st Century*, Stanford: Stanford University Press: 1–25.

Paul, T. V. (2005) 'Soft Balancing in the Age of U.S. Primacy', *International Security*, 30 (1): 46–71.

Paul, T. V., Wirtz, J. J. and Fortmann, M. (2004) (eds) *Balance of Power: Theory and Practice in the 21st Century*, Stanford: Stanford University Press.

Pauly Jr., R. J. (2005) 'French Security Agenda in the Post-9/11 World', in T. Lansford and B. Tashev (eds) *Old Europe, New Europe and the US*, Aldershot: Ashgate: 3–17.

Pedersen, T. (1998) *Germany, France and the Integration of Europe: A Realist Interpretation*, London: Pinter.

Pedersen, T. (2002) 'Cooperative hegemony: power, ideas and institutions in regional integration', *Review of International Studies*, 28 (4): 677–696.

Perthes, V. (2004) 'Syria under Bashar al-Asad: Modernisation and the Limits of Change', IISS, *Adelphi Paper* 366.

Petersberg Declaration (1992) Bonn: Western European Union. Online, available at: www.weu.int/documents/920619peten.pdf (accessed 5 February 2008).

Peterson, J. (2003) 'The US and Europe in the Balkans', in J. Peterson and M. A. Pollack (eds) *Europe, America, Bush*, London: Routledge: 85–98.

Piening, C. (1997) *Global Europe*, Boulder: Lynne Rienner.

Pipes, R. (1997) 'Is Russia Still an Enemy?', *Foreign Affairs*, 76 (5): 65–78.

Podeh, E. (2005) 'Between Stagnation and Renovation: the Arab System in the Aftermath of the Iraq War', *The Middle East Review of International Affairs*, Vol. 9: 3, September.

Pollack, M. A. (2003a) 'Unilateral America, multilateral Europe?', in J. Peterson and M. A. Pollack (eds) *Europe, America, Bush*, London: Routledge: 115–127.

Pollack, M. A. (2003b) 'The Political Economy of Transatlantic Trade Disputes', in E. U. Petersmann and M. A. Pollack (eds) *Transatlantic Economic Disputes: The EU, the US and the WTO*, Oxford: Oxford University Press: 65–118.

Pond, E. (2003) *Friendly Fire: The Near-Death of the Transatlantic Alliance*, Washington DC: Brookings Institution Press.

Popper, K. R. (1959) *The Logic of Scientific Discovery*, London: Routledge.

Popper, K. R. (1989) *Conjectures and Refutations: The Growth of Scientific Knowledge* (5th edn), London: Routledge.

Posen, B. (2003) 'Command of the Commons', *International Security*, 28 (1): 5–46.

Presidency Conclusions (2000) Nice, Nice European Council: ANNEX I to ANNEX VI. Online, available at: www.consilium.europa.eu/ueDocs/cms_Data/docs/pressData/en/ec/00400-r1.%20ann.en0.htm (accessed 5 February 2008).

Press-Barnathan, G. (2005) 'The Changing Incentives for Security Regionalization: from 11/9 to 9/11', *Cooperation and Conflict*, 40 (3): 281–304.

Prizel, I. (1995) 'Warsaw's Ostpolitik: A new Encounter with Positivism', in A. A. Michta and I. Prizel (eds) *Polish Foreign Policy Reconsidered*, London: Macmillan.

Quandt, W. B. (1993) *Peace Process. American Diplomacy and the Arab-Israeli Conflict since 1967*, Washington DC: The Brookings Institution/Berkeley and Los Angeles: University of California Press.

Ra'anan, U. and Martin, K. (1995) *Russia: A Return to Imperialism?*, Boston: Institute for the Study of Conflict, Ideology, and Policy, Boston University.

Radio Free Europe (2007) SCO To Hold Largest Military Exercises To Date, *Radio Free Europe*. Online, available at: www.rferl.org/featuresarticle/2007/08/b04ccf5d-9cbd-4df6-b07e-9454ecc7324d.html (accessed 8 August 2008).

Rees, W. (2006) *Transatlantic Counter-terrorism Cooperation*, London: Routledge.

Rees, W. and Aldrich, R. J. (2005) 'Contending cultures of counterterrorism: transatlantic divergence or convergence?', *International Affairs*, 81 (5): 905–923.

Reinicke, W. H. (1996) *Deepening the Atlantic*, Gütersloh: Bertelsmann Foundation Publishers.

Remington, T. (2003) 'Taming Vlast', in R. R. Kelley (ed.) *After Communism*, Fayetville: The University of Arkansas Press: 89–118.

Resende-Santos, J. (1996) 'Anarchy and the Emulation of Military Systems: Military Organization and Technology in South America, 1870–1914' in B. Frankel (ed.) (1996) *Realism: Restatements and Renewal*, London: Frank Cass: 193–260.

Ria Novosti (2006) Russia–Belarus single currency to simplify gas payments – source, *Ria Novosti*. Online, available at: http://en.rian.ru/world/20060428/47024147.html (accessed 28 April 2006).

Rich, N. (2003) *Great Power Diplomacy since 1914*, New York: McGraw-Hill.

Robinson, N. (2003) 'The Politics of Russia's Partial Democracy', *Political Studies Review*, 1: 149–166.

Rogel, C. (1998) *The Breakup of Yugoslavia and the War in Bosnia*, London: Greenwood Press.

Rose, G. (1998) 'Neoclassical Realism and Theories of Foreign Policy', *World Politics*, 51: 144–172.

Rosecrance, R. (2001) 'Has Realism Become Cost-Benefit Analysis?', *International Security*, 26 (2): 132–154.

Rubin, B. (2006) 'Why Syria Matters', *The Middle East Review of International Affairs*, Vol. 10: (4), December.

Rubin, B. and Rubin, J. C. (2003) *Yasir Arafat. A Political Biography*, London: Continuum.

Russel, W. (1995) 'Russian Relations with the "Near Abroad"', in P. Shearman (ed.) *Russian Foreign Policy Since 1990*, Boulder: Westview Press: 53–70.

Rynning, S. (2005) *Nato Renewed*, New York and Houndmills: Palgrave.

Rynning, S. and Guzzini, S. (2001) *Realism and Foreign Policy Analysis*, Working Papers 42/2001, København: Copenhagen Peace Research Institute.

Sabelnikov, L. (1996) 'Russia on the Way to the World Trade Organization', *International Affairs*, 72 (2): 345–355.

Sadowski, Y. (1993) 'The New Orientalism and the Democracy Debate', in J. Beinin and J. Stork (eds) *Political Islam: Essays from Middle East Report*, Berkeley: University of California Press

Said, E. W. (1995) *Peace and its Discontent, Gaza-Jericho 1993–1995*, London: Vintage.

Schweller, R. L. ([1994] (1995)) 'Bandwagoning for Profit: Bringing the Revisionist State Back In' in M. E. Brown, S. M. Lynn-Jones and S. E. Miller (eds) (1995): *The Perils of Anarchy – Contemporary Realism and International Security*, Cambridge, Massachusetts: The MIT Press: 249–284.

Schweller, R. L. (1998) *Deadly Imbalances*, New York: Columbia University Press.

Schweller, R. L. (2003) 'The Progressiveness of Neoclassical Realism', in C. Elman and M. F. Elman (eds) *Progress in International Relations Theory*, Cambridge, Massachusetts: MIT Press: 311–347.

Schweller, R. L. (2004) 'Unanswered Threats: A Neoclassical Realist Theory of Underbalancing', *International Security*, 29 (2): 159–201.

Schweller, R. L. (2006) *Unanswered Threats*, Princeton: Princeton University Press.

Schweller, R. L. and Priess, D. (1997) 'A Tale of Two Realisms: Expanding the Institutions Debate', *Mershon International Studies Review*, 41: 1–32.

Sergounin, A. (1998) 'The Russia Dimension', in H. Mouritzen (ed.) *Bordering Russia: Theory and Prospects for Russia's Baltic Rim*, Brookfield, VT: Ashgate: 15–78.

Shad, T. I. and Boucher, S. (1995) 'Syrian foreign policy in the post-Soviet Era', *Arab Studies Quarterly*, Vol. 17: 1/2, Spring: 77–84.

Shearman, P. (1995a) *Russian Foreign Policy Since 1990*, Oxford: Westview Press.

Shearman, P. (1995b) 'Russian Policy Toward Western Europe: The German Axis', in P. Sharman (ed.) *Russian Foreign Policy Since 1990*, Boulder, San Francisco, Oxford: Westview Press: 93–110.

Sheikh, N. S. (2002) 'Book review of Birthe Hansen: Unipolarity and the Middle East', *Cooperation and Conflict*, Vol. 37, No. 2: 233–236.

Shimkus, John (2006) 'Changes in the forward deployment of the United States' military and the effects on the transatlantic alliance', *063 DSCTC 06 E*, NATO Parliamentary Assembly. Online, available at: http://nato-pa.int/Default.asp?CAT2=0&CAT1=0&CAT0=576&SHORTCUT=922 (accessed 5 February 2008).

Sidorenko, T. (2004) 'Foreign Trade in Post-Communist Russia and Some Problems Related to Its Adhesion to the World Trade Organization', *Foro Internacional*, 44 (4): 656–689.

Sinai, J. (1997) 'Libya's Pursuit of Weapon of Mass Destruction', *The Nonproliferation Review*, Spring–Summer 1997: 92–100.

Singer, D. (1987) 'Reconstructing the Correlates of War Dataset on Material Capabilities of States, 1816–1985', *International Interactions*, 14 (1): 115–132.

Singer, D., Bremer, S. and Stuckly, J. (1972) 'Capability Distribution, Uncertainty, and Major Power War 1820–1965', in B. Russett (ed.) *Peace, War and Numbers*, Beverly Hills: Sage: 19–48.

Sloan, S. R. (2005) *NATO, The European Union, and the Atlantic Community*, Lanham: Rowman and Littlefield.

Smaghi, L. B. (2004) 'A Single EU Seat in the IMF?', *Journal of Common Market Studies*, 42 (2): 229–248.

Smith, M. and Steffenson, R. (2005) 'The EU and the United States', in C. Hill and M. Smith (eds) *International Relations and the European Union*, Oxford: Oxford University Press: 343–363.

Snyder, G. H. (2002) 'Mearsheimer's World – Offensive Realism and the Struggle for Security: A Review Essay', *International Security*, 27 (1): 149–173.

Snyder, J. (1991) *Myths of Empire: Domestic Politics and International Ambition*, Ithaca and London: Cornell University Press.

Soskice, D. (1998) 'Openness and Diversity in Transatlantic Economic Relations', in B. Eichengreen (ed.) *Transatlantic Economic Relations in the Post-Cold War Era*, New York: Council on Foreign Relations: 8–35.

Stake, R. E. (1995): *The Art of Case Study Research*, Thousand Oaks: Sage.

Steinberg, G. M. (2001) 'Israel and the United States: Can the Special Relationship Survive the New Strategic Environment?', in B. Rubin and T. Keaney (eds) (2001) *US Allies in a Changing World*, London: Frank Cass: 145–180.

Stålenheim, P., Perdomo, C. and Sköns, E. (2006) 'Chapter 8: Military expenditure', in *SIPRI Yearbook 2006*, Oxford: Oxford University Press.

Stirk, P. M. R. (1996) *A History of European Integration since 1914*, London: Pinter.

Surry, E. (2006) 'Appendix 9A. The 100 largest arms-producing companies, 2004', in *SIPRI Yearbook 2006*, Oxford: Oxford University Press: 419–427.

Takeyh, R. (1998) 'Qadhafi and the Challenge of Militant Islam', *The Washington Quarterly*, 21 (3), Summer: 159–172.

Tardy, T. (2003/2004) 'France and the US – The inevitable clash?', *International Journal*, Vol. 59, No. 1: 1–22.

Taylor, A. R. (1991) *The Superpowers and the Middle East*, Syracuse: Syracuse University Press.

Telhami, S. (2003) 'An Essay on Neorealism and Foreign Policy', in A. K. Hanami (ed.) *Perspectives on Structural Realism*, Houndmills: Palgrave Macmillan: 105–118.

Tellis, A. (2006) 'The Evolution of U.S.-Indian Ties: Missile Defense in an Emerging Strategic Relationship', *International Security*, 30 (4): 113–151.

Tervarent, P. de S. de (1997) 'The Creation of the Common Foreign and Security Policy', in E. Regelsberger, P. de S. de Tervarent and W. Wessels (eds) *Foreign Policy of the European Union*, Boulder: Lynne Rienner: 41–63.

Thakur, R. (1995) 'Russian Foreign Policy Toward India: A Relationship on Hold', in P. Shearman (ed.) *Russian Foreign Policy Since 1990*, Boulder, San Francisco, Oxford: Westview Press: 225–246.

The White House (2002) *National Security Strategy*. Online, available at: www. whitehouse.gov/nsc/nss.pdf (accessed 5 February 2008).

The NATO-Russia Archive (2005) 'Russia and the CFE Treaty', *The NATO Russia Archive* (18 November 2005).

The Voice of America (1999) Russia/Belarus. Online, available at: www.fas.org/ news/belarus/991208-belarus1.htm (accessed 8 December 1999).

Toft, P. (2002) *Magtpolitik & Alliancer – Realistisk Allianceteori og Polens Vej fra Warszawa-pagten til NATO*, MA Thesis, Department of Political Science: University of Copenhagen.

Toft, P. (2006) 'The Way of the Vanquished: Fallen Great Powers and Responses to Collapse 1815–2004', *PhD Dissertation*, Copenhagen: Faculty of Social Sciences, University of Copenhagen.

Toft, P. and Oest, K. N. (2007) 'The Shanghai Cooperation Organization: A Threat or Opportunity for Europe?', *working paper*, AP 2007/01, Department of Political Science, University of Copenhagen. Online, available at: www.polsci.ku.dk/forskning/publikationer/2007/AP_2007_01.pdf (accessed 20 March 2008).

Toje, A. (2005) 'The 2003 European Union Security Strategy: A Critical Appraisal', *European Foreign Affairs Review*, 10 (1): 117–133.

Transparency International (2005) 'Transparency International Corruption Perceptions 2005', *Transparency International*. Online, available at: www.transparency.org/ policy_research/surveys_indices/gcb/2005 (accessed 20 March 2008).

Treisman, D. (2002) 'Russia Renewed?', *Foreign Affairs*, 81 (6): 58–72.

Treisman, D. and Schleifer, A. (2000) *Without a Map: Political Tactics and Economic Reform in Russia*, Cambridge, Massachusetts: MIT Press.

Trevan, T. (1999) *Saddam's Secrets: The Hunt for Iraq's Hidden Weapons*, London: Harper Collins Publishers.

Tripp, C. (2007) *A History of Iraq* (3rd edn), Cambridge: Cambridge University Press.

United Press International (2005) 'Russia, China boost joint defense plans', *United Press International*. Online, available at: www.washtimes.com/upi-breaking/20050207–045504–8153r.htm (accessed 8 February 2005).

Urban, M. (2003) 'Social Relations and Political Practices in Post-Communist Russia', in R. R. Kelley (ed.) *After Communism*, Fayetville: University of Arkansas Press: 119–142.

Valdez, J. (2000) 'The Near Abroad, the West, and National Identity in Russian Foreign Policy', in 'The making of Foreign Policy in Russia and the new States of Eurasia'.

Van Evera, S. (1997): *Guide to Methods for Students of Political Science*, Ithaca and London: Cornell University Press.

Van Evera, S. (1999) *Causes of War*, Ithaca and London: Cornell University Press.

Vasquez, J. A. (1997) 'The Realist Paradigm and Degenerative versus Progressive Research Programs: An Appraisal of Neotraditional Research on Waltz's Balancing Proposition', *American Political Science Review*, 91 (4): 899–912.

Wallace, W. (1983) 'Less than a Federation, More than a Regime: The Community as a Political System', in H. Wallace, W. Wallace and C. Webb (eds) *Policy Making in the European Community*, New York: Wiley: 403–436.

Wallace, W. (2001) 'Europe, the Necessary Partner', *Foreign Affairs*, 80 (3): 16–34.

Walker, M. (1993) *The Cold War*, London: Vintage.

Walt, S. M. (1987) *The Origins of Alliances*, Ithaca: Cornell University Press.

Walt, S. M. (1988) 'Testing Alliance Formation: The Case of Southwest Asia', *International Organization*, 42 (2): 275–316.

Walt, S. M. (1989): 'U.S. Grand Strategy: The Case for Finite Containment', *International Security*, 14 (1): 5–49.

Walt, S. M. (2002a) 'The Enduring Relevance of the Realist Tradition' in I. Katznelson and H. Milner (eds) (2002) *Political Science: The State of the Discipline III*, New York: W. W. Norton: 197–230.

Walt, S. M. (2002b) 'Keeping the World "Off-Balance": Self-Restraint and U.S. Foreign Policy', in G. J. Ikenberry (ed.) *America Unrivalled*, Ithaca and London: Cornell University Press: 121–154.

Walt, S. M. (2005) *Taming American Power*, New York: W. W. Norton and Company.

Waltz, K. N. (1979) *Theory of International Politics*, New York: Random House.

Waltz, K. N. (1981) 'The Spread of Nuclear Weapons: More May Be Better?', *Adelphi Papers*, London: International Institute for Strategic Studies, 171 (1): 1–31.

Waltz, K. N. (1986) 'Reflections on Theory of International Politics: A Response to My Critics', in R. O. Keohane (ed.) *Neorealism and Its Critics*, New York: Columbia University Press: 322–345.

Waltz, K. N. (1988): 'The Origins of War in Neorealist Theory', in R. I. Rotberg and T. K. Rabb (eds) (1988) *The Origin and Prevention of Major Wars*, USA: Cambridge University Press: 39–52.

Waltz, K. N. (1993) 'The Emerging Structure of International Politics', *International Security*, 18 (2): 44–79.

Waltz, K. N. (1996) 'International Politics is Not Foreign Policy', *Security Studies*, 6 (1): 54–57.

Waltz, K. N. (2000) 'Structural Realism after the Cold War', *International Security*, 25 (1): 5–41.

Waltz, K. N. (2002) 'The Continuity of International Politics', in K. Booth and T. Dunne (eds) *World in Collision*, New York: Palgrave Macmillan: 348–353.

Waltz, K. and Sagan, S. (2003) *The Spread of Nuclear Weapons: A Debate Renewed*, New York: Norton.

Webber, M. (2007) *Inclusion, Exclusion and the Governance of European Security*, Manchester University Press: Manchester.

Webber, M. and Sakwa, R. (1999) 'The Commonwealth of Independent States, 1991–1998: Stagnation and Survival', *Europe–Asia Studies*, 51 (3): 379–415.

Wilson, J. (2004) *Strategic Partners: Russian–Chinese Relations in the Post-Soviet Era*, Armonk, New York: M. E. Sharp.

Wishnik, E. (2001) 'Russia and China: Brothers again?', *Asian Survey*, XLI (5): 797–821.

Wivel, A. (2000) *The Integration Spiral. International Security and European Integration 1945–1999*, Copenhagen: University of Copenhagen.

Wivel, A. (2004) 'The Power Politics of Peace: Exploring the Link between Globalization and European Integration from a Realist Perspective', *Cooperation and Conflict*, 39 (1): 5–25.

Wivel, A. (2005a) 'Explaining why state X made a certain move last Tuesday: the promise and limitations of realist foreign policy analysis', *Journal of International Relations and Development*, 8 (4): 355–380.

Wivel, A. (2005b) 'The Security Challenge of Small EU Member States: Interests, Identity and the Development of the EU as a Security Actor', *Journal of Common Market Studies*, 43 (2): 393–412.

Wohlforth, W. C. (1995) 'Realism and the End of the Cold War', in S. M. Lynn-Jones., S. E. Miller, and M. E. Brown (eds) *The Perils of Anarchy: Contemporary Realism and International Security*, Cambridge, Massachusetts and London: The MIT Press: 3–41.

Wohlforth, W. C. (1999) 'The Stability of a Unipolar World', *International Security*, 24 (1): 5–41.

Wohlforth, W. C. (2002a) 'U.S. Strategy in a Unipolar World', in G. J. Ikenberry (ed.) *America Unrivalled*, Ithaca and London: Cornell University Press: 98–118.

Wohlforth, W. C. (2002b) 'Russia', in R. J. Ellings and A. Friedberg (eds) *Strategic Asia 2002–03: Asian Aftershocks*, Seattle: National Bureau of Asian Research.

Wohlforth, W. C. (2004) 'Revisiting Balance of Power Theory in Central Asia', in T. V. Paul, J. J. Wirtz. and M. Fortman (eds) *Balance of Power: Theory and Practice in the 21st Century*, Stanford, CA: Stanford University Press: 214–238.

Wolfowitz, P. (2000) 'Statesmanship in the New Century', in R. Kagan and W. Kristol (eds) (2000) *Present Dangers*, San Francisco, California: Encounter Books.

Woods, N. (2003) 'The United States and the International Financial Institutions: Power and Influence within the World Bank and the IMF', in R. Foot, S. N. MacFarlane and M. Mastanduno (eds) *US Hegemony and International Organizations*, Oxford: Oxford University Press: 92–114.

World Trade Organisation, *The Organisation*. Online, available at: www.wto.org/english/thewto_e/whatis_e/inbrief_e/inbr02_e.htm (accessed 5 February 2008).

Wyllie, J. H. (2006) 'Measuring up: the strategies as strategy', in R. Dannreuther and J. Peterson (eds) *Security Strategy and Transatlantic Relations*, London: Routledge: 165–177.

Yin, R. K. (1994) *Case Study Research: Design and Methods* (2nd edn), Thousand Oaks: Sage.

Zakaria, F. (1990) 'The Reagan Strategy of Containment', *Political Science Quarterly*, Vol. 105: 3.

Zakaria, F. (1998) *From Wealth to Power: The Unusual Origin of America's World Role*, New Jersey: Princeton University Press.

Zisser, E. (2001) *Asad's Legacy: Syria in Transition*, New York: New York University Press.

Zisser, E. (2003) 'Does Bashar al-Assad Rule Syria?', *The Middle East Quarterly*, Winter.

Index

For Product Safety Concerns and Information please contact our EU
representative GPSR@taylorandfrancis.com
Taylor & Francis Verlag GmbH, Kaufingerstraße 24, 80331 München, Germany